KRAV MAGA

Combat Mindset and Fighting Stress

KRAV MAGA

Combat Mindset & Fighting Stress

HOW TO PERFORM UNDER ALARMING AND STRESSFUL CONDITIONS

Master Eyal Yanilov and Dr. Ole Boe

Meyer & Meyer Sport

Dekel Publishing House

KRAV MAGA
Combat Mindset & Fighting Stress

Copyright © 2020
Dekel Publishing House
www.dekelpublishing.com

ISBN: 978-965-7178-34-8

Technical editing: Richard Bejtlich
Initial editing: Merete Ruud
Language editing: Katie Roman
Concluding editing: Liz Evans

Photography: Rami Sinai
Graphic design: Giulio Venturi
Cover design and Layout: Orgad Studio
Proof reading: Dory Morik & Pnina Ophir

For information contact:
Dekel Publishing House
P.O. Box 6430, Tel Aviv
6106301, ISRAEL
Email: info@dekelpublishing.com

Published in the United Kingdom
by Meyer & Meyer Sport (UK) Ltd.
Member of the World Sport
Publishers' Association (WSPA)
Email: info@m-m-sports.com

British Library Cataloguing in Publication Data
A catalogue record for this book is available from the British Library

KRAV MAGA: Combat Mindset & Fighting Stress
Maidenhead: Meyer & Meyer Sport (UK) Ltd., 2020
ISBN: 978-1-78255-203-1

Dedicated to Grandmaster Imi Sde-Or (Lichtenfeld),
Founder of Krav Maga (1910-1998),
our memorable teacher for life.

In Memory of Israel and Tuvia Yanilov,
fighters, educators and family people

WARNING

The authors, the editor, and the publisher are not and will not be responsible, in any way whatsoever, for any use made by anyone, whether proper or improper, of the information contained in this book. All use of the aforementioned information must be made in accordance with what is permitted by law, and any damage liable to be caused as a result thereof, will be the exclusive responsibility of the user.

It is the duty of every person planning to train in the techniques described in this book, to consult a licensed physician in order to obtain complete medical information on his or her personal ability and limitations. In addition, he or she must adhere strictly to the safety rules contained in the book, both in training and in actual implementation of the knowhow presented herein.

For professional support:
KMG - Krav Maga Global
P.O. Box 3711, Kadima,
6092000 Israel
www.krav-maga.com

Table of Contents

Foreword

In summer 2001, shortly before September 11, we were the first to publish a book about Krav Maga, the Israeli renowned self-defense system. It was titled *How to Defend Yourself against Armed Assault*, and authored by Krav Maga's founder, Grandmaster Imi Sde-Or (1910–1998), and Eyal Yanilov, his foremost follower and direct successor.

Although at that time Krav Maga was barely known outside Israel, the book proved to be a huge hit, resulting in numerous editions and translations into German, Dutch, French, Spanish, Italian, Czech, Hungarian, Polish, Japanese, Korean, and Chinese.

Since then, several hundred different Krav Maga titles have been published by various instructors all over the world, who have tried their best to follow our pioneering work. Over the years, we have often been asked when the next volumes in our authentic Krav Maga Series are due to appear.

Another interesting query has been whether Krav Maga, like many other fighting systems, also has a spiritual facet that connects the physical and psychological sides of the fighter—or is it a purely technical self-defense discipline? As Grandmaster Imi's disciple, assistant, and friend for over thirty years, I can testify that he was always absorbed in improving the fighter's mindset, which he referred to as Mental Training, and he had a holistic view of human beings as combined body and spirit.

After Imi Sde-Or (Lichtenfeld) passed away, this significant aspect of Krav Maga was enhanced and thoroughly developed by Eyal Yanilov, head instructor of KMG (Krav Maga Global). Yanilov and his student and friend, KM expert instructor Dr. Ole Boe, have authored this innovative book after long years of intensive research.

They offer their invaluable knowledge not only to warriors, who must efficiently function in extreme conflicts, but also to all people who need to cope with stressful situations, whether they work in the medical professions, corporations, emergency agencies, competitive sports teams, and even at home with their families.

I must confess that while editing the book for over a year, the knowledge it contains has proved to be extremely useful for me as, coincidentally, I have faced unforeseen challenges at work and at home. I am most grateful to the authors for the insight and support their book has offered me during this difficult time.

Publishing such a comprehensive book is the obvious result of a teamwork, and I would like to express my deep gratitude to the following people who contributed their energy and expertise to attain the best possible final product: First and foremost, my old friend and Krav Maga teacher, Master Eyal Yanilov, who initiated this cutting-edge approach and coauthored the book. Despite his demanding teaching responsibilities as head of KMG, Eyal relentlessly kept advancing the book, solving unexpected problems while encouraging us from start to finish, for which I am most grateful and deeply indebted.

Coauthor Dr. Ole Boe contributed his vast knowledge and experience as an expert Krav Maga instructor, and as a professor at the University of South-Eastern Norway, Bjørknes University College, the Norwegian Military Academy, and the Norwegian Defense University College. Thanks to his admirable composure, patience, and understanding, our collaboration was both friendly and fruitful.

To Meyer & Meyer, especially its publisher, Mr. Martin Meyer, a seasoned professional who encouraged us along the way with his polite consideration and enthusiasm. Thanks also to the most professional editorial director, Ms. Liz Evans, who gave the book her thoughtful final touch.

Mr. Yuan Boyang, martial arts editor of Beijing Science and Technology Publishing Co., whose brilliant suggestions and professional insight early on greatly helped us improve the book.

Our excellent language editor, Ms. Kathleen Roman, reviewed the book in its initial stages and prevented us from running wild with the English language.

Our graphic artist, Sigalit Orgad-Doron, diligently and bravely tackled the book's layout without complaint, even during upsetting air raids on her border hometown.

Last but not least, my wife, Pnina, who, shortly after recovering from her severe spinal injury, courageously resumed her proofreading work with my son Dory—thank you!

Zvi D. Morik, publisher
Dekel Publishing House
Tel Aviv, March 2020

Preface

For every confrontation, you need mental resources and the ability to retrieve information, analyze it, and make decisions, all under some level of stress. It is obvious that soldiers in war or law enforcement officers policing downtown streets need mental abilities and resources to manage and deal with violence and to mitigate danger. However, those same resources and capabilities are also needed by managers in the corporate sector, politicians running for office, public figures, artists performing on stage or in the media in front of a crowd of fans, lecturers and teachers who have to appear and practically act in front of their students, as well as those same students when taking an important exam. The same resources enable doctors to calmly make decisions that can mean life or death in the operating room, or even enable housemakers to multitask eighteen hours per day and juggle hundreds of household missions.

We decided to share our acquired extensive knowledge of stress management and decision making with a larger audience, with people from all walks of life, and various professions, ages, cultures, and countries. We first tried it in personal training sessions and workshops, and now we openly present it in this book, the first of its kind.

A Real-Life Story: From Soldiers to Warriors

In the mid-1980s, we started teaching an undercover anti-terror unit. The candidates who wished to be admitted to such units were young men with solid soldiering skills who had previous service in the infantry or other fighting units. Most of them had performed three years of regular Israel Defense Forces (IDF) service. Some were officers who had served about four to five years and been commanders with varying responsibilities. Many of the troops had fought in the 1982 Lebanon War. Overall, they were good candidates to enter a three-month anti-terror course that aimed to educate security officers to serve in Israel's national and international airports and border terminals.

The first course started with thirty-three participants. Eleven graduated. The main mission was to prepare them to be fighters able to deal with high-risk situations, and to function under stress in dangerous, violent confrontations against terrorists. Their opponents could use firearms, explosives, or sharp objects to create maximum damage and political effect on civilian populations, Israeli and foreign politicians, and other targets.

This warriors course focused on training in the use of small firearms, Krav Maga techniques, fitness, and applicable regulations and laws. The main factor that made the difference in turning soldiers into warriors was the integrated mental, physical, and technical training that elevated their courage, aggression, perseverance, self-control, and fast decision making. The drills and training methods in this book were the foundation of the training delivered to those warriors.

When preparing trainees, officers, corporate managers, and the general public to handle stress, we use different ways that are best suited to that specific audience. We introduce methods, training drills, and simulations of different natures and kinds. Some of them are physical, and others are not. We use Krav Maga (KMG), the fighting science of the forces we have been training over the years, as a vehicle to cultivate mental capabilities such as courage, determination, the application of controlled aggression, focus, and self-control. We use KMG to manage destructive emotions like anger, fear, and frustration. We also use other methods that we either developed internally in different units and organizations or took from eastern or western ways. Some involve psychological methods or ancient teachings, which we adapted to respond to the specific needs of various groups and individuals.

The real challenge is to create a realistic, true-to-life training format that raises problems and induces stress for the trainee without creating the actual situation or exposing the defender to a real life-threatening condition.

Krav Maga (KMG), as a realistic, integrated, tactical, and technical system, is faced with the question of how to train a person to deal with life-and-death situations. Needless to say, we don't have the privilege or the option to deal with truly real situations, get seriously injured if we fail, or even die, and then miraculously return to our previous uninjured condition in order to repeat the exercise and correct any mistakes.

Therefore, we should use basic and advanced technical, tactical, and simulation training, all under relatively safe conditions and in a reasonably controlled environment.

It is clear that all the "regular" practices in other professions—outdoor workshops for corporate directors; autopsies for medical students; brainstorming, conversations, and simulations for teachers, artists, and politicians; physical self-defense, fighting, and protection of others for officers and civilian trainees—contribute significantly and improve the ability to handle a confrontation or accomplish a mission. This mental preparation is mainly due to the fact that while we are training physically or doing simulations, our mind is being exercised too.

But, in addition to this "regular" training, and in order to further improve ourselves, there is an evident need for special preparation that expands our mental capabilities and additionally enhances our mental and psychological resources. In this book, we present that knowledge, experience, and methodology to benefit our readers whom we also encourage to seek personal guidance from qualified instructors.

Train well and keep safe,
The authors
KMG-HQ, Kadima, Israel
March 2020

Note: Today the words "Krav Maga" no longer describe one system, as it was originally meant to do. There are numerous variations and some remote imitations of the original Israeli Krav Maga system that was founded by Grandmaster Imi Sde-Or (1910-1998) who, after his departure, was succeeded by Eyal Yanilov.

The acronym KMG refers here to the original and evolved system of Krav Maga, with a direct lineage to the origin, which is now taught as an integrated technical and tactical system, as well as to its corresponding organization, **Krav Maga Global**.

Introduction

Fear and stress are conditions that we all experience from time to time. A life without any stress at all would look very strange and somewhat dull. It is natural for humans to feel stressed when confronted with physical danger but also when something new, difficult, or unforeseen comes up, or even when someone is judging or testing us. Being stressed is the brain and body's natural way of trying to take care of us in situations where we feel or perceive that we have stepped outside our normal routine.

Stress also happens when you are bombarded with many small, nonthreatening "missions." You receive several text messages at once, with an expectation for fast responses. You find three dozen emails in your inbox, all of which seem to require your immediate attention. You answer one phone call, while another beeps in the background. You pick up an object that fell to the floor while your child cries in the next room, or the boss calls you to her office.

The intensity of the stress you feel changes according to your perception of demand (i.e., the nature of the emergency or the missions at hand). Stress levels vary according to your experience and your ability to manage your physical and mental resources, concentration, and focus.

In many cases, you feel stress when you are suddenly confronted with a task that you are not sure that you can handle. If you perceive the situation to be very problematic, dangerous, or frightening, you may also feel fear.

The intensity of your fear changes according to how stressful you perceive the situation to be and according to your levels of experience and mental training. Yes, you can train yourself to better manage stress and fear. Through specifically designated mental training, you can change your perception of a situation, and simply function better. You can learn not to feel the same degree of anxiety or stress as before.

The aim of this book is to impart to the reader, based on our knowledge and experience, how to improve decision making under stressful conditions. We also explain how to enhance and recruit all needed mental resources to deal with violent and nonviolent confrontations, as well as how to manage the mind when it is flooded with information during stressful missions.

This book focuses on three areas of mental training: **combat mindset**, which includes attributes such as courage, determination, mental toughness, and aggression; **relaxation and defusing destructive emotions** such as fear, anger, antagonism, and frustration; and **focusing, concentration, and self-control**. These three areas are integrated and there are also overlapping sections. Be aware that even though this is a book on mental training, some of our physical training drills are definitely not easy! We provide demanding drills and techniques in order to develop better combat mindset and mental capacities. Body and mind cannot be separated. They are the two dual parts of a whole, a human being, separable only when the physical entity dies.

Greater than any other calling, the life of the warrior requires mental skills in combination with physical or mechanical skills. Yet, mental training is an area which has been long neglected in the fields of conflict management and force application.
—Wes Doss, an internationally recognized firearms, tactics, and use of force instructor with over thirty years of military and law enforcement experience.

This book is a result of decades of training and study, development, testing, and conducting research into different areas of combat mindset and training for mental conditioning. We combined many years of experience and tens of thousands of hours of practical training with the study of numerous articles, papers, and books. Our research areas included mental toughness, mental preparation, D-MUS (decision making under stress), warrior mindset, fighting spirit, focus, mental preparation and enhancement, mental skills, and mental training.

We chose "Combat Mindset and Fighting Stress" as the title because these words most accurately describe what we do and what we present to our readers, regardless of their chosen professions and backgrounds. Our training methods are unique in the way that they integrate technical, tactical, physical, and mental aspects. This is the way KMG (Krav Maga Global) trains. Within KMG, we offer an instructor education course called the Combat Mindset and Mental Conditioning Instructor Course (MCIC). The purpose is to teach participants how to acquire for themselves and how to instruct others to develop combat mindset and mental capacities and conditioning.

However, the MCIC and other workshops, periodic training sessions, and regular and intensive lessons are also suitable for commanders, officers, and instructors in governmental units of military, security, and protection services, for law enforcement, martial arts instructors and trainees, and these days especially for corporate executives, managers, and coaches, and to other private, corporate, and government audiences.

In this book, we further develop our thinking and elaborate on all aspects of combat mindset and mental conditioning. We describe how a person should develop and integrate mental, tactical, physical, and technical aspects; how to instill a proper mindset to accumulate mental capacities; and how to experience and conduct correct training and conditioning.

A Real-Life Story: The Lady Who Hid at Home

Like all the stories we share, the following is a true one. A talented and beautiful woman, who was in her forties, was attacked and raped by several men. Because she was living in a calm and prosperous European country, she was totally shaken and could not believe such an attack could happen. For her, such a gang rape was something that belonged in Hollywood movies or in a documentary about a third-world country. She shut herself in her apartment for a couple of years and refrained from interacting with the outside world.

One of her friends convinced her to leave her home for the first time after her terrible trauma for some physical activity. He believed that KMG training might help her overcome her fear and anxiety and begin rebuilding her life.

The training hooked her mind and body. She fell in love with the activities. She started going to sessions several times a week. She joined different seminars and workshops in other countries and even travelled to Israel for training camps. Her confidence grew, her physical capabilities strengthened, her mind fortified. She totally changed her life with training that rested on four dimensions: mental, physical, technical, and tactical.

After three years of training, she graduated from a four-week instructor education at the KMG headquarters in Israel. Her goal is now to share her knowledge with other women and young people. She wants to empower those in danger, whether via a physical attack or through the mental stresses of modern life.

KMG uses four dimensions—mental, technical, physical, and tactical—to guide practitioners in training. Figure I-1 explains how these aspects of KMG training relate to one another.

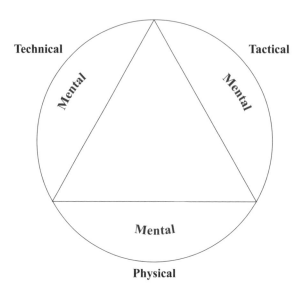

Figure I-1. Relationship between the four different aspects of KMG training.

If the body is like a car, the mind is the driver. It may be a luxury brand with a supercharged engine, but once the driver makes the wrong decision, the consequence is inevitable.

Practicing only the technical, the physical, and the tactical elements of an art may take you a long way, but it is not enough. You also need to practice the mental components; this is the message of Figure I-1. This book shares the mental benefits of KMG training with a large selection of exercises to develop combat mindset, focus, concentration, and relaxation. The goal is to defuse destructive thoughts and emotions, and to elevate mental conditioning. Many exercises also contain physical components, which expand the benefits of mental training.

Combat mindset has been known by many different names, such as "mental toughness," "grace under fire," and "nerves of steel." The mental and physical are two sides of the same coin, and cannot be divided. Our unique combination of theory and practical drills, functional games, techniques, and training methods from KMG enhance the synthesis of mental, technical, physical, and tactical skills.

If you are a practitioner of martial arts, a corporate manager, an officer of the law, or a combat soldier, you may be familiar with some technical, physical, and tactical aspects from different disciplines. KMG incorporates mental training into every aspect of training, even though students may not be aware of it! Within our system and organization, we focus on developing the mental, technical, physical, and tactical capabilities of the trainee while instilling a proper combat mindset through correct conditioning.

Whether you are a KMG practitioner, an officer serving in the military or the police, a business leader, a martial artist, or a corporate employee in a position that requires you to make quick and efficient decisions, you can benefit from this book. You can learn how to improve your mental capabilities, including combat mindset (controlled aggression, perseverance and determination), visualization, focus, relaxation and breathing, body language, self-talk, and the ability to overcome destructive emotions through correct conditioning.

This is only the first step; you must start practicing and implementing this knowledge! It may be compared to reading a book about fitness—you cannot improve your pull-ups and squats just by reading about it! The same is true of ancient books like *The Art of War* or the *Kama Sutra*.

What Professionals Say about These Techniques

Some time ago, we had the privilege to train some of Norway's most experienced police officers. None of them had less than fifteen years of hard-earned experience, from crowd control to entering houses where armed and dangerous people were waiting for them. During their training, we used several of the techniques described in this book. The experienced police officers said the training was extremely useful. They wanted more. The Norwegian Police University College was also interested!

The techniques, drills, and combat mindset training were a perfect match for these experienced people. It is rewarding to hear positive feedback from people who on a daily basis face fear and stress. We had the same experience with cadets at the Norwegian Military Academy where Ole Boe used to work. Even very experienced combat veterans say that they benefit greatly from this type of training. Working with the Israeli military and SWAT officers, Argentinian, Polish, German, and British police units, and Singaporean, Swedish, Australian, and Norwegian armed forces, and with different special units, the authors have heard that the combat mindset training these groups received has helped them stay alive and function much better in the streets of Kabul, Afghanistan, or East Jerusalem to downtown Chicago, Buenos Aires, or Berlin.

George S. Patton, the famous US Army general and a participant in the 1912 Olympic modern pentathlon, once said, "Now if you are going to win any battle you have to do one thing. You have to make the mind run the body. Never let the body tell the mind what to do. The body will always give up. It is always tired morning, noon, and night. But the body is never tired if the mind is not tired. When you were younger the mind could make you dance all night, and the body was never tired... You've always got to make the mind take over and keep going."

Patton said this during World War II. It was true then, as it is true today.

If you are a newcomer to a competitive martial art, these mental skills help you reduce the fear you might otherwise experience in a tournament. The same mental skills help you if you happen to get into a situation where you need to apply some preventive measures, avoid the situation, or apply self-defense skills. As a bonus effect, these skills help you better cope with other difficult, stressful, but nonviolent situations too, as your mind no longer perceives them as being so dangerous.

You may not be a martial artist, or a soldier, or a police officer. Your challenge might involve facing two hundred people listening to you give a presentation, or arguing with a colleague who does not want to listen to you, or preparing to talk to the boss about a pay raise. You fight many battles every day, which never include physical conflicts or contact. You surely need mental training so that you have mental resources to win your nonviolent battles.

A correct combat mindset is closely related to the concept of being a warrior. What does it mean to be a warrior? The warrior "aims to follow his heart, to choose consciously the items that make up his world, to be exquisitely aware of everything around him, to attain full control over self, then act with total abandon. He seeks, in short, to live an impeccable life." A warrior is not only someone who is in the military. A warrior is anyone fighting to improve several aspects of his or her life and who does not give up when facing difficulties. Decide if you want to be a warrior too. If you already are a warrior, we believe and know that you should be proud of yourself. This book can help you continue on your chosen path in life.

Throughout the book, we explain the unique way that we think, practice, and train within KMG, and how this transfers to educating people of all backgrounds. The book is divided into three parts.

Part One addresses the theoretical side of mental training and why you should practice it. It introduces mental training, discusses stress, mental toughness, and coping theory, and examines how stress affects your performance. This part concludes with a chapter on character, self-regulation, and willpower.

Part Two draws you into the combat mindset with practical aspects of physical and mental training. It covers controlled aggression, perseverance and determination, strength and power drills, and functional games. This part offers dozens of figures to illustrate the drills that can help you develop a combat mindset. The final chapter provides resources on Krav Maga training for special units, law enforcement, and security personnel.

Part Three deals with enhancing your mental resources and capacities by addressing visualization and anchoring different mental states, focus and attention span, and relaxation and breathing. This part also describes how you can make body language a positive force in your life, and how you can minimize destructive emotions and improve self-talk. It concludes with a powerful exercise called "accepting defeat," which is designed to minimize stress and encourage success.

At the end of the book, there is a multitude of references to the literature that we have researched. Within many chapters there are also real-life stories that illustrate and enhance our understanding of the use and the effects of the mental state, mental training, and preparation.

How to Use This Book
If you are interested in first learning more about what lies behind the techniques and the more theoretical aspects and explanations of mental training, who uses it, and why, then start with Part One.

If you want to start practicing the mental and physical techniques right away, go to Part Two.

If you want to start training on enhancing your mental resources and capacities, start with Part Three.

Our recommendation is to take a comprehensive perspective of the book. We think that you will benefit more if you have an understanding of the theories behind the practical exercises. As we see it, "theory without practice is for professors; practice without theory (and values) is for thugs." In short, learn both theory and practice, and you will gain the most benefit.

We know that the techniques presented here are easy and quick to learn, and that they lead to better perception and understanding of how to perform more efficiently under stressful conditions.

One final point: Take the time to do the exercises in this book. As we say in the military, making decisions is not difficult, but finding the correct time to make a decision is more challenging. This means that you can read the book and put it away, or you can make decisions as you go along, practicing diligently and methodically. We can easily compare it to weight lifting—if you wish to become stronger and grow your muscles, you must train and practice every day and for a long time.

If you choose to walk the path of a warrior, whatever your profession is, you have the freedom to choose where your steps take you. There can be many different paths to choose from, but there is only one "way." As a warrior, you accept total responsibility for your thoughts and emotions, your behavior, your deeds, and your actions. This is known as decision making. It generally takes sixty-six days to create a new habit, after which time you still need to work to maintain it. Such persistence is a sign of a good character. The decision how to benefit from this book is yours.

Part One
Overcoming Stress

When the going gets tough, the tough get going...

Knute Rockne, a Norwegian-born American football player (1888-1931)

Chapter 1

Mental Training

Mental training is a collection of methods and techniques to develop both psychological and physical capabilities. Psychological capacities, among others, can be improved through concentration exercises, whether applied to general pursuits or specific mission requirements. Physical performance can be improved through visualization exercises, such as imagining successful completion of a track and field high jump. It has been stated that well-developed psychological skills are a prerequisite for being able to perform at a high level, regardless of the type of performance. Mental training helps you leverage your resources to achieve peak performance. Training requires working purposefully, systematically, and regularly over time. Similar to physical training, mental training requires long-term commitment. You cannot expect to be a good runner or fighter after one training session, or even achieve significant improvement in only one session; the same is true with mental training.

The Necessity of Mental Training

Why do military special units, law enforcement units, top athletes, firefighters, corporate executives, and martial artists practice mental training? The answer is simple: Mental training works! Successfully accomplishing critical missions requires mental preparation. What is the difference between the following: the gold and silver Olympic medalist; a person who defends himself or herself efficiently in a violent confrontation, and one who does not; a soldier who functions well on the battlefield and one who does not; a police officer who solves a crime and one who does not; and a company manager who handles a difficult employee or co-worker and one who does not?

With respect to top athletes, winning or losing can often be attributed to either good mental preparation or a lack of mental preparation. An athlete can mentally overcome an opponent before the contest physically begins. Observe an athlete before a competition starts. You can almost see what the athlete is thinking. Often the athlete goes through a series of motions similar to those they are going to perform during the contest. They visualize the upcoming competition and see themselves winning. The sports world has practiced mental training for many years, and mental training has been attracting more and more attention from other professional areas during the last few decades. In the 1980s, the United States Army Green Berets (an element of the US Army Special Forces) started a unique mental training program called Project Jedi. The aim was to enhance operators' mental capacities and make them become better warriors. Project Jedi included a practice called **neuro-linguistic programming** (NLP). It suggests that there is a connection between neurological processes ("neuro"), language ("linguistic"), and your behavioral patterns that have been learned through experience ("programming"). The thinking is that these can be changed to achieve specific goals.

Eyal Yanilov pioneered the use of NLP and other forms of mental training in the Krav Maga system, beginning in the 1980s. NLP and other forms of mental training have been used in everything from parachute jumping to shooting and close combat. NLP trainees appear to function better when they are facing difficult and stressful situations. NLP and mental training with visualization have also been used in other governmental organizations, such as, of all places, tax authorities.

Your "regular" physical practice, such as self-defense, fighting, and protection of others, contributes to your ability to mentally handle a confrontation. Other physical activities also help build a better mindset. When you train your body, you also train your mind. Mental training reduces stress, improves concentration, sharpens focus, and accelerates information processing. Mental training also helps you make better decisions and gain control of your direction in life. If needed, mental training makes you more decisive, aggressive, and determined. After working with several thousand people over many years, we have seen the positive effects of mental training first hand.

Imi Sde-or (Lichtenfeld), founder of Krav Maga, demonstrates a knife-fighting situation with Michael Hertzig, PhD, while training at the IDF's School of Combat Fitness in the mid-1960s.

A soldier may be facing a life-and-death situation, but mental strength is essential for both the battlefield and peacekeeping missions. Grandmaster Imi and Moshe Kats, PhD, at the same place and time.

Developing a Combat Mindset

When you are exposed to demands on your brain and body, you react with a combination of defensive and adaptive measures. This combination is referred to as a stress reaction. This stress reaction is the total of the psychological and physiological processes that happen within you. Social, physical, or mental stressors can elicit stress. Stressors are stimuli that create a stress reaction. Examples of physical stressors are loud sounds, cold temperatures, or seeing a person with a weapon. Mental stressors include feelings of anxiety or fear. Social stressors can develop in situations where you feel that other people are criticizing or judging you. The greatest fear a soldier experiences on a battlefield is not that of dying or being killed, but rather of letting his friends down by not performing the right actions.

During a fight, participants need to constantly readjust, make new decisions, and act in order to overcome the aggressor. This is the essence of the OODA loop as specified below.

This book introduces you to a suite of mental tools and tactics to improve mental and physical performance. You can develop a clear sense of the mental and physical reactions that you experience in a nonviolent conflict as well as in a self-defense or fighting situation. You can understand how to improve your "**OODA loop**," that is your ability to observe–orient–decide–act, and how to avoid "**attentional rubbernecking**," meaning the drawing of your attention to stimuli with a strong emotional aspect. You can learn practical methods and drills for training concentration, focus, neutralization of destructive emotions, minimizing stress, reducing negative self-talk, and improving attention skills.

The well-known mindfulness teacher Kabat-Zinn states that tension in the muscles can be relieved by directing nonjudgmental attention toward them. This muscle tension is also referred to as somatic anxiety, which is the worry caused by the perception of, and judging of, your bodily reactions to a situation. **Mindfulness training** may help reduce these feelings by transferring awareness to the present moment, away from the negative stress reactions themselves. For example, research shows that the perception of stress is dramatically reduced in people who practice mindfulness training before, during, and after parachute jumping. Being "here and now," or focusing on current events, is an important skill that enables more advanced mental training.

Self-confidence is another benefit of mental training. B.K. Siddle describes self-confidence as a mental condition where anxiety, fear, and self-doubt are not present. When you lack confidence, your body experiences stress and anxiety. The more confidence you feel and project, the better you perform.

Five training strategies enable the development of mental capabilities. These include visualization, goal setting, positive self-talk, combat mindset (courage, determination, and aggression), and relaxation. Utilizing these five main strategies, we develop confidence and commitment, and we learn to control our attention and physical responses. You may start your mental training by building a "**mental attack plan**." Consider how, when, and where you will train, and which stages and methods you will use.

Your developing mental skills are transferable to other walks of life, including how to deal with aggression and violence. If you practice **Krav Maga** or some type of close combat training, chances are high that you will function better in other stressful situations. For example, for three weeks a group of soldiers trained in highly stressful close combat exercises. A control group did not practice any close combat training. Both groups later rappelled down a 30-meter high (100 feet) water tower. Examiners measured their pulse rates when they put on the equipment on top of the tower, when they were ready to rappel from the tower, 1 meter (3.3 feet) down the tower, and finally 3 meters (10 feet) down the tower. The close combat group had lower pulse rates at both 1 and 3 meters down the tower compared to the control group. Close combat training helped reduce the stress in another difficult situation. Stopping negative thoughts, also known as "**self-talk**" or "**internal monologue**," is key to successes like these. It is vital to be aware of your own negative thoughts and know how to transform them into positive thinking instead. Having a positive attitude and repeating affirmations like "I can do this" to yourself are effective strategies.

Visualization is another powerful mental tool. Some military professionals refer to visualization as "**strategic vision**," or "**tactical performance imagery**." We have used visualization to improve the performance of Krav Maga students and corporate directors—indeed the technique offers benefits well beyond physical confrontation scenarios.

A Real-Life Story: Visualizing a Self-Defense Technique against a Gun Threat

We wanted to test the power of visualization and integrate it into physical training. During a Krav Maga summer camp, we divided participants into two groups of roughly thirty people each. One group had approximately a year of Krav Maga experience, while the other had several years of experience. The group with a year of experience had never practiced any gun defense techniques before. No one in either group had seen or practiced the technique we taught that day.

We showed each group a high-level gun defense technique against a threat with a handgun. The threat involved an attacker approaching from behind and putting a gun to the side of a victim's head while grabbing him around the chest with the other arm. The demonstration took about four minutes.

We showed the technique ten times slowly to the first group. Then we asked the group to go to a different room and to practice the gun defense technique by themselves (without a partner). They were told to practice the technique with their eyes closed, and to visualize themselves doing the movements. We gave them around five minutes to practice.

Next, we ordered them to return, lined them up, and started to test the first person in the line. An instructor came up from behind, put the gun to a person's head, and grabbed him around the chest. About half of the participants managed to perform the technique correctly the first time, and the other half showed a tolerable, but not perfect, technique. We only let each person try the technique once.

We repeated the procedure with the more experienced group. Almost all of the participants managed to do the technique correctly the first time.

Even with the additional pressure of being observed and singled out to perform a technique they had never seen or practiced before, half of the first group and almost everyone in the second group performed very well, given only four minutes of observation and five minutes of visualization. Without two control groups of inexperienced and experienced practitioners who did not use visualization, we cannot yet isolate the effects of visualization in a scientific manner. Anecdotally, the performance of the two groups in this scenario was superior to other exercises where we did not instruct students to apply visualization to their learning process.

In a future experiment, we could compare groups in a different manner. A set of students with similar experience levels could be divided into four groups and exposed to a Krav Maga technique. One group would not practice at all. A second group would only conduct physical practice. A third group would only conduct visualization practice. A fourth group would conduct both physical and visualization practice. Our hypothesis is that the fourth group would perform best, given the power of visualization to improve the training and performance experience.

Mental Challenges

Military, police, and civilian leaders frequently encounter challenges, known as **in extremis** leadership situations or simply the "unforeseen." Even though you may not work in "protect-and-serve" organizations, your daily life may not be predictable. Your job working at the tax office may be challenging when a visitor disagrees with his assessment. A colleague may surprise you with his aggression or attitude. Another driver may swerve toward you on the highway. Your spouse may be irritated because you came home late or forgot to buy one of the ingredients for dinner, not to mention a birthday gift...

When these situations occur, we have some aces up our sleeve thanks to mental, physical, and tactical training. From recent research, we know that character strengths can be developed through increased awareness and effort, and that these strengths are phenomena that coexist with goals, interests, and values. In KMG training, character strengths are built and enhanced via partner, group, and individual training that are composed of mental, physical, and technical ingredients. You can find in this book some specific drills as strength exercises that enhance confidence and trust, or passing through crowd drills that build courage and controlled aggression while the set goal is to pass between the "aggressors" and fulfill a specific mission.

The officer is facing a sudden attack with a machete and has no opportunity to shoot the aggressor.

The officer blocks the deadly strike with his weapon and first counterattacks with a simultaneous kick.

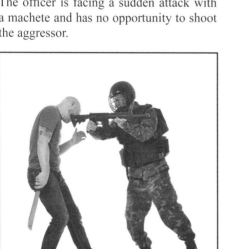

The officer then counterattacks with the weapon, using a horizontal butt strike.

Additional strikes with the weapon are common practice. The next phase of action depends on the situation.

For military officers, soldiers, police officers, and firefighters, challenging and unexpected situations are common. You need sufficient subject matter expertise, combined with social and personal proficiency. Social and personal proficiency means being able to react to and communicate with other people, and to sense what is going on inside another person's head.

In order to function optimally under stress, several properties are required from an individual. Properties within an individual's personal proficiency include assertiveness, willpower, determination, self-efficacy, mental resilience, and mental stamina. For instance, higher degrees of psychological characteristics such as mental toughness, goal setting, imagery, realistic performance evaluation, and commitment have been found to be the difference between a medal winner in the Olympics and those who do not win any medals.

Individuals with a high degree of **self-efficacy** are more apt to believe that they can meet different challenges despite the weight of different stressors. Self-efficacy is a concept developed by the famous psychologist Albert Bandura in 1977. Self-efficacy is the extent or strength of your belief in your own ability to complete tasks and reach goals. **Mental toughness** can be described as having a natural or a developed psychological edge. This psychological edge enables you to cope better than your opponents with the many demands that are placed upon you as a performer. More specifically, having mental toughness means that you are more consistent and perform better than your opponents, thanks to your determination, focus, and confidence when under pressure.

Unexpected changes in life can create unpredictability and uncertainty, and both are considered major sources of stress. If you are a business leader or manager, many of the concepts used for top-level athletes can help you cope with daily stress. At least seven aspects of mental toughness are directly transferable to the business world: flexibility, responsiveness, strength, courage and ethics, resiliency, and sportsmanship. These aspects of mental toughness are similar to the twelve character strengths required to become a better military leader. These include leadership, integrity, persistence, bravery, teamwork, open-mindedness, social intelligence, self-regulation, creativity, fairness, love of learning, and perspective.

Developing these twelve character strengths requires you to emphasize different aspects of mental training. You need to work on your controlled aggression, persistence, determination and courage, relaxation, body language, your ability to focus and to concentrate, and attention span. A link has also been established between those who tend to score high in these twelve character strengths and those who tend to score high in rating their own mental toughness.

Research demonstrates that training on aggression and aggression control can create soldiers that can be described as "**monsters with brakes**." Soldiers can be aggressive when needed, but they are still able to be in control and regulate their emotions. Evidence further suggests that regulating emotion is a critical factor of military performance. Regulating emotion is important for people outside the military as well. On a related note, Eccles and Feltovich have pointed out that psychological skills such as managing self-talk, a form of regulating emotion, are highly important for performance.

Acharai la'tzanchanim, Hebrew words for "follow me to the paratroopers," is written on this decoration. This is a tribute to the famous command, "**follow me**," that is used by IDF officers instead of "**charge**" as they lead by their own example.

Leadership Qualities

We know from many years of experience in educating soldiers, military, police officers, security branch officers, KMG practitioners and instructors, martial artists, and ordinary civilians that to take control over your own thoughts and feelings is crucial to success. Only after learning to lead yourself, you can lead other people. From working with managers over many years, we know many of them dread having "**the difficult talk**," a conversation with an underperforming employee. How can mental training prepare a manager for this disturbing discussion of job performance?

A Real-Life Story: The Difficult Talk

We led a series of two-day workshops on stress management for middle managers of the tax authority in Norway. There were approximately twenty managers in each workshop, and one or two section leaders always participated as well.

During the first workshop, it became very clear that these managers were facing many of the same challenges as military officers, but one challenge was particularly salient. Their worst fear was to have "the difficult talk." For example, they did not know what to do with employees who were just waiting for retirement in a few years, and who were clearly not interested in doing their jobs. Another example involved an employee who had become an alcoholic and had problems complying with the demands of work.

We worked on several mental strategies, including a technique we call "accept defeat," breathing, concentration drills, neuro-linguistic programming, and how to anchor different mental states. The "invest in loss" technique let the managers' minds experience what would be the worst outcome of a situation.

In the managers' minds, before using this technique, it seemed that things would go terribly wrong during a difficult talk with someone. After using the "invest in loss" technique, they found out that the worst-case scenario was not so bad, and it was not so likely to happen either. When you condition your mind to feel the worst outcome, it does not seem so bad or frightening anymore. We did not, however, spend much time on the worst scenario, but quickly moved toward better outcomes.

The idea is to teach your brain how to win instead of how to lose. This is the reason you should spend a lot more time visualizing winning or positive outcomes than the opposite. In the case of these managers, we did not want them to think of winning against an employee, but rather reaching a positive outcome for both. It was not a fight for life or death with an opponent or enemy. If this had been the case, we would have told them to win at all costs.

We continued to work on different breathing techniques, starting with practicing breathing deeply in and out a couple of times. We also worked on several concentration drills with the aim of enhancing the ability to understand the meaning of what the other person said. We used several techniques from neuro-linguistic programming to teach the managers to find out what different types of body language, words, pitch, and tone of voice could indicate. We also taught them how to anchor a positive feeling (and an aggressive feeling if this was needed for some reason) in their bodies and how to retrieve this before a difficult talk took place.

After the workshops were conducted, the section leaders evaluated the benefit of the sessions. It became clear that the work environment in the different sections had changed for the better, and that the middle managers had told their section leaders that they felt much more confident about having these difficult talks. The sections functioned more efficiently and managers felt less stressed.

Transformational Leadership and Mental Training

James MacGregor Burns, who created the theory of **transformational leadership** in the 1980s, said "leadership is one of the most observed and least understood phenomena on earth." Transformational leadership can be said to positively affect the achievement of results in both service-oriented and in production-oriented organizations. Research has shown that leaders who have a personality characterized by kindness and little aggression achieve higher efficiency and fewer errors with their teams. For instance, the efficiency of aircrews was found to be dependent upon the captain's personality. Crews with captains who were warm, friendly, had good confidence, and were able to withstand pressure had the lowest number of errors. Crews with captains who were arrogant, hostile, boastful, selfish, passive aggressive, or dictatorial committed more and graver mistakes.

Research has revealed that high energy and sound decision making are the personality traits that best predict rapid career advancement. Other predictive personality traits include the ability to withstand uncertainty and stress (emotional stability), intrinsic work discipline (conscientiousness), a wide interest (openness to new experiences), as well as a desire to advance. Although not mentioned directly in these studies, leaders need to improve their ability to withstand uncertainty, stress, and pressure. Mental training is a key to this process.

Based on the theory of transformational leadership that was developed by Bass and Avolio, researchers at the Swedish National Defence College developed a model called **Developmental Leadership**. The Swedish model aims to provide a comprehensive picture of leadership and is referred to as a "holistic leadership model." It is based on an interactional person versus situation perspective. Both personal and contextual characteristics are taken into account when looking at a person's leadership behavior. The **Developmental Leadership** model consists of three main components: leader characteristics describing the leader's personal aptitudes; contextual characteristics of the environment that affect the leader's thoughts, feelings, and behavior; and three leadership styles. The first and desired leadership style is **developmental leadership**, where the leader acts as a role model and raises questions of morals and ethics while observing core values. A developmental leader also provides inspiration and motivation to promote participation and creativity, and shows personal consideration by providing support, but also opposition, if this is beneficial for the individual and organization. The second leadership style in the model is **transactional leadership**. Here the positive sides of transactional leadership, that is, to seek agreements and to take necessary measures, are desirable, but the negatives sides of transactional leadership, such as over-control and to reward other people if and only if they perform what is required, is less desirable. The third leadership style in the model is **non-leadership**, which is a leadership style that should be avoided. In non-leadership, the leader is present but not active in leading. An example here could be a conflict between two or more employees at a workplace where the leader sees this, but where he does not do anything to help solve the conflict. The leader is connected to the environment in which he operates, and this affects his leadership style and behavior in a situation.

Leader characteristics are divided into basic prerequisites consisting of physical-, psychological-, and view-of-life-related aspects. They can further be divided into desirable competencies such as task-related competence, management-related competence, social competence, and capacity to cope with stress. The Developmental Leadership model has been used at the Norwegian Military Academy for many years, with benefits observed by the cadets. They learn to adapt their leadership behavior to the circumstances, and they also improve their ability to interact with other people. Cadets practice mental training techniques to enhance task-related competence, management-related competence, social competence, and the capacity to cope with stress. We have applied the Developmental Leadership model to several other organizations outside the military—from tax authorities and municipal employees to business organizations and the health sector—with similar positive results.

Most of the research conducted previously has shown that certain psychological skills are critical if an expert is going to be able to perform at his maximum in a variety of tasks and contexts—in other words, to be able to cope. Being an expert simply means that you have practiced to such a degree that you master one or several areas. How do you become an expert in something? You practice repeatedly until you master it.

Psychological Skills and Self-Efficacy

Bandura launched a theory called Social Cognitive Theory in his 1986 book **Social Foundations of Thoughts and Action**, elaborating on the concept of **self-efficacy** that he invented in 1977. Self-efficacy can be defined as the "beliefs in one's capabilities to organize and execute the courses of action required to produce given attainments." This is not about the abilities and skills you possess, but about what you consider **attainable** with the skills you possess.

Self-efficacy in Bandura's theory is fundamentally about our faith in or our genuine conscious or unconscious beliefs about our own ability to cope; that is, the belief in our capacity or ability to implement and master an impending task. Self-efficacy affects how we think, feel, and motivate ourselves, and when and how we act. A key question that arises for any theory that deals with cognitive regulation of motivation, affect, and action is causality. Does self-efficacy really act as a causal factor for our impending function and performance? The findings of a wide scope of different tests of causality, where self-efficacy has been systematically varied, consistently demonstrate that there is a clear connection between self-efficacy, motivation, and achievement. Self-efficacy has proved to be negatively related to perceived stress and psychological imbalance, known as distress. If your self-efficacy is high, you experience less stress and distress. Also, self-efficacy has proved to be positively related to self-ranking of your own health. The higher self-efficacy you think you have, the better you think your health is. Having a high degree of self-efficacy may in turn be a significant predictor of decreased mortality.

Self-efficacy is an individual's ability to organize and carry out the activities required to achieve desired results. Bandura believes there are four factors that promote a better subjective self-efficacy. The four factors are enactive mastery experiences, vicarious experiences, verbal persuasion, and physiological and mental states.

Enactive Mastery Experiences

Enactive mastery experiences have the most impact on self-efficacy. The actions you have mastered before are likely to influence whether you are able to solve similar tasks. The successful, but also unsuccessful, coping experience is stored in your memory, so they later may affect your self-efficacy belief. Repeated success strengthens self-efficacy while repeated failure weakens it. Wes Doss also places great emphasis on enactive mastery experiences in order to build belief in yourself and your abilities. He explains that this is one of the most effective ways to boost your confidence and increase faith in your abilities. Doss thus supports Bandura's thinking and emphasizes that it is important for both soldiers and instructors to understand that success comes from being confident in your skills.

The attacker intends to execute a forearm chokehold from behind.

Sensing the danger early, the defender starts turning, bringing his chin to his shoulder.

The defender grabs and pulls the aggressor's palms to his sternum, bends and removes his head from the chokehold.

The defender gets his head out, steps to the aggressor's side, and knees him in the groin.

On the other hand, performing very simple tasks over time may result in small defeats, creating cracks in your self-efficacy. Therefore, it is important to find a balance between difficult and easy tasks. Imagine a military cadet who serves as a company commander on an infantry exercise. She masters this role in a satisfactory manner and fulfills her goals. In the next exercise, the cadet serves as a platoon leader. The cadet had a good experience from her previous leadership role and, therefore, feels confident in her ability to perform as a platoon leader.

Vicarious Experiences

Vicarious experiences, or seeing others succeed, is the second factor involved in building self-efficacy. Living vicariously persuades an observer that he is capable of performing a task as well as, or better than, the observed party. If you are able to identify with the performer, the impact is even greater. However, this way to build self-efficacy is not thought to be as powerful as enactive mastery experiences. Imagine a military cadet who is about to take her close combat exam. The cadet sees a peer perform in an outstanding manner throughout the test. The cadet may think that she is as capable as her peer in other endeavors, and thus convince herself that she can achieve the same result.

Verbal Persuasion

The third factor in increasing self-efficacy is verbal persuasion, hearing praise or encouraging comments. Bandura explains that positive feedback at work or when performing a task encourages you to make a greater effort if the encouragement is realistic. In order for you to feel that the encouragement is real, the feedback must be within the limits of what is feasible for you. Experiencing failure because you were encouraged to take on more responsibility than you thought was realistic could have a negative impact on your self-efficacy. Negative comments also weaken self-efficacy. An instructor or supervisor might refrain from giving negative feedback, but there should be feedback to address deficiencies. Correct feedback and encouragement causes the focus to be turned away from what is difficult and shifted to how you should do your best to resolve the challenges. In many situations it is more important that the person giving the feedback addresses the process than its outcome and results.

For example, a company leader encourages an employee to take on a position with more responsibility. The leader explains that the employee is loyal, fair, and full of effort and should therefore take on the task. The employee feels that the leader has credibility, and therefore this feedback increases the belief that he can cope with additional responsibilities.

Physiological and Affective States

The fourth factor in increasing self-efficacy is physiological and affective states. When you judge yourself and your skills, you often consider information that comes from cognitive and emotional impulses. These can include stress and anxiety, or other characteristics such as butterflies in your stomach, a positive mood, or increased heartbeat. These cognitive and emotional impulses may over time evolve such that you have difficulty functioning in a normal way, or that these impulses improve the way you function. Consider a platoon leader who is highly stressed before a mission. These feelings can weaken self-efficacy for this mission, and the feeling of stress returns in similar situations. To counter these feelings, the development of personal coping strategies and techniques help win back control and achieve better self-efficacy.

The aggressor applies a typical attack against long-haired people that keeps them at a distance and, therefore, vulnerable to strikes. The defender overcomes this hair-grab by turning and kicking the aggressor.

Self-efficacy is not just about controlling your actions and surroundings, but mainly about being able to control your own thought process, motivation, and physiological state and emotions. Your individual perceived competence in defined domains or activities is linked to your degree of both self-perception and self-efficacy. If you feel that you are very competent in a certain area, you most likely also have a high degree of self-efficacy in the same area. Self-efficacy is considered a "personal moderator" because the support comes from within yourself. On the other hand, there may be a correlation between general low self-esteem and lack of self-efficacy on a larger scale across many situations and areas.

The terms self-efficacy, self-esteem, and self-concept theoretically cannot simply be mixed together. Other related concepts affect the idea of self-efficacy, such as "self," "self-esteem," and "self-evaluation." "Self-concept" is another term to ponder, and researchers debate how these concepts are related to one another. Other terms frequently encountered in articles and books on self-efficacy include "hardiness" and "resiliency." The idea of "coping" introduces terms like "social support," the meaning of self in relation to others, referred to as "mattering," and "stress mindset." In this book, we discuss these concepts, but we focus on the concept of self-efficacy and its relation to stress.

There is not much research on which specific psychological skills are the most effective in the military. The need for more research using sports psychology to understand a soldier's physical performance has been requested in the past. Researchers Janelle and Hillmann point out that through knowing the underlying mechanisms of achievement at high levels in athletes, we may also gain insight into the factors that underlie effective practice, instruction, and support networks necessary for facilitation of performance and learning in military contexts.

Investigations on a physically demanding selection program in the US Special Forces show that the effect of social support, meaning that you matter to other people, and self-efficacy are important factors regarding whether the soldiers complete the selection or not. A study conducted on personnel in an American Stryker brigade shows that soldiers with well-developed psychological skills perform better on physical tests than soldiers with less developed psychological skills. Another study conducted on soldiers and self-efficacy looks into whether a correlation exists between theory and practice regarding Bandura's four factors of how to increase self-efficacy. The aim was to find out if Bandura's theoretical aspects of self-efficacy are transferable to real situations. The four investigated factors are enactive mastery experiences (meaning your own experiences from performing something), vicarious experiences (meaning you see others have success), verbal persuasions and allied types of social influences (meaning feedback from people you trust), and physiological and affective states. The four factors have previously been found to influence self-efficacy. The results show that in general there was a high correlation between how military cadets perceived Banduras theory on self-efficacy and the four factors' importance in practice.

CONCLUSION

Now you have some background on the theory and rationale of mental training. You should also understand why you need mental training and, in principle, how to build a combat mindset. We propose that you start your mental training by building a "mental attack plan." Focus on some of the leadership qualities that we find valuable for all leaders and managers. It is also important to understand the link between transformational leadership and mental training, and the four factors contributing to self-efficacy—that is, enactive mastery experiences, vicarious experiences, verbal persuasion, and physiological and mental states.

Chapter 2

Stress, Mental Toughness, and Coping Theory

You need to know what stress is, be aware of it, and know how it manifests itself in your brain and body before you can fix it. Stress is the pressure you feel when you have too much to do and not enough time to do it. Stress is caused by stressors, internal or external influencers with social, physical, or mental origins. Worrying about what other people think about you is a social stressor. Heat, cold, pain, fatigue, and violent confrontations are physical stressors. Negative thoughts concerning the outcome of a situation, such as not winning an athletic competition or losing your job, are mental stressors. Feeling stress does not mean you are "broken." Rather, learning to mitigate stress helps you perform and feel better when facing ordinary or extraordinary challenges.

Stress and Performance

If you suddenly experience a stressor and you think and feel that this stressor is threatening, your body reacts by producing the stress hormone cortisol. This leads to an increased heart rate and respiration, as well as tensed muscles and increased perspiration. In addition, your blood flow is drawn away from digestion and directed toward your muscles so that you can use them to run away or to fight. You feel stress when you believe that you lack the resources, will, skills, or abilities to handle a situation, whether a violent confrontation or a nonviolent one. Perceived competence within clearly defined domains or activities has been found to be the main factor in both self-perception and self-efficacy. Research shows that performance may be affected by the degree of perceived anxiety. The more anxiety, the worse your performance. Your performance is in turn affected by various factors, such as your activity and level of achievement. Your coordination, cognition, and memory may be impaired. You may suffer tunnel vision, loss of hearing ("auditory exclusion"), and a distorted perception of time and space. Several of these impairments are related to your heartbeat. At certain heart frequencies, it is difficult to perform fine motor movements, to hear what another person tells you, or to follow someone with your eyes. In a threatening situation, your hand-eye coordination decreases. Small, fine movements become almost impossible to perform, especially those requiring use of the fingers. An example of degraded fine motors skills are sometimes seen when police officers shoot themselves in the leg or fire into a car door while trying to draw their weapon in a stressful situation. Your activity and achievement levels can be changed through physical training, visualization, breathing, concentration, and focusing practice.

A group of military static-line jumpers waiting to climb into the airplane and take off.
Courtesy of Torbjørn Kjosvold, Norwegian Armed Forces.

The Federal Bureau of Investigation's (FBI) Law Enforcement Officers Killed & Assaulted (LEOKA) Report from 2004 reveals that 594 police officers were killed in the United States during the ten-year period leading to 2004. Most of these killings involved a short distance between the officers and the perpetrator or perpetrators. A total of 545 of these officers were killed by handguns, and 268 (49.2%) of the officers were killed at distances of 1.5 meters (5 feet) or less. A total of 107 officers (19.6%) were killed at distances of 1.8–3 meters (6–10 feet). In total, 440 officers (80.7%) were killed at distances of less than 6 meters (20 feet), and 47 officers (8.6%) were killed at distances of 6.3–15 meters (21–49 feet). Finally, 41 officers (7.5%) were killed at distances greater than 15 meters (49 feet), primarily due to sniper action. With the remaining 17 officers that were killed, the distance to the perpetrator or perpetrators was not reported. The majority of these officers probably experienced extreme stress and reacted with an inappropriate action, such as freezing. When they fired their guns, most of the shots missed—even when the distances were very short. As a result of the stress involved and inappropriate actions taken, these officers were killed by the attackers. The 2016 LEOKA Report reveals that 7,829 federal officers were reported to have been assaulted, and 7 of these officers were killed between 2012 and 2016. During the same period, 622 federal officers were attacked with personal weapons such as hands, fists, or feet; 104 were assaulted with firearms; 99 were assaulted with vehicles; 40 were assaulted with knives or other cutting instruments; and 26 were attacked with blunt instruments. Again, we see that a lot of these reported attacks often occurred at short distances.

A Real-Life Story: "An Iron Ball in a Pinball Machine"

We once taught a course to an undercover antiterrorism unit responsible for the security and safety of passengers in airports. A special obstacle course required trainees to climb ropes and ladders, jump over and under hurdles, navigate other barriers, and then fight single and multiple attackers. After one pass, we observed that half the trainees had completion times twice as long as the other half of the group.

We decided to give all participants a ten-minute lecture, telling each person to try his best, and not worry about the consequences or his personal safety. We told the trainees to fulfill the mission as if they needed to rescue a loved one, such as a parent or sibling. There was no alternative; no one else could do the job. We next invited the trainees to visualize themselves as iron balls buzzing around a pinball machine. We then asked them to make a "mental video clip" showing a bowling ball rolling powerfully and hitting the pins.

About fifteen minutes later the trainees took a second pass through the course. The result was astonishing—the faster group improved their times by only a few seconds, but almost everyone in the slower group had just about cut their times in half. We had not changed the vehicles (the physical bodies of the trainees), only the drivers (their minds). Their minds became more immune and resistant to stress and fears. The result was the vehicle performed much better.

Most of the physiological changes that occur during stressful situations are caused by the human body's sympathetic nervous and adrenal-cortical systems. The sympathetic nervous system is part of the autonomic nervous system, and it is activated to prepare you to fight or flee. The psychological and physiological reactions you experience in a threatening situation create your "psycho-physiological pattern of reactions." You may find it difficult to differentiate between the psychological and the physiological reactions you experience in a traumatic situation. The intensity of these reactions vary from individual to individual, and from situation to situation. By increasing your knowledge about how and why you react as you do when you are exposed to fear and stress, you increase your chance of performing better. You can be your own worst enemy or your own best friend. The Chinese philosopher and military general Sun Tzu captured this sentiment in 490 BC when he wrote, "So it is said that if you know others and know yourself, you will not be imperiled in a hundred battles; if you do not know others but know yourself, you win one and lose one; if you do not know others and do not know yourself, you will be imperiled in every single battle."

The specific sort of training found in this book can help you understand yourself, how you react to different stressors, and how you should train in order to improve your abilities.

Differing Views on Stress

Most definitions view stress as an imbalance or disturbance that causes physiological and/or behavioral responses. Stress researchers Levine and Ursin consider stress to be a multi-dimensional concept, consisting of stress stimuli, processing systems (including the subjective experience of stress), and stress responses. Other researchers, such as Burton, Weston, and Kowalski, see stress as a psychobiological process, because stress consists of both physical and psychological components and consequences. Stress can be defined as "…any circumstances that threaten or are perceived to threaten one's well-being and that thereby tax one's coping abilities." The activation of the stress reaction is caused by a person's perception of a situation as threatening. It is, therefore, logical to imagine that this perception of a situation is influenced by a person's psychological resources. People with a high degree of psychological resources perceive a situation as less threatening than people who have a low degree of psychological resources. A soldier who believes that he has the resources to get through stressful combat-related situations and complete a mission successfully experiences less stress. Experience at the Norwegian Military Academy demonstrated that while participating in international operations helped stress management on active duty, visualization could also be used to prepare future officers for challenging situations.

Coping with Stress

The scientific literature leaves no doubt that stress and related stress reactions have a definite effect on human health and performance. One study shows that the majority of the British military personnel deployed to the Falklands War in the 1980s used positive thinking as their primary coping strategy. A meditation exercise that emphasizes mindfulness was found to have a documented effect on neurological activation, breathing, and heart rate. Another study demonstrates that an individual's concentration, attention, and ability to tolerate negative emotions increases thanks to mindfulness exercises. In situations like these, you do not stop responding to negative events, but your stress reaction fades faster and you do not ponder inappropriate action strategies.

Instinctive alarmed response against a lethal attack.

Research has not yet determined exactly which mental training strategies enhance a military member's ability to cope with stressful events. Only a limited number of studies have explored the connection between stressors, coping strategies and military performance. However, Milgram, Orenstein, and Zafrirs' study of Israeli soldiers in the Lebanon War is a significant exploration of the impact of stressors and coping strategies on military performance. These studies found that social support as a coping strategy has a positive impact on military performance. In another study, by measuring stress, coping strategies, and military performance before and after deployment to Afghanistan, researchers found that social support is the most important predictor variable of military performance.

A Real-Life Story: Playing Chess under Heavy Shell Fire in the 1973 Yom Kippur War

Roughly a week after the Yom Kippur War started in October 1973, Zvi—who was then a twenty-six-year-old university student—found himself drafted as a reserve soldier in the Signal Corps battalion of an IDF armored division, and stationed with a small team of radio operators on top of the Mitla Pass, a 480-meter-high (about 1600 feet), winding passage in the Sinai Desert.

Due to its strategic significance, the Mitla Pass was the site of major battles between the armies of Egypt and Israel during the wars of 1956, 1967, and 1973, until the two countries finally signed a peace treaty.

As the Yom Kippur War developed and intensified, the small communication base on the mountain became the target of heavy shelling from the already besieged Third Egyptian Army. Several times a day, they launched well-directed 130-millimeter mortar shells at the few Israeli soldiers based there.

During each attack, Zvi and his fellow soldiers rushed to the reinforced trenches that had been dug there beforehand, which provided them with reasonable shelter. During the first of these attacks, a nineteen-year-old cadet, who had joined the battles in Sinai with his platoon from the officers' academy, suggested that Zvi join him for a game of chess, as he had brought along a chess board and all the pieces.

Zvi, who loved playing chess, asked the young cadet how he could concentrate on playing chess while being under lethal shell fire. The cadet reasoned that as long as they did not suffer a direct hit, nothing could happen to them, and if they unfortunately were hit, whether they were playing chess or not at the time wouldn't matter.

From that day until the end of the war, they enjoyed playing "under-fire chess" together, which greatly helped them overcome the natural fear evoked by such a stressful situation.

Indeed, we are better off living in the moment, dealing with what we can control, and avoiding focusing on what is beyond our influence.

Outside the military, much research shows that social support reduces stress and helps people to recover. Social support has been shown to protect people against unexpected stressors and physical illness and has proven to be significant when it comes to recovering from injuries. Social support is regarded in the literature as a so-called "environmental moderator," since the support comes from outside yourself.

A person's mental stamina and hardiness is thus the sum of mental resilience and a good physical capacity along with adaptability, the will to change, flexibility, discipline, empathetic and analytical skills, and conscientiousness. To succeed with this requires a good deal of mastery of different situations. Personal mastery (sometimes also referred to as subjective mastery) can be explained as "what I can do with my skills under certain conditions"—in other words, how you cope with stressful events. To get a glimpse of how good you perceive your psychological skills to be at the moment, we advise you to take a look at the testing tools described in pages 56 and 57 of this book. We have utilized this tool, referred to as mental toughness and psychological skills profile (MTPSP), for many different groups of military officers, police officers, people in the security businesses, firefighters, company leaders and managers, KMG instructors and practitioners, and martial artists with great success. The success is basically because of the tool's ability to deliver a clear graph of eight different psychological skills measuring your mental toughness. When you can see your score on the different psychological skills, it is easier to decide where to start. In a study using the MTPSP, it was found that if military officers scored high on twelve character strengths, they also scored high on several aspects of mental toughness. These results explain why it is important to work on both your psychological skills (mental skills) and your character strengths, as they are connected. Practice one, and you gain the other one, and vice versa.

Leadership Development and Coping with Stress

As a leader in a business organization, you are responsible for many things. Included in this is taking care of the people you lead, and increasing the company's profit. If you are an officer in the military, you have to fulfill the mission and take care of your men and women. How can you make your leadership better? A good way to enhance your leadership skills is to work with your own leadership development, that is, why and how you think and behave as a leader. At the Norwegian Military Academy, a new leadership development concept has been constructed. In order to find out if this new concept is valid, a research and development (R&D) project has been launched. The purpose is to examine what character is, what specific character strengths are particularly relevant for military officers to develop, and if and how character strengths can be developed in cadets. A spin-off of this project is that the same developmental tools can be used by other people as well—that is, business leaders, martial artists, police officers, fire officers, and others facing challenging situations. Previous attempts to identify suitable character and to predict performance in the military and in other high-risk organizations have usually been based on measurements of personality. One challenge with this is that personality is about differences between individuals when it comes to how one reacts to circumstances, while character is about the values that govern individuals' actions and behavior.

The "Character in Military Leaders" project aims to answer both which specific character strengths that are important to develop in leaders, and how these properties can be developed. Several of the mental training techniques from KMG provided in this book have been used for many years at the Norwegian Military Academy in order to develop military leaders with strong character. The outcomes from this show very good results and the techniques will be further incorporated into the character project. We assume that our training methods are equally valuable for people outside the military system, as character is important if you want to achieve any goal. If you do not have any character—that is, you lack persistence, discipline, and stamina—you will find it hard to achieve any goal you might have.

A Real-Life Story: Effect of Stress on the Health of Reserve Soldiers in the 1982 Lebanon War

In early June 1982, Zvi—who was then a newlywed reserve soldier—was drafted along with his Signal Corps battalion to serve as part of their armored division in the Lebanon War that had suddenly broken out.

After three weeks of fighting, a ceasefire was declared, but the brigade was to remain stationed in Lebanon for an undetermined amount of time.

Most of the IDF reserve soldiers felt bored and stressed; they had left behind worried families, jobs, and small businesses that needed their personal attention and care. Besides, the traumatic memory of their five-month-long service during the dramatic Yom Kippur War, barely nine years earlier, was still at the forefront of their minds.

After one month of service in Lebanon, many of the battalion's soldiers started developing all kinds of maladies, each of them different from the other—from a severe cold to gastrointestinal disorders, which the usual available medical treatment could hardly treat.

Zvi, a *bon vivant*, who believed in having a good time in any occasion, had brought a suitcase full of "emergency equipment" consisting of prime edible products, cooking ingredients, spices, and invigorating liquors. His team of radio operators began cooking delicious dishes under his culinary guidance, and they enjoyed hilarious gourmet evenings with food, drinks, singing, and jokes. Surprisingly, most of the soldiers on Zvi's team remained in good health until they were all finally discharged to return to their ordinary civilian lives a few weeks later. This clearly demonstrates the strong link between state of mind and the physical body.

Tools for Measuring Your Mental Toughness

Mental toughness is critical for dealing with stress. We developed a questionnaire—the Krav Maga Global Self-Efficacy, Decision Making, and Stress Management Questionnaire (KSDSQ)—for use by all KMG practitioners. The purpose of this questionnaire is to give the user an indication of his current levels of decision making skills, self-efficacy, and stress management skills. The questionnaire can also be used to measure improvements over time as a result of practicing the KMG system.

The questionnaire consists of seventeen statements. The first five are related to self-efficacy, the next five are related to decision making skills, and the final seven are related to stress management abilities. Each statement starts with, "With reasonable certainty, I can say that I…." A statement then follows.

Table 2-1 (see page 54) gives an overview over the seventeen statements.

Table 2-1. The KMG Self-Efficacy, Decision Making, and Stress Management Questionnaire (KSDSQ).

With reasonable certainty, I can say that I…	Your answer
1. *am a person who can handle practicing KMG.*	
2. *am able to mobilize the energy needed to work hard during my KMG training.*	
3. *am able to handle new challenges in my KMG training.*	
4. *will manage to get a good result in the next level test in KMG.*	
5. *will handle my KMG training session well.*	
6. *will quickly learn new KMG techniques.*	
7. *am confident in my ability to make correct decisions when practicing KMG.*	
8. *am able to make correct decisions when practicing **new** KMG drills.*	
9. *can process new information while practicing KMG.*	
10. *function well while doing different sparring and fighting drills.*	
11. *am able to remain cool under stress when practicing KMG drills of 4 vs. 1.*	
12. *adapt quickly to new stressful and unknown scenarios presented in a KMG session (such as 4 vs. 1, variations on scenarios from curriculum, CQB, public transport, and others).*	
13. *can think straight when I am being stressed in a KMG training and sparring scenario.*	
14. *can calm myself down if I become too stressed during KMG training.*	
15. *can control myself when training gets physically tough.*	
16. *can control myself when my partner hits me, accidently or not, while practicing a basic technique.*	
17. *can control myself when my partner hits me during a sparring session.*	

The scale used in the KSDSQ ranges from 1 (totally disagree) to 100 (totally agree). The higher the score for each of the questions, the better.

Your mission:
Answer the statements for yourself now, even if you are not a KMG practitioner. Just substitute KMG with your own martial art, or your position at work, or your work assignments. For example, you can use **my colleague insults me during a private meeting** instead of **my partner hits me** in question number 16. In question number 17 substitute a **board meeting** for "a sparring session."

Use the scale from 1 (totally disagree) to 100 (totally agree) and put down the number that is most suitable for each statement.

The KSDSQ was given twice to all participants at KMG training camps in Israel in the summer of 2015. The camps were divided according to the ranks of the participants: Practitioner (0.5–3 years of training), Graduate (2.5–6 years of training), and Expert (5–15 years of training). The purpose was to measure whether there were differences in the participant's decision making skills, self-efficacy, and stress management skills before and at the end of a challenging five to ten days of training. We also wanted to measure differences in the level of decision making skills, self-efficacy, and stress management skills dependent on the participants' KMG ranks. We expected that the Experts would show better decision making skills, self-efficacy, and stress management than the Graduates, and that the Graduates would show better decision making skills, self-efficacy, and stress management skills than the Practitioners.

Thus far we analyzed data from the Practitioner, Graduate, and Expert camps. We measured an increase in the participants' perception of their decision making skills and stress management skills. However, their perceived levels of self-efficacy did not improve significantly. The participants may have already possessed a high degree of self-efficacy before the camp. The ability to handle stress and new situations was the skill that increased the most.

The KSDSQ is based on research conducted at three Norwegian military academies. The original self-efficacy scale for use in a military context has been found to have a good internal consistency. For those statistical-oriented people out there, this means that Cronbach's alpha was at .89. *Cronbach's alpha* is a measure of internal consistency, that is, how closely related a set of questions are as a group. It is considered to be a measure of scale reliability and this indicates that the scale measures self-efficacy to a high degree. You can find the original self-efficacy scale in table 2-2.

Your mission:

Remember that this self-efficacy scale was developed for military use, so change military academy student to university student, studies to working, military academy to work or company, or something else, and write down your answer directly after the question.

Table 2-2. The self-efficacy scale.

The questions use a 7-point scale from 1 (totally disagree) to 7 (totally agree). After answering, total your scores.

With reasonable certainty, I can say that I...		Your answer
1.	*am a person who can handle being a military academy student.*	
2.	*am able to mobilize the energy needed to work hard at my studies.*	
3.	*am able to handle difficult moments while studying.*	
4.	*will manage to complete the military academy.*	
5.	*will achieve a result I can be proud of.*	
6.	*will achieve results above average among my peers after completing the military academy.*	
7.	*will receive a service report above average after completing the military academy.*	
	My self-efficacy score	

The highest possible score you can get is forty-nine, and the lowest you can get is seven. If you are not a cadet at a military academy somewhere, this test is not 100% valid. However, no matter where you work or study or what you do, this test can give you an idea of what your general self-efficacy is at the moment. You can take the test later to see if you improve your self-efficacy.

If you want to continue to explore your perceived ability to cope with stress, consider the Mental Toughness Psychological Skills Profile (MTPSP) questionnaire developed by Asken, Grossman, and Christensen. The MTPSP measures eight psychological skills within the area of mental toughness. The MTPSP was originally developed for military and police personnel, but we know it works well for all people training to cope with uncertain and stressful situations.

The MTPSP consists of seven questions for each skill, with a total of fifty-six questions. The eight psychological skills are listed in table 2-3. Search for

MTPSP on the internet and you can quickly find an online version that you may take in order to get some feedback on your mental toughness.

Table 2-3. The eight different psychological skills measured by the MTPSP.

1.	*Confidence describes the degree of belief you have in your ability to respond effectively in any situation.*
2.	*Physical arousal represents how positive your physical and psychological arousal is during a mission.*
3.	*Attention control describes how well you believe you can stay focused during your mission and response.*
4.	*Arousal control reflects the degree to which you can control the effects of the adrenaline rush, so that they do not interfere with your performance during a mission.*
5.	*Imagery use describes the degree to which you can use mental imagery or mental rehearsal to prepare yourself for responding in various aspects of an assignment as a means of preparation for that mission.*
6.	*Commitment refers to your degree of satisfaction and positive involvement with being a leader.*
7.	*Self-talk relates to a specific psychological performance factor that affects how your thinking (manifested in internal monologue) influences your performance during a mission.*
8.	*Physical condition is a brief measure of how well you act to optimize your fitness level.*

We have identified four attributes that make up the belief system of mentally tough performers. The four beliefs are: (1) an unshakable self-belief in achieving goals; (2) an inner arrogance; (3) a belief that you can get over any obstacle; and (4) a belief that your desire will ultimately result in fulfilling your potential. Inner arrogance may sound like an odd quality, but here we see it as a contribution to the belief that success is achievable. People with this inner arrogance can look at their talents and truly know that they have what it takes to achieve at the highest levels. They believe that they can accomplish the things they set their mind on doing. This book can help you become mentally tougher. Understanding the basics of coping theory can help.

Coping Theory

The starting point for the coping theory is based on how humans relate to stress. The theoretical explanations for the source of and ways of dealing with stress can be broadly categorized based on three considerations, respectively a response-based, a stimulus-based, or a transaction-based account.

The basis for coping theory was created by Hans Selye in his book **The Stress of Life** in 1956. As a doctor, Selye was concerned with inflammatory reactions in patients. He stated that the skin reactions he observed apparently had no causal link to the original sufferings of the patient. Thus, he defined stress as being response-based, but his approach was to alleviate the symptoms, i.e., the inflammatory reactions.

During the 1960s, stress was increasingly explored from a more psychological consideration. Stress reactions were now perceived as a result of external change and influence. This gave rise to a stimulus-based approach to stress, where external events were seen as the cause of stress reactions. From Masuda, Holmes, and Rahes's research in 1967, a scale was published to judge whether stressful events were leading to disease. The scale is known as the Holmes and Rahe Stress Scale or the Life Change Index Scale. The higher your life change score, the harder you have to work to get yourself back into a state of good health. You can easily find the test on the internet if you are interested in checking yourself.

During the 1970s, researchers began to assume that we all react virtually identically to stimuli such as high altitude, noise, or a sudden illness. However, toward the end of the 1970s, research revealed that we react differently to the same situation, and that such a normative approach had little relevance.

Aggression and determination in chasing with attacks, while the escapee runs away under elevated stress.

Stress is thus a result of both internal and external events, leading us forward to the transaction-based approach. The most influential scientist of this approach was L.R. Lazarus, whose classic definition of coping reads as follows: "Constantly changing cognitive and behavioral efforts to manage specific external and or internal demand, that are appraised as taxing or exceeding the resources of the person." Coping is considered an individual process-oriented phenomenon, and not a result of a particular stimulus and/or response. This also distinguishes coping from other behavior that has been learned or automatically adopted.

Coping may involve efforts to minimize, avoid, tolerate, change, or accept the stressful situation, while at the same time trying to master or handle your surroundings. As the theory stands today, coping is conceptualized as an attempt to change the perception of the source of stress (threat), or handle the stress emotions. This approach is known as either emotion-based coping or problem-focused coping. The Norwegian Special Forces soldier and mental coach Tommy Fjeldheim notes that it is not enough to think positively, but we also have to think constructively, i.e., we need to be constantly looking for possible solutions to those challenges. Only then can we definitely have a better chance of succeeding.

Another way to describe this approach is that of a "**stress mindset**," one that sees stress as an enhancement factor. You consider challenges as solvable problems, not threats. Fjeldheim reported that a "**stress-is-enhancing mindset**" was associated with moderate cortisol reactivity (that is, less stress hormones in the blood stream) and a high desire for feedback under stress. Crum, Salovey, and Achor concluded that the stress mindset is a distinct and meaningful variable when it comes to determining people's stress response. This book seeks to instill a stress-is-enhancing mindset, which we refer to as a combat mindset.

The following real-life story describes the mindset needed to process a lot of information and function as a leader.

A Real-Life Story: A Young Commander and Leader

The Israel Defense Forces (IDF) provides amazing opportunities for young people. Eyal Yanilov's initial service, after the first infantry training and boot camp, was in the field of communication. He was first assigned to a course to be a radio operator. The course commanders in the IDF's school of communication assessed him as a talented operator so they decided to keep him as an instructor in that school. Eyal joined a month-long instructor's course and then started to teach his first platoon. As a high-school graduate with majors in physics and mathematics, as well as a rather experienced Krav Maga instructor (since the age of sixteen, Eyal taught and ran groups of teenagers and adults), this was really a piece of cake. In the middle of the course they pulled Eyal out for a higher course for NCO (non-commissioned officer) radio operators. After that course, he stayed in the department to teach the next courses. The experienced instructors there were soon to finish their service, so he found himself, at the age of nineteen-plus, commanding and responsible for high-level courses, with soldiers that had higher ranks than his and missions that were very demanding.

The highlight of Eyal's two-month course was field drills in communication, simulating a war type of situation where you need to establish radio and telephone line communication among several small units. This exercise required two to three days and nights of planning with close to zero time to sleep; drawing tons of equipment from the storage facilities and warehouses of the school, including ten to fifteen vehicles of different kinds, together with their drivers; and basic food supply for couple of days. Eyal was to activate and monitor the fifteen to twenty trainee-commanders that were taking the course, as well as about thirty to fifty additional young soldiers who also took part in the drill.

This challenging experience provided Eyal with the opportunity to exercise high responsibility as a young sergeant.

CONCLUSION

Stress is an inevitable part of life and people handle it differently. Stress and stress reactions have a clear effect on your mind, body, health, and performance, and controlling your stress level leads to enhanced performance. Learning to identify and cope with difficult and challenging situations is vital in most walks of life. Using the tools provided in this chapter can help in giving you a clear picture of your mental toughness, self-efficacy, decision making skills, and your level of stress management, thus contributing to your ability to understand and handle stress.

Chapter 3

How Stress Affects Your Performance

As we discussed in chapter 2, stress occurs from either social, mental, or physical stressors, or a combination of these. Stress is an activation of the autonomous nervous system, part of the sympathetic nervous system. Stress is a reaction to something that happens around or in you; your brain and your body then mobilize to cope with the situation. The techniques in this book develop self-control in order to experience less stress, i.e., your stress reaction is smaller than it would be without training.

A Real-Life Story: A Close Protection Assignment

Ole Boe was once assigned as a bodyguard (close protection specialist) to a high-ranking military officer, to whom we refer here as "the VIP." The VIP's mission was to attend a meeting with a local warlord, and to negotiate safe passage through his territory. The VIP was accompanied by an assistant, which was not a routine occurrence. The close protection team drove the VIP and assistant to the warlord's location, established a secure perimeter, entered his house, and prepared for the meeting on the second floor of the building.

An hour later, Ole heard a gunshot and screams from somewhere below the second floor. The warlord and his goons started to freak out. Ole could tell that they wanted to draw their weapons. Ole grabbed the VIP and retreated into a corner, shielding him with his body. Ole used breathing techniques and self-talk to maintain control, and mitigated the VIP's stress by telling him what to do. The rest of the team inside the house took up new positions and did what they were trained to do. Ole could hear them giving one another orders and information about what happened.

Suddenly Ole saw the VIP's assistant standing right in the middle of the big room, with eyes like big balloons. He looked at Ole, who could tell that the assistant was not really seeing him. Clearly the assistant was having a severe stress reaction; the gunshot and screaming had temporarily paralyzed him.

Ole had planned to have a close protection team member take responsibility for the assistant, but at this moment the team had enough to struggle with—trying to secure an escape route from the house while controlling the warlord and his goons. Half of the inside team was working their way down the stairs and the other half was around the VIP, securing him and controlling the warlord. The assistant just stood there, not hearing commands to "clear" and "move."

Ole dragged the VIP toward the assistant and slapped his face, saying, "Move toward the stairs and get out." As if the assistant's brain had been reactivated, he started to move in the right direction. Ole's focus returned to the VIP. They arrived at the stairs, and one of the team members took care of the assistant while Ole concentrated on getting the VIP safely out of the house. They managed to escape without further incidents. However, the team refused to bring the assistant with them to future meetings.

Perception

Stress results from the gap between the demands set upon an individual and his or her ability to meet those demands. This definition contains a psychological element, the cognitive process, meaning your thinking process. In stressful situations, an individual's cognitive interpretation is more important in assessing the threats' intensity than the objective situation. In other words, it is how you perceive the threat that matters, and not the threat itself. Your perception is, of course, a result of your previous experiences, knowledge, and training, and how you managed previous challenges and situations.

Imagine entering a room and seeing a gun on a table. By itself, the gun is not dangerous. Rather, your perception is the factor that affects your decision making process. If you feel that the situation demands more than you can handle, you experience stress. If you feel that you are able to meet the demands of the situation, you do not experience stress. It is likely that you would react to the gun-on-the-table scenario according to your occupation. If you are a police or military officer, your perception would probably be less intense than others. In movies, "bad guys" tend to put guns on tables during a confrontation in order to intimidate their opponents.

Imagine walking into your boss's office to discuss your latest project. Things get a bit heated, and suddenly your boss pulls a gun from the drawer in his desk and puts it down hard on the table, staring at you. What would you think and feel at this moment?

Imagine a less extreme scenario. Instead of pulling out a gun, he clenches his fists, rises from the chair, and stares at you. Or, your boss picks up some papers and points and shouts at you. You can see that his hand holding the papers is shaking and you sense that he is not in control of himself. For most people, situations like this are very uncomfortable; they have not been trained to cope with other people's aggression, and humans have what Grossman refers to as "a universal phobia toward violence." So, how do you handle the stress that starts building inside you?

Three Types of Decision Making Situations

It is generally possible to distinguish between three types of decision making situations:

Decision making without time pressure regarding body movement, balance, mobility, and power.

1. **Decision making without time pressure and with a low level of stress.** In this situation, you use the frontal lobes of your brain. You are able to think rationally. You have time to think through the consequences of your

choices. One example is the period before you buy a new car, when you ponder alternatives in a leisurely manner.

2. **Decision making with time pressure and a high level of stress.** In this type of situation, you experience a phenomenon called the fear response and you unconsciously start using a part of the brain known as the amygdala in order to make a quick decision to either fight, if it becomes necessary, or flee. The amygdala is a part of your brain involved with emotions and aggression. An example is seeing someone approach you while threatening you with a knife in his hand.

3. **Decision making with time pressure and an extremely high level of stress.** This scenario is similar to the previous one, except the opponent has a handgun and he is actually shooting at you. It simply becomes too much for your brain to handle. You may experience a phenomenon referred to as the survival stress reaction. You freeze and do not react. Your ability to make a decision depends on the strength of this reaction. Your heart rate is an indicator of the effect of this phenomenon.

Imagine you are walking home after a good physical training session. You are simultaneously tired and less observant than normal, but you also feel stimulated thanks to the endorphins released during training. It is dark, and you find yourself on a poorly lit street. You know that you shouldn't take this route, but it is shorter than the alternatives.

You do not notice three guys leaning against a wall a bit farther ahead until they spread out in front of you. How do you react? Do you notice their movement? Do you freeze, run, feel fear, or have time to think about whether you should try to defend yourself if necessary?

A Real-Life Story: Shooting a Farmer with an AK-47

During the beginning of a long military training course in close protection, Ole Boe's team was conducting walking drills with a VIP. The objective was to protect the VIP and respond correctly to whatever happened. After several hours, Ole felt exhausted.

At one point, Ole was walking as the last man in the formation. The team had just passed one of the instructors when he started to shout at them and point to a barrel beside a house. He moved toward the barrel and picked up an AK-47, a Russian assault rifle. Ole immediately felt threatened and shot him twice in the chest using his firearm with plastic bullets.

The instructor stopped the scenario and gave Ole hell for shooting him. The instructor had picked up the gun from the barrel with one arm, clearly holding it by the muzzle and as far away from his body as possible. The gun was hanging from his hand, so it shouldn't have been seen as a threat just then.

The instructor was just playing an innocent farmer who wanted to show them what he had found. He was no threat. Ole felt like an idiot for "shooting" the "farmer," but he learned a lot about dealing with stressful situations.

Life is not always as stressful as the scenario described earlier. It was Ole Boe's perception that made it stressful, and the perception was clearly wrong.

Exercise- and Hormone-Induced Activation of the Nervous System

Your maximum heart rate is approximately 220 beats per minute (BPM) minus your age. However, this is only true if you exercise hard, or run as fast as you are capable. The strain and stress you then expose yourself to is called **exercise-induced activation (EIA)** of the nervous system. In contrast, **hormone-induced activation (HIA)** of the nervous system is the stress experienced when you are being shot at, or when somebody screams at you, or when someone runs toward you with a knife. HIA can raise your heart rate in the blink of an eye.

Your heart rate increases as a response to a potentially violent situation, and the more threatening you perceive the situation to be, the higher your heart rate and the more hormones released in your body. If you want to function as effectively as possible during a stressful situation, it is not enough just to develop endurance or physical ability. It is also necessary to practice with hormonal stress or fear response, as this is the main type of stress reaction that you experience in a fight or even in a nonviolent, verbal confrontation.

Stress-Induced Behavior (FFF): Fight–Flight–Freeze

Sensory data—what you see, feel, hear, taste, or smell—is transferred to a part of the brain called the thalamus. The thalamus then relays sensory and motor signals to another part of the brain called the cerebral cortex. When stressed, sensory data goes to the amygdala, a part of your brain that has a primary role when it comes to your memory, decision making, and emotional reactions. The amygdala, or more correctly, the two amygdalae, are considered to be a part of your limbic system, also known as your "primitive brain." It determines whether what you see, feel, hear or smell is dangerous. In other words, the amygdala does a quick threat assessment and if it finds that the sensory data shows danger, it blocks your regular, logical, and "slow" thinking process done in the cortex. Figure 3-1 gives a graphic overview of how the brain processes information during stressful situations.

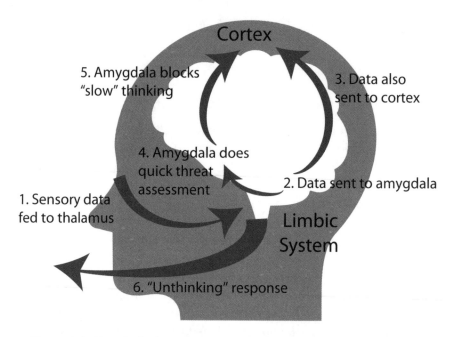

Figure 3-1. How the brain processes information during stressful situations.

The brain is a complex system. Stress is one of the factors that influences where the brain stores information. In stressful situations, the brain calls on its more primitive regions, such as the amygdala. This is the area available to the brain when the body is being threatened. In less stressful situations, the brain interacts with its higher or more logical regions, such as the frontal lobe. The higher regions are available when the body is more peaceful, allowing time for reflection and deeper thinking.

Cadets in line to jump from a plane. Their thoughts are racing and their heart rates are skyrocketing.

The cadet in front jumps first. Typically at this moment, stress levels are highest.

The moment just after jumping.

Between heaven and earth, the cadet is checking his parachute. Is it functioning? Has it deployed properly?

A fraction of a second before touchdown.

Finally, collecting the parachute.

The consequences of this process are profound. If you train effectively under stressful conditions, your brain learns how to cope with danger. It stores pertinent information in its primitive regions, rather than in its logical regions. When confronted by a real-life threat, your brain automatically reaches into those primitive regions and finds ways to efficiently manage the danger. However, if you train under more pleasant circumstances, your brain stores those experiences in its **more developed** regions. When confronted by danger, your brain still reaches into its primitive areas, but it finds very little data there. The brain is not capable of searching the frontal lobes due to the body's stress reactions. Thus, you are likely to "freeze," or otherwise fail to come up with a relevant solution based on previous memory and experience, because there is none to be found by your pleasantly-trained brain that now has little idea how to respond.

The Fear Response

Very often stress is accompanied by negative undesirable consequences. These frequently appear in four main elements: 1) the cognitive element, what you are thinking about; 2) the somatic element, what happens in your body; 3) the emotional element, what you feel; and 4) the behavioral element, what you do or do not do, otherwise known as the fight-or-flight response. As you can see, two elements are mental and two are physical.

Table 3-1 gives a short overview of the four reactions in your brain and body. These consequences may be negative and undesirable; as a result, they can affect you and may lead to a decrease in performance, a decrease in decision making skills, morale, commitment, safety, and your ability to cope with the situation you find yourself in. This process of perceiving a situation as negative is known as the **fear response** and can be described as consisting of four elements.

Table 3-1. The fear response. What happens in your brain and body during a confrontation.

1.	Cognitive elements: what you are thinking
2.	Somatic elements: what happens in your body
3.	Emotional elements: what you feel
4.	Behavioral elements: what you do

When we experience danger, the different processes that take place in the brain are called the fear response. The purpose of the fear response is to give you the option to flee or fight. The whole fear response, from the moment you perceive a danger until you do something, normally takes 0.7–1.5 seconds, assuming you are aware and have trained to deal with threats. If you are not sufficiently trained or aware, or if you are not able to recognize the threat, the fear response can take up to 4–5 seconds.

The primitive parts of your brain, especially the amygdala, have a simple mission: determine if what you see or sense is dangerous. The brain searches for similar previous experiences. If you have never been in such a situation, the brain looks for experiences as similar as possible. If you have been exposed to many stressful situations, the whole fear response process may take 0.25 seconds or even less. If you have never experienced something like what you are facing, you might become paralyzed.

The intensity you feel is dependent on the situation. If you are being verbally threatened by a colleague, the intensity might be lower during the fear response than, for instance, if the same colleague suddenly starts pushing you, or attacking you with a baseball bat, or shooting at you with a handgun. The level of intensity is also related to your heart rate. The higher your heart rate becomes under stress, the more intense the fear response is perceived. This is a phenomenon known as the **survival stress reaction**. Your response to a threatening situation or confrontation is known as the **fight-or-flight response**. Recently, the fight-or-flight response has been extended to include five more responses: freeze, submit, posture, choke, and the death grip. In some situations, you might do nothing because of information overload, and you might freeze.

Cognitive Elements

The cognitive elements of fear consist of your expectations of an impending or imminent danger. A cognitive process simply means that you try to perceive, process, store, or retrieve information. The formation of sensory impressions and ideas is part of a cognitive process. When three people suddenly stand in your way, you create a picture of the situation. The signals from your sensory organs, the eyes, and possibly the ears, if you hear any sounds, reach the amygdala. The amygdala quickly examines the data to discover anything that can be perceived as dangerous and threatening. Certain parts of your memory systems are activated to retrieve the most relevant memories and knowledge concerning the current situation.

If you have no previous similar experiences, your brain may not perceive the situation as dangerous. If the brain recognizes the situation as something to fear, the amygdala reacts with lightning speed by sending alarm signals to all the other parts of the brain. The brain then sends signals to release about thirty different stress hormones to prepare the body for the imminent danger.

Another part of the brain, known as the gray matter, consists of nerve cells that control the muscles. Under stress, these nerve cells are commanded to start to release adrenaline and other hormones to make your muscles tighten. Even the muscles of your vocal cords tighten, leading to your voice becoming higher and thinner when you are afraid. The hormone noradrenaline rushes through your brain, increasing your propensity to react and resulting in a sharpening of your senses. Very often, you are not aware of being afraid, because most of these changes take place at a subconscious level. Your brain also releases dopamine, fixing your attention on what caused you to become afraid. The amygdala also sends signals to the visual processing area in the back of your brain, causing your eyes to focus on the most relevant thing in the present situation. When these signals have been sent away from your brain, fear starts to take hold.

Somatic Elements

The reactions and changes that occur in your body are referred to as the somatic elements of the fear response. They can be divided into two groups: external and internal changes. Table 3-2 gives a short overview of external changes that may occur during a stressful situation.

Table 3-2. External changes in a fear-induced stressful situation.

Your forehead sweats and wrinkles.
Your eyebrows are pulled upward and toward each other.
Your lips start to shake.
Your lips also tighten and start to withdraw, revealing your teeth.
Your facial muscles start to tighten.
Your eyes widen and the pupils dilate.
Your skin becomes pale.
Your mouth begins to open.
The palms of your hands become moist.

If you are able to stay calm, you may be able to see these changes in another person. Changes can also occur in the skin—it may become pale, as the blood is drawn away from the face toward internal organs in order to protect them. These facial changes can increase other reactions of fear in the body.

In addition to these external changes, several changes occur within the body. Table 3-3 presents some of the different internal changes that can take place in your body when you experience fear.

Table 3-3. Internal changes in a fear-induced stressful situation.

Your blood sugar level increases.
You develop tunnel vision.
Your bone marrow produces more white blood cells.
Production of saliva and mucus decreases.
Your digestion decreases.
The airways to your lungs expand.
The air volume increases when you breathe in.
Larger amounts of carbon dioxide are removed when you exhale.
The release of endorphins leads to a higher tolerance of pain.
Your blood clots more quickly and easily.
Your spleen produces more red blood cells.

When you perceive a potential threat, the resources of your body are quickly mobilized. Your brain sends signals to release the hormone adrenaline into the bloodstream. The adrenaline flows through your body and reaches the heart, lungs, and muscles. The different parts of the body then start creating the changes necessary to react to the perceived threat. Your muscles need more oxygen to either fight or flee. A result of this is that your muscles tighten. Your breathing becomes faster and deeper to be able to receive the extra oxygen needed for action. Your blood vessels dilate to carry more blood around faster. Your heart then beats faster because it wants to pump the blood through your body. In those areas of the body where oxygen is not needed, the blood vessels restrict themselves. Tissue inflammation decreases, and digestion and the production of saliva and mucus also decrease.

Training of Norwegian Special Forces.
Courtesy of Torbjørn Kjosvold, the Norwegian Armed Forces.

The extra resources make it possible for you to throw yourself away from an oncoming car, or start defending yourself, either by running away or by fighting your adversary. When you perform an action that is appropriate to the situation, you use and exploit the chemical changes that your body has produced to deal with it. When the danger is over, your body then tries to return to a normal state, a phenomenon known as homeostasis.

When a **fear response** starts but there is no need to fight or flight—like during a verbal confrontation in a corporate boardroom where there is no need for physical actions—your body does not use the chemical changes and substances released into it. You are usually in a sitting position, at work, home, or school when the effects of stress hit you. The results are highly hazardous to the mental and physical health of those who are not trained to neutralize stress.

Emotional Elements

In addition to bodily changes, fear is also closely related to strong emotional elements: fear, feelings of sickness, fits of shivering, creeping sensations in the body, and the feeling of having a lump in the stomach. These sensations are usually the first signs of fear, and they follow the cognitive and somatic changes that have already taken place in your body and brain. Table 3-4 shows how World War II combat pilots experienced different symptoms of fear, offering insight into how the emotional elements manifest during stress.

Table 3-4. Symptoms of fear during combat flying (in %).

During combat missions, did you feel...?	Sometimes	Often	Total
A pounding heart and rapid pulse	*56*	*30*	*86*
That your muscles were very tense	*53*	*30*	*83*
Easily irritated or angry	*58*	*22*	*80*
Dryness of the throat or mouth	*50*	*30*	*80*
Nervous perspiration or cold sweat	*53*	*26*	*79*
"Butterflies in the stomach"	*53*	*23*	*76*
A sense of unreality	*49*	*20*	*69*
A need to urinate very frequently	*40*	*25*	*65*
Trembling	*53*	*11*	*64*
Confused or rattled	*50*	*3*	*53*
Weak or faint	*37*	*4*	*41*
That right after a mission you were unable to remember details of what happened	*34*	*5*	*39*
Sick to the stomach	*33*	*5*	*38*
Unable to concentrate	*32*	*3*	*35*
That you had wet or soiled your pants	*4*	*1*	*5*

It is highly probable that these symptoms of fear are higher for people involved in close combat than for combat pilots. The feeling of unreality can sometimes result in what is called an **"out-of-body-experience."** You may perceive yourself standing outside your body, watching yourself being shot.

Behavioral Elements

Finally, we have the opportunity to either run away from the threatening situation, or stay and defend ourselves. These patterns of behavior are known as the fight-or-flight response to a perceived threat. The whole sequence, from the moment you became surprised when you see the three guys standing in front of you, to your feeling of uncertainty, further to worry, and finally to the feelings of fear and the mobilization of the resources in your body to fight or flee, can take as little as 0.15–0.20 seconds. Of course, obtaining a quick reaction time like this is dependent on the premise that you have pre-planned a response to the threat. Eventually we have to do something about the situation that we find ourselves in. This means that we have to act even though we are filled with fear. The last element of the fear response is the behavior that we display after the cognitive, somatic, and emotional components have taken place. We can divide this behavior into two parts: classical conditioned responses and instrumental responses. Classical conditioned responses are involuntary reactions to the situation. An example of this is the **startle reflex**, meaning that you blink and pull your head away from a punch. Instrumental responses are voluntary attempts to improve the situation, like blocking a punch or running away. These basic reflexive reactions have to be trained in order to be more functional and efficient. It is the instrumental responses you work with when training in close combat, or when you train to change a firearm's magazine during a conflict.

Re-examining the Fight-or-Flight Response

The fight-or-flight response has seven possible outcomes: fight, flight, freeze, submit, posture, choke, and the death grip.

Fight response here refers not only to physical fighting but also to standing your ground and confronting your opponents verbally. For soldiers, this physical response behavior is one of their most important goals. Soldiers drill fighting responses to stay mentally alert and to increase the likelihood that they can fight when necessary. A high degree of mental alertness results in automatic fighting, while a low degree of mental preparation and alertness leads to paralysis or escape reactions. If your level of training and alertness before you enter a threatening situation is too low, and the situation suddenly escalates too fast, it is possible that you can freeze.

Flight responses can be divided into two types: Either you run away or you avoid the situation. Eighty percent of all human beings are biologically preprogrammed to run away from a confrontation. Unfortunately, there are many situations where you do not have the opportunity to walk or run away. You may have someone with you whom you do not want to leave. One of your team members may be injured, or you may be with someone you cannot leave—your wife, husband, child, sibling, elderly parent, colleague, friend, etc.—who is unable to move at the desired speed.

The other type of flight response is called avoidance response behavior. To succeed with this option, you must have knowledge about types of problems and dangers, and ensure that you have enough time to avoid these situations

The defender stops the aggressor at a distance.

before something negative happens. Proactive skills are key. For example, in a restaurant, do you sit with your back against the wall where you can see most of the restaurant, especially entrances and escape routes? Again, this is a mental skill, and you can develop these skills by learning from others and training with others, as well as through visualization or self-talk.

Also consider practicing "what-if thinking." What if someone suddenly entered the restaurant holding a knife or a gun; what would you do? What if the three men at the next table start staring hard at you; what would you do? Think through as many possible scenarios as you can, and find solutions. Some may find this type of thinking a bit paranoid, but we prefer to call it **"healthy paranoia."**

Freeze response means your brain and body suddenly cannot cope. You often hesitate before you make a decision, especially if your level of alertness is too low. During extreme stress—for instance, when someone is firing at you, or you are attacked by someone with a knife, or just when someone such as an aggressive boss is yelling at you—your brain does not function rationally. Results from catastrophes, such as earthquakes, reveal that 70% of people do not do anything immediately after the earthquake. A total of 15% of people act irrationally and do things that do not help them or other people; for example, these people start to pick up rocks or flowers. The last 15% act rationally and do something that is meaningful in the situation; they try to help.

The defender is frozen, unable to act in the face of danger.

Which behavioral pattern you will reveal in a life-threatening situation is really difficult to predict. If you practice mentally and physically to handle threatening situations, your chances of overcoming, winning, or just escaping alive significantly increase. Results from surveys of Israeli soldiers show that the degree of perceived control under stressful conditions increases after a period of training where the soldiers have experienced the same or similar situations. You can "vaccinate" yourself so that you can tolerate more stressful situations.

When you **submit**, you surrender in hope that your opponent will not begin to hit you, or that he will stop attacking or hurting you if he already started. Submitting behavior includes turning your back to an opponent, lowering your head, shrinking your whole body, going to the ground, or bending down or away from an opponent. You think that if you do nothing to hurt or annoy your attacker, the attacker will stop. Unfortunately, you do not know what is going on inside the aggressor's mind. He might think that it is even easier to attack you when you do these things. Some people are actually triggered by submissive behavior—that is, their predatory behavior is triggered.

Two men **posture**, standing very close to each other, exposing their throats and genitals, making their chests bigger, both trying to convince the other one that he is dominant. Add some shouting and gestures into this situation, and you have a better picture of what is called posturing. Posturing sends a signal to the other person that you are not afraid of him, and that you are so very confident of yourself that you can stay very close to him even with your most tender areas exposed.

The defender (on the left) orders or threatens the aggressor while in the appropriate posture after initial warning contact has been made.

Do not engage in this type of behavior. If you meet someone who is a good fighter, you will be exposing the vulnerable parts of your body in very close proximity. Some people use this type of behavior to trigger you to fight. If you feel that the only correct response is to fight, then fight; otherwise, keep your distance or leave. You can also grab a bottle, break it, and start jumping around and shouting like a crazy ape. Most people do not wish to fight with a crazy animal, so this response might work. However, are you faking craziness in order to avoid the physical confrontation, while still being willing to fight—which is the way it should be—or is your posturing a bluff?

Your posture response may only be a pretense. It might look like a fighting pose, with your hands up and in front of you. A closer look might reveal that you weight is backward instead of forward, a stance that may reveal your true intentions to your opponent. You may also make the mistake of saying, "If you take one step forward, I will hit you." A more confident (or stupid) opponent may take one step forward. If you step backward, your opponent knows you are just bluffing. You are not in control of this situation, and you may trigger the opponent's predatory behavior.

The **choke response** is a feeling that you are not able to swallow or breathe. The brain cannot deal with the simultaneous internal and external changes. This reaction is similar to the freeze response. The brain interprets muscle tension in the neck area as breathing difficulty.

The **death grip** response involves holding an object very tightly, such as a doorknob or someone's arm or jacket. A police officer may have to break a person's fingers, or knock him unconscious, in order to loosen that grip, which is a result of a strong fear response. When stressed, you become "more primitive" and some people react in this way. The problem is that if you are going to save a person from a burning house, or from drowning, or from an attacker, or start to fight to protect yourself, you may have to loosen his grip first.

The Survival Stress Reaction

The **survival stress reaction** (SSR) describes a condition where a perceived threat stimulus automatically activates the sympathetic nervous system. The sympathetic nervous system is part of the autonomic nervous system, and the changes occur without your being aware of them. The SSR was discovered in the 1930s. Two examples from combat situations demonstrate the SSR in action. Soldiers sending Morse code performed much better in the classroom than in combat. When stressed, the Morse operators' fine motor skills deteriorated, resulting in mistakes and difficulty interpreting signals. Fighter pilots in the Vietnam War suffered similar problems when their heart rates rose; tunnel vision made it difficult to read their instruments.

People who find themselves in a fighting or self-defense situation suffer from SSR, and they lose the ability to function as their heart rate increases. Table 3-5 gives an overview of hormone-induced heart rate increase and related physical and mental processes that take place when the heart rate goes up due to stress or fear.

Table 3-5. Hormone-induced heart rate increase and related physical and mental processes.

Heart rate	Effects of hormone-induced heart rate increase
60–80	*Normal resting heart rate*
115	*Fine motor skills start to break down*
115–145	*Zone of optimal survival and combat performance for:* *Complex motor skills* *Visual reaction time* *Cognitive reaction time*
165	*Complex motor skills start to break down*
175	*Thinking processes start to break down* *Loss of peripheral vision (tunnel vision)* *Loss of depth perception* *Loss of near vision* *Auditory exclusion (tunnel hearing)*
175–220	*Critical incident amnesia* *Visual tracking becomes difficult* *Irrational fighting or fleeing* *Freezing* *Submissive behavior* *Vasoconstriction (reduced bleeding from wounds)* *Voiding of bladder and bowels* *Gross motor skill (running, charging etc.) at highest performance level* *Hypervigilance (impulsive and disorganized), leads to hyperventilation.*

The zone of optimal survival and performance is 115–145 BPM. In this zone, complex motor skills, visual reaction time, and cognitive reaction are at their best. Your cognitive reaction deals with the ability to perceive a potential threat and to make a decision about what to do. Your hand-eye coordination is also at its best in this zone. You are able to see what is going on and make quick and correct decisions. The goal of training both physically and mentally is to increase the zone in which you perform well.

Studies have shown that humans can perform well up to 179 BPM, meaning that the zone of optimal survival and performance may be expanded from

115–145 to 115–179. However, increasing your range of performance to this level takes a lot of training. In order to work well, activities should not be too complicated or complex. This process of increasing your range of performance is often referred to as "**pushing the envelope**." To push the envelope is used figuratively to mean "**to stretch the boundaries**."

As your brain and body become more stressed, they try to make your life simpler. When you reach 145 BPM, unless you are very well trained, your body starts to behave symmetrically. If you put your left hand out in front of you to stop someone from reaching you, chances are high that your right hand does the same. You push with both hands, or you pull with both hands.

This is considered to be one explanation for why police officers sometimes shoot without the intention to do so. In a fight with a criminal, the police officer draws his weapon. If he has the trigger finger inside the weapon, changes are high that if the police officer grabs the criminal with one hand, a shot is fired, as the fingers of the other hand also clenched. This problem can be avoided by following the simple rule of holding your finger outside the trigger until you are ready to shoot. Unfortunately, people sometimes break this simple rule.

At 175 BPM, your thinking degrades. Your ability to process information and to make decisions starts to suffer, unless you are a very well-trained person. When your hormone-induced heart rate increases due to the stress response to 175 BPM or more, it is difficult to remember what happened in a stressful situation. Soldiers and police officers often have difficulty counting the number of shots fired during a stressful situation. Of course, there are techniques for coping with this—tactical reloads, using transparent plastic magazines so that it becomes easier to see how many rounds are left in the magazine, or different ways of counting the rounds you have fired, and so on. As time goes by, professionals get better and better at remembering the number of shots fired, what happened, and so on. At 175 BPM, it is difficult for you to correctly recall how long things took or the sequence of events in a stressful situation. The same goes for those who suddenly have to fight for their life. Trying to remember the number of hits and punches exchanged in a fight is quite hard. After a critical incident where you have to fight for your life, it is not unusual that you only correctly remember 30% of the incident during the first twenty-four hours. After forty-eight hours, you remember about 50%, and after seventy-two to one hundred hours, you remember about 75–95% of the incident. Afterward, your memory gradually degrades.

When, due to the stress response, your heart rate is 185–220 BPM, your brain more or less shuts down. Tunnel vision is extreme, about 2–3% of normal field of vision, because of lack of oxygen to the eyes. Fine motor skills disappear. One study showed that police officers tended to use the simplest baton techniques under stress, even if they had practiced more complex techniques. Under extreme stress you fail to remember how to respond correctly.

To address these conditions, KMG basic self-defense techniques consist of only two to three actions. These basic techniques are founded on natural responses, meaning the beginning of the technique is identical to the beginning of your natural reaction under stress, and the whole technique itself is very similar to that response. As a result, your brain retains the ability to remember these actions under stress. When training, KMG instructors gradually increase the stress level, making the scenarios more complex and difficult for their trainees.

When you reach a heart rate of about 175 BPM, suddenly it also becomes difficult to see two or more attackers. It even becomes difficult for you to use your vision to follow a moving person. The pupils start losing their ability to focus at this heart rate. The decreased supply of oxygen to the eyes leads to tunnel vision. Focus is directed toward the most relevant cues, i.e., a person's hand that is holding a weapon. This is described in the cue-utilization theory. You see (and hear) the criminal in front of you, screaming that he is going to rob you, but you do not see his criminal friend approaching from your right side with a baseball bat. This perceptual narrowing is a result of fixation on a specific aspect of the situation, such as the criminal in front of you. This fixation may also be "burned" into your memory, and it is very easy for you to describe details, such as the face of or objects held by a person attracting your attention, but your memory of other aspects of the situation is not accessible.

At somewhere around 185–220 BPM, you find yourself in a condition known as **hypervigilance**. You act in inefficient ways. You may continue to pull the trigger of an empty gun, or push at a door that only opens toward you, or you may simply freeze. Hypervigilance is sometimes also referred to as the "brain fart" mode. Your brain simply does not work anymore, and as a result of this nothing happens.

Another way to consider the effect of heart rate on the mind and body is shown in Table 3-6. Here the point is to think of the different heart rate zones as connected to different colors.

Table 3-6. Levels of alertness and related hormone-induced heart rates.

Condition	Heart rate (BPM)
White	Around 70
Yellow	Up to 115
Red	115–145
Gray	145–175
Black	175–220

In a completely neutral situation, you operate near your resting heart rate, in condition white. If you perceive that you may be confronted by a threat, you can mentally imagine yourself in condition yellow. When a threat materializes, you know that your optimum response to danger occurs in condition red. As the intensity increases, you understand that your ability to handle challenges degrades as you escalate from condition gray to condition black. The trick here is to think of yourself as being in one condition, for instance condition yellow, and then quickly change to condition red when needed.

Stress Effects Summarized

Figure 3-2 summarizes the effects of stress on the body. Seven systems are affected. Following the figure you will find some short explanations according to the numbers you see in Figure 3-2. Under stress, your nervous system switches to using the sympathetic nervous system so that you can face the threat that you experience. Under stress, you lose your ability to perform complex or fine motor skills, and you are only able to perform simple gross motor skills. You may suffer from what is known as **attentional rubbernecking**. This means that your attention is drawn to stimuli that have a strong emotional aspect. A lot of changes also take place in the nervous system, as well as in the respiratory, musculoskeletal, cardiovascular, endocrine, gastrointestinal, and reproductive systems.

Figure 3-2. How key body systems react to stress.

1. Nervous system
If you are being stressed by a social, physical, or a mental stressor, your body redirects its energy resources toward fighting the perceived threat. The fight-or-flight response kicks in and the sympathetic nervous system sends signals to the adrenal glands, so that adrenaline and cortisol can be released into the blood stream. Adrenaline and cortisol make your heart beat faster, and your blood pressure rises. In addition, the digestive process is affected and the glucose levels in your bloodstream increase. At this instant you do not have the time to eat a banana, for example, but if you did, this would increase your glucose levels, too. When the situation is not dangerous anymore, the systems in your body gradually return to their normal state.

2. Musculoskeletal system

Your muscles start to tense up and contract under stress. If this tension goes on for a long period of time, the result may be chronic conditions in your musculoskeletal system. Examples of these conditions are tight muscles or the feeling of cramped muscles, as well as tension headaches and migraines.

3. Respiratory system

Under stress, you breathe rapidly and more shallowly. This may lead to hyperventilation and can cause panic attacks in some people. Hyperventilation may occur if the rate and quantity of ventilation of carbon dioxide exceeds the amount your body produces. Ventilation is synonymous with breathing and just means the air you breathe in and out.

4. Cardiovascular system

Sudden or acute stress leads to contracted muscles and an increased heart rate. This means that the blood vessels that direct your blood to the heart and to the large muscles in your body are contracted. As a result, the amount of blood that is pumped into and away from the heart and the large muscles increases. If this is repeated over time, you may suffer from an inflammation in the coronary arteries. The end result may be a heart attack.

5. Endocrine system

The endocrine system consists of glands that release hormones into your circulatory system. The purpose is for these hormones to be carried toward other organs in your body. Your stressed brain sends signals to the hypothalamus. The hypothalamus provides a link between your nervous system and your endocrine system. The signals sent from the hypothalamus cause the adrenal cortex to produce the stress hormone cortisol and the adrenal medulla to produce epinephrine. Epinephrine is also known as adrenaline. Under stress, your liver produces more glucose due to stress hormones being released into your blood stream. This glucose is a blood sugar that releases energy that you can use to either fight or flee if you need to.

6. Gastrointestinal system

The gastrointestinal system is involved in consuming and digesting food, in absorbing nutrients, and in expelling waste from your body. During stressful times, you may find yourself eating too much or too little.

If the stress in an acute situation becomes too much for you, you may feel as if you have "butterflies" in your stomach. You might even feel pain or nausea. If the stress is extreme, you may even vomit. The stress you feel can even affect your digestion and which nutrients are absorbed by your intestines. The level of stress you feel can also have an effect on the speed at which food moves through your body. You can end up with diarrhea or the opposite, constipation, so that not much leaves your body.

7. Reproductive system

Being exposed to the stress hormone cortisol over a period of time may have some unwanted effects on your reproductive system. Chronic stress in men can impair the hormone testosterone and the production of sperm. Worst case, severe stress can cause impotence, known as erectile dysfunction, which is the inability to achieve or to sustain an erection that is suitable for sexual intercourse. Chronic stress in women can lead to irregular or absent menstrual cycles, or more painful periods. A reduced sexual desire may also be an outcome of chronic stress.

The bottom line is that the stress response that is genetically designed to make you fight or flee can also harm you if the various changes in your body are not used for what they were intended.

A Real-Life Story: Self-Induced Stress during a Parachute Jump

During an operation deep inside Cambodia, Ole Boe was supposed to parachute jump from a helicopter. He decided to inspect the parachutes before the jump and saw that they had been used a lot. They looked worn out, with loose threads. Ole took a parachute, trying to convince himself that he chose the best one. He started to feel stressed.

After partnering with his jump buddy, Ole and the team approached the Russian helicopter that would be their jump platform. One of the Cambodians stepped forward and started praying in Cambodian. Suddenly everyone was praying. Ole went along with the prayers, doing what everyone did but not understanding a word that was said.

When the prayer was finished, Ole asked his Cambodian jump buddy what the group was praying for. He said that the prayer was to make sure that everyone survived the jump. That almost freaked Ole out; he wanted to ask if people usually died from jumping, but the signal to move to the helicopter interrupted him.

Ole's mind was racing, thinking about the worn-out parachutes. He was the last person to board the chopper, meaning he would be the first to get out after turning toward the open exit door. The helicopter took off and Ole looked into the cockpit. He saw two pilots who looked like kids— too young to fly a helicopter. Everything inside the cockpit was written in Cyrillic, an alphabet Ole could not read at the time. It all looked very strange, very different, and very wrong.

Ole decided he needed to take control of himself, so that he could perform a correct parachute jump. He concentrated on breathing correctly, thinking positively, and mentally reviewing the emergency procedures for his specific type of parachute.

Feeling some sense of control, Ole decided to talk with the jumpmaster. He asked how many jumps he had done. He smiled at Ole, showing gold teeth, and then he gave Ole a number. Ole froze; the number was much lower than he would have expected from an experienced jumpmaster.

Ole felt an immediate increase in his heart rate, and he focused again on breathing correctly in order to lower it. He started talking to himself, saying, "You will do fine...you have done this before," and so on.

Ole got a signal from the jumpmaster indicating that there was one minute to the jump. The helicopter started to hover. The go signal came and Ole jumped out of the door. The jump went perfectly, and the parachute opened as it was supposed to.

Before the jump, Ole had considered that his group might land on cows, on barbed wire, on old houses, on people riding small motorcycles, on rocks, or in a big hole in the ground. As he descended, Ole noticed children running around, and he thought he might even land on them!

When landing, he rolled to the side and cut open one of his forearms. Blood was pouring out, but he did not notice anything. Feeling stressed before the jump, he had forgotten to roll down his sleeves. A medic helped him recover.

Looking back at this jump, Ole realized that there really was nothing to be stressed about. Yes, the parachutes were worn, but he knew they would be thoroughly checked and packed properly before being laid out. The prayer was just a traditional way to prepare before jumps. The pilots were well educated and the Russian-built helicopter was generally rock solid. The jumpmaster was good enough. Ole felt stress because he was in a situation that looked different from what he expected and what he was accustomed to. The second jump was completely different, thanks to feeling more in control, but that is another story.

CONCLUSION

Stress is often a result of your perception. Practicing making better decisions is important, and this is possible to do by working on your perception skills. Your nervous system can be activated through either exercise- or hormone-induced activation or a combination of both. In difficult situations, you may experience a stress-induced behavior known as fight–flight–freeze. The fear response is a model for what happens in the brain and body during a confrontation. The fight-or-flight response has seven possible outcomes: fight, flight, freeze, submit, posture, choke, and the death grip. The survival stress reaction (SSR) is a model that is used to describe how your heart rate is linked to various reactions in your brain and your body. Also, the stress affects seven systems in the body. Knowledge about phenomena that may occur under stress is important for you to be able to improve your performance under stress.

Chapter 4

Character, Self-Regulation, and Willpower

Prussian general and military theorist Carl von Clausewitz emphasized the need to keep your head at times of exceptional stress and violent emotion. Clausewitz used the terms "character" or "character strengths" to describe this capability. He further stated that a strong character is one that stays balanced even while experiencing the most powerful emotions.

Clausewitz also wrote about willpower, explaining that when you are under pressure you tend to give in to physical and intellectual weakness. Only great strength of will leads to achieving the objective. In brief, "your will must be harder than anything it comes up against."

Character, self-regulation, and willpower are the three topics we explore in this chapter. They interact to form a combat mindset that can overcome stress and achieve your missions.

Classifying Character

Thoughts on the importance of virtues and how you perceive courage in leaders are found in Aquinas and Aristotle (who said, "Courage is the first of human qualities because it is the quality which guarantees the others"), but it was not until around the year 2000 that a classification system on character and virtues started to emerge within psychology. This new trend was the positive psychology paradigm, and since its birth, it has grown a lot as a new psychology paradigm. Embedded within the positive psychology paradigm you can find a lot of research on different character strengths. Character strengths can be developed through an increased awareness, practice, and effort, and are phenomena that coexist with goals, interests, and values. Therefore, they are worth exploring, because developing your character strengths is for everyone, as we all experience temptations, challenges, and problems from time to time. Being able to develop your character strengths resonates well with our thinking around how to develop your combat mindset. Building a solid combat mindset is demanding and tasks a lot of your different character strengths—for instance, integrity, persistence, and self-regulation.

Peterson and Seligman classified twenty-four character strengths within six main virtues in their 2004 book **Character Strengths and Virtues: A Handbook and Classification**. They suggest that these twenty-four character strengths are universally valued across cultures. Virtues represent "core characteristics valued by moral philosophers and religious thinkers. [They] are universal, perhaps grounded in biology through an evolutionary process that selected for these aspects of excellence as means of solving the important task necessary for survival of species." Character strengths are "the psychological ingredients—processes or mechanism—that define virtues." They are distinguishable routes to displaying one or another of the virtues.

Table 4-1 gives a short overview of the six virtues (referred to as A-F) and the accompanying twenty-four character strengths (referred to as 1-24) as classified by Peterson and Seligman. The six virtues are wisdom and knowledge, courage, humanity, justice, temperance, and transcendence. Under each virtue, you can find the character strengths related to that specific virtue.

Table 4-1. An overview of the classification of character strengths and their related virtues.

A.	Wisdom and knowledge: cognitive strengths that entail the acquisition and use of knowledge	1. *Creativity*, originality, ingenuity 2. *Curiosity*, interest, novelty seeking, openness to experience 3. *Open-mindedness*, judgment, critical thinking 4. *Love of learning*, mastering new skills 5. *Perspective*, wisdom
B.	Courage: emotional strengths that involve the exercise of will to accomplish goals in the face of opposition, external or internal	6. *Bravery*, valor 7. *Persistence*, perseverance, grit, industriousness 8. *Integrity*, authenticity, honesty 9. *Vitality*, zest, enthusiasm, vigor, energy

C.	Humanity: inter-personal strengths that involve tending and be-friending others	10. *Love*, valuing close relations with others 11. *Kindness*, empathy, generosity, nurturance, care, compassion, altruistic love, niceness 12. *Social intelligence*, emotional intelligence, personal intelligence
D.	Justice: civic strengths that underlie healthy communi-ty life	13. *Teamwork*, social responsibility, loyalty, citizenship 14. *Fairness*, treating all people the same according to notions of fairness and justice 15. *Leadership*, encouraging a group of which you are a member to get things done
E.	Temperance: strengths that protect against excess	16. *Forgiveness and mercy* 17. *Humility and modesty* 18. *Prudence*, being careful about your choices 19. *Self-Regulation*, self-control, regulating what you feel and do
F.	Transcendence: strengths that forge connections to the larger universe and provide meaning	20. *Appreciation of beauty and excellence*, awe, wonder, elevation 21. *Gratitude* 22. *Hope*, optimism, future-mindedness, future orientation 23. *Humor*, playfulness 24. *Spirituality*, religiousness, faith, having coherent beliefs about the higher purpose and meaning of the universe

According to Peterson and Seligman, these virtues and character strengths can be found in all cultures and they are thus regarded as universal. When you look at the twenty-four character strengths described in Table 4.1, you probably immediately feel that some of them or perhaps many of them are important to you. This says something about your underlying values system. This means that you might have a different set of core values than other people. In addition, the culture you live in also has an impact on your values, and hence which character strengths are the most important to you. Not all of the twenty-four character strengths are of equal importance to those dealing with extremis leadership, the unforeseen, or facing different challenging situations. Looking at the military forces of various countries, we find several common character strengths.

Character Strengths in the Military

An officer leads under extreme conditions. What separates military leadership from leadership in most other organizations is the need to acquire the ability to face and cope with extreme situations where your own life and the lives of those you lead are in danger. Under these demanding conditions, an officer has to make decisions that may result in both taking lives and risking lives. The Norwegian Armed Forces document on leadership states, "It is about doing the uncomfortable and being able to cope with it, to overcome powerlessness, and to avoid emotional breakdown. Military leadership requires a robustness in order to think clearly and effectively, and cope with one's feelings when facing complex and difficult situations."

The US Army doctrine on leadership contains a leadership requirements model. Three categories of leader competencies described in the model are the leader serves 1) to lead others; 2) to develop the environment, himself, others, and the profession as a whole; and 3) to achieve organizational goals. The leader attributes described in the model are character, presence, and intellect. Character captures the values and identity of the leader. Presence captures the leader's outward appearance, demeanor, actions, and words. Intellect captures the mental and social faculties the leader has to apply while he is leading.

The Greek historian and soldier Xenophon pointed out that the true test of a leader is whether others will follow him (or her) by their own free will in times of "immense hardship." A military leader plays a key role when it comes to the soldier's moral and character development. A business leader also has the same effect on his employees. The British prime minister Winston Churchill's physician, Lord Moran, stated that the practical implication of leadership is your capacity to frame plans that will succeed and the ability to persuade others to carry them out in the face of death.

Individual character strengths have proved to be able to predict success when it comes to the selection of personnel into so-called high-risk organization (those involving unpredictable, difficult, stressful and also dangerous situations). By high-risk organizations, we mean organizations in which personnel may have to face highly dangerous, unpredictable, difficult, and stressful situations in their daily work. Put another way, personnel must be able to handle situations that occur suddenly and surprisingly, the unfamiliar, and the unexpected, where outcomes of actions are characterized by a low degree of predictability. Researchers Gayton and Kehoe found that successful applicants to the

Australian army's Special Forces chose teamwork, integrity, and persistence as their top three character strengths. The applicants who did not include any of those three character strengths in their top ranking of character strengths all failed to complete the selection process.

The officer's posture, his body language, and the look in his eyes show a confident leader and warrior. Courtesy of Petter Brenni Gulbrandsen, the Norwegian Armed Forces.

Character Strengths in the Corporate Sector

The conditions that corporate leaders may find themselves in are normally less extreme than in the military. However, several of the same character strengths that are important for the military are also important for corporate leaders. For instance, the top ten character strengths in ranked order expressed at work have been found to be integrity, open-mindedness, perspective, fairness, persistence, love of learning, leadership, vitality, curiosity, and social intelligence.

In addition, other character strengths have also been found to be important for corporate leaders. The character strengths of honesty and integrity, bravery, perspective, and social intelligence studied in top-level executive leaders of for-profit companies showed that each of these strengths was important for performance, but that honesty and integrity most contributed to explaining executive performance. A study investigating character strengths at work revealed that curiosity, vitality, hope, gratitude, and spirituality are associated with work satisfaction. This was found across different occupations. In another study, specifically vitality was found to be associated both with greater life and work satisfaction.

Understanding Self-Regulation

The character strength of self-regulation plays an important role in developing your combat mindset. Self-regulation is the ability to govern your emotions and rule your behavior, your desires, your responses, your thoughts, and your actions when facing different demands. Self-regulation is a character strength whereby you can consciously adjust what you feel, think, and act. It is your ability to consciously control your own responses to achieve what you want, or to live up to some standard, such as the expectations of others, norms in a situation, or moral standards. Responses include your thoughts, feelings, impulses, desires, achievements, and actions. Self-regulation is a conscious and deliberate process.

As stated by the American billionaire J. Paul Getty, founder of Getty Oil and the world's richest private citizen in 1966, "The individual who wants to reach the top in business must appreciate the might and force of habit. He must be quick to break those habits that can break him—and hasten to adopt those practices that will become the habits that help him achieve the success he desires."

You have to control yourself (thoughts, emotions, and actions) to maximize your achievements and results in any kind of action; better your behavior; have excellent relations with other people, whether family, friends, or colleagues; handle bullies or deal with life-threatening attacks by violent aggressors; or deal with dangerous actions executed by business competitors. You need to analyze and weigh situations, circumstances, and outcomes, make the appropriate decision, and take action.

Willpower, Self-Regulation, and Self-Control

Your mental state is strongly influenced by outside conditions. It is also influenced by what is under your skin, i.e., your physical health. What is outside your skin can also lift your spirits, such as driving a new car, wearing a new shirt or dress, or owning a new diamond ring or wristwatch. Unfortunately, you may also feel miserable if your car is scratched, your shirt or dress is stained, or your ring or watch is lost.

The high-level warrior, the fighter of life, stays calm. He is not influenced emotionally by the outside conditions and materialistic artifacts. He analyzes, decides, and acts, solving the situation at hand no matter how dangerous, disturbing, or rewarding it is. In other words, his ability to observe–orient–decide–act (known as the **OODA loop**) is excellent. Exercises in later parts of this book can help you develop the character trait of self-regulation.

Willpower has been the subject of research since the 1960s. However, it is just during the last few years that it has been possible to clearly document the positive benefits of strong willpower. There is a robust and predictive association between the degree of willpower and a wide range of life consequences. The ability to rationally control your actions is particularly important, and willpower is a key component in achieving this. Some consider willpower to be the most important of all human virtues, as it manifests in the character strengths of persistence and self-regulation. The concepts of willpower, self-control, and self-regulation often are used interchangeably in literature, whatever the context, but they all refer to the same mental process. Other overlapping concepts include performance control, "executive control," self-discipline, grit, postponement of reward, and ego strength.

A leader exercising self-control is more likely to stay calm, promote confidence in his subordinates, and make good decisions. One explanation for why leaders with a high degree of self-control make better decisions in stressful situations than those with low self-control may be that leaders with high self-control become less ego-depleted. Ego-depletion here simply means that your self-control or your willpower draws from a limited pool of mental resources. The point is that these resources can or will be used until there is nothing left. It has been suggested that making decisions is ego-depleting, because you are using a lot of your resources. Individuals exhibiting self-control may be drawing on a larger reservoir of willpower. The need to develop willpower is important in a person's development process, because the development process includes cognitive, emotional, and behavioral efforts. Longitudinal studies of preschool children revealed that willpower is a good predictor of later academic achievement and planning ability. Willpower is also a good predictor for the ability to cope with frustration and exercise stress management, as well as general self-control when the children became older.

Some call willpower a "moral or mental muscle" because it gives you the power to do what is right. Several studies have shown that when individuals lose their willpower, they become more dishonest and cheat more often. Other studies have shown that lack of willpower is involved in prejudice and violence. Research on military populations shows the same patterns. For example, those with the lowest self-control are also responsible for the most misconduct in the US Navy.

Developing Willpower

The physical, technical, and mental drills in this book require determination, aggression, focus, and concentration. Many are not easy. They require work, practice, self-control, and willpower. For now, consider the following drill: At least once a day, force yourself to do something you really dislike. It can be finishing your shower with cold water for a minute or two; doing a physical exercise that you don't like but know is good for your fitness level; skipping that sweet dessert after lunch; interacting with a person who makes you feel small or nervous; sitting down and writing part of the work you have been postponing for weeks; fixing the drainage problem on the roof of your

Participants waiting for the command to charge and pass to the other side, through the passage marked by the kick shields and the other group.

house; mending your child's bed; or adding twenty minutes of focusing and concentration drills to your daily training schedule. Make the decision not to eat lunch, or leave work, or go to bed before you finish the selected task. Never miss it unless your life is on the line, and maybe even then you should think about doing it!

Making these small changes takes you a huge step forward in building your character strengths of self-regulation and willpower. If you want an even bigger challenge, consider the practice of becoming "comfortable with the uncomfortable." This has proven to be the most important factor for building self-discipline, self-control, and willpower. US Navy SEALs practice this approach in their training. Short of training with the SEALs, we recommend starting with the drills and exercises in this book.

CONCLUSION

This chapter has discussed character strengths, self-regulation, and willpower as components of your combat mindset. There are several character strengths that are important for you to further develop. You have to find out for yourself which ones to improve according to your needs. In the military, several character strengths have emerged as important in order to succeed as an officer. Willpower is also an important component of your combat mindset. Character strengths and willpower aid in overcoming stress and help you fulfill your missions in life. A key component of developing a stronger combat mindset is to work on your ability to self-regulate. This means working on and adjusting what you feel, think, and do. The exercises presented later in this book can help you to achieve this.

Part Two
Combat Mindset

Never give in, never give in, never, never, never, never—
in nothing, great or small, large or petty—never give in
except to convictions of honor and good sense.

Sir Winston Churchill (1874-1965)

Without struggle, no progress and no result.

George Ivanovitch Gurdjieff (1872-1949)

Chapter 5

Controlled Aggression, Perseverance, and Determination

Part One provided a foundation for the concepts essential to developing a combat mindset and the pursuit of mental perseverance and conditioning. We introduced a few physical exercises, but for the most part we focused on biology, reactions, and theory. In Part Two, we instruct you how to leverage technical drills and physical training to build your combat mindset.

We agree with Aristotle, who said that "courage is the first of human virtues because it makes all others possible," and with Lau Tzu, who wrote that "a man with outward courage dares to die; a man with inner courage dares to live." Our goal in this chapter is to share drills that develop mental skills and capabilities relevant for martial artists, fighters, sport competitors, military or law enforcement officers, as well as for managers in any type of organization. The drills you choose, their intensity, frequency of usage, and practice depend on the person you are, your job, and the nature of the group you are training.

Chasing Games

You develop courage by overcoming adversity. Both courage and controlled aggression are tools that help you meet challenges, both mental and physical. We start this process with drills and games involving chasing people. Divide the training group into pairs, where one person is the attacker, and the partner is the defender or "escapee." During the drills, the chasing attacker tries to stay close to the escapee. There is a risk of collisions, tripping, and falling in these drills. Instructors and trainees must pay attention and train with the appropriate intensity and safety measures.

The first chasing game begins with fast walking. The attacker touches the middle of the escapee's back. The escapee has to move away at a fast walking pace to disconnect himself from the attacker's hand.

The second chasing game increases the speed from fast walking to a light jog.

The third chasing game replaces the touching of the back with straight strikes and hammer strikes to mark (no impact) the defender's back. If any contact occurs it may only be with the defender's shoulder blades, and not his spine or neck.

The fourth chasing game involves the escapee holding an object, such as a kick shield, on his back, while being pursued by the attacker. The attacker chases him while delivering rather strong and hard strikes to the pad. A variation of this drill involves chasing and kicking a pad that is held lower, covering the buttocks of the escapee.

The final variation of these chasing drills offers the option of rapidly switching roles. The running defender, on the instructor's command, steps sideways and turns to become the attacker. The attacker assumes the role of escapee. Without protective equipment, strikes should only mark the target. With a body protection vest, trainees can deliver strikes that connect with the target. All these drills, especially the last two, mentally turn the defender into an aggressive escapee that moves between obstacles and difficulties with a strong spirit and an aggressive mindset.

As an attacker, you learn to focus on your target and develop controlled aggression, determination, and persistence. You practice overcoming frustration and controlling your anger while chasing and attacking the escapee, especially when you miss your target.

As an escapee, you rather immediately encounter panic as a result of escaping what seems to be, for your subconscious, a life-threatening incident (being chased and attacked from behind). Your subconscious assumes that you are running to save your life. Stress levels rise as you need to analyze a lot of information, especially in order to calculate escape routes and to try to avoid crashing into other people. As an escapee, you do not want to find yourself, in the last fraction of a second, responding to a person that is only few inches away and about to crash into you. This is a tactical requirement to which you have to recruit mental resources—you need to be calm, focused, and use your peripheral vision.

Breathing techniques, unfocused peripheral vision, and concentrating on the mission help you "survive" the event.

This drill improves your ability to deal with stress, develop courage, and quickly activate and deactivate a high level of aggressive response and attitude. It makes you work on your determination and perseverance, as well as teach yourself how to overcome anger and frustration and how to reduce panic and fear.

This is a physically demanding drill, and you may feel tired after less than half a minute. We usually start with seventy-five–second rounds, depending on trainee fitness levels. In a KMG session for beginners or a workshop for managers, this family of exercises is practiced with very light and controlled contact. A training session for special forces equipped with protection gear rapidly becomes an extreme event! For more advanced practitioners, as well as for kids' groups, we present different chasing drills. For all practical purposes, they belong to the same family of innovative and functional games; however, they differ in requirements and demands, and they aim to elevate additional skills. For example, we may ask attackers to hold a knife while chasing an escapee. Alternatively, third parties may add to the confusion by also attacking the escapee.

Tag Games

Kids may love playing tag, but adults can also use modified versions of this game to develop combat mindset and controlled aggression. The goal of the attacker is to touch as many people as possible in the time allowed. If the attacker touches another trainee, the trainee needs to perform a physical task, like a push-up or a sit-up, after which he can continue evading the attacker. A variation involves the touched trainee becoming a new attacker.

In the first version of this drill, there is one attacker in the group. The next variation invites multiple attackers to participate, either by selection or by touching. This scenario forces trainees to divide their attention, constantly searching for attackers and escape routes.

The third version of the drill introduces KMG-related missions. For example, an attacker armed with a training knife tries to chase and "stab" the other trainees. The types of attacks should match the knowledge, experience, and capabilities of the defenders: straight stabs, circular attacks, and slashes are most appropriate. Escapees defend themselves using the most appropriate KMG techniques.

Ideally, escapees are not touched by the knife. KMG techniques use hand defenses to actively stop or deflect the knife hand, and body defenses to move the target from the line of attack. Trainees "cut" by the knife need to complete a task, such as push-ups, or freeze until a group member frees them. This may require the trainee to perform another KMG technique, such as a release from a choke or headlock.

The following figures depict some of these drills.

Walking chase with the hand placed between the shoulder blades of the escapee.

Jogging chase with the hand placed between the shoulder blades of the escapee.

Chasing with strikes that look and feel vicious, but are only **marking attacks** on the escapee's shoulder blades.

Chasing with stronger attacks to a pad held on the escapee's back. The strike does not penetrate deep into the target, to avoid injuring the escapee.

The attacker is chasing and attacking with a knife. The escapee should experience the escape and overcome the panic response, and at the next phase apply the most appropriate technique (solution) for defending and counterattacking.

Chasing and attacking with a knife, with the possibility of a second aggressor also interfering and attacking.

Introducing multiple armed attackers increases the difficulty level to a high degree and, accordingly, the trainees' stress levels. When you ramp up the strain of the training, you ramp up the capacities of the trainee, mentally, tactically, technically, and physically.

Attacker–Disturber–Target (ADT)

The following drills and games develop aggression, determination, courage, focused attention, and perseverance. They help trainees overcome fear in order to protect others, ignore thoughts about personal consequences, enable each person to focus on his (or her) own mission without being disturbed by thoughts and emotions like "What will happen to me?" or "I am afraid to get hit; I don't want to be in this dangerous area." They also teach trainees to control and overcome anger, frustration, and other destructive emotions. These capacities and skills are needed by everyone living in the fast lane of the twenty-first century, whether you are a manager, soldier, officer, university student, teenager, martial artist, or competitive athlete.

Divide trainees into groups of three. The first trainee is the attacker, who tries to **constantly** strike a target. The second trainee is the disturber, whose goal is to prevent the attacker from reaching the target. The attacker should land 10–20% of his strikes while being frustrated by the disturber. The third trainee holds a pad or a kick shield, which is the "target." The combination of the attacker–disturber–target forms the acronym for this set of drills: ADT.

For the first drill, the disturber holds the attacker from behind with his hands, a belt, or a rope around the attacker's waist. The attacker strives to constantly hit the target while the disturber pulls him backward and sideways. The target holder can stay in place or move in different directions; we recommend the latter.

The next variation requires the disturber to come to the front of the attacker and serve as a buffer, push the attacker, and disrupt his ability to reach the target. As the drill progresses, and with the instructor's consent, the disturber can grab and try to hold the attacker. The physical load and stress applied to the attacker should be adequate to his fitness level, as well as to the technical and mental abilities of the trainee.

In both drills, the disturber functions as a defender of the target. The disturber tries to keep his "VIP" from being injured. Disturbers as defenders experience destructive emotions, such as anxiety, fear, frustration, anger, and so on. Disturbers learn to confront those emotions when fulfilling their mission as protectors while they experience physical fatigue and mental stress.

In the next phase, we divide the whole group into teams of four. The missions for the first three remain attacker, disturber, and target, but the fourth person assumes different roles. The fourth trainee may motivate the attacker or the disturber. He may try to motivate the attacker to reach the target, to strike harder, or he may try to motivate the disturber with words like "Save your mother!" or "Help your friend!" or "Push harder!" and so on. To elevate stress and difficulty, the fourth person can also disturb, block, or strike the attacker. Attacks can be low-impact strikes with boxing gloves, or light slaps or kicks to different parts of the body. The attacker can have the mission to ignore or to defend against those attacks. In higher level training, mainly directed at special forces and advanced KMG trainees, the attacks are heavier and harder.

ADT drills are also very physically demanding. Trainees may feel exhausted after less than half a minute. We usually start with seventy-five–second rounds, depending on trainee fitness levels, and even with untrained managers of a corporation, we ask for a similar length of training, but at low intensity.

The following figures depict some of these drills.

One trainee guards an object on the ground, pushing the attacker and blocking his way and ability to touch the target.

While the disturber holds the attacker from behind, the attacker tries to repeatedly strike a target.

The disturber positions himself between the attacker and the target.

The disturber positions himself between the attacker and the target, blocking the way and pushing the attacker.

Sometimes the attacker manages to bypass the disturber.

The attacker repeatedly strikes the target until the disturber recovers and manages to push him away.

A fourth trainee encourages the attacker.

The fourth person encourages the disturber, who practically acts as a protector, as the ADT drill continues.

ADT with a fourth trainee who is striking the   A fourth trainee lightly kicks the attacker.
attacker to enhance the difficulty of the drill.

Passing through a Crowd

We developed the following drills for anti-terror and special units. A fighter with the mission to go forward as part of an intervention or anti-terror unit may face a crowd streaming in the opposite direction, away from the problematic area. These drills develop and elevate courage, aggression, grit, determination, alertness, and early response, even in the face of danger. We present multiple drills because exercising only one variant leads to trainee's "acclimation." You need to "play" different "functional games" to continue building your capabilities.

These drills do not convey technical or tactical approaches to passing through a crowd of people. They aim to build mental capacities and capabilities. Consider how frightening it is to have two groups of people storming toward each other. Do you really need to clash with them? In real life, you may not, but in these drills, the goal is to collide, to "smash."

You must overcome fear and stress, and ignore the thoughts that you may get hurt. These thoughts deplete you mentally and physically. You need to focus your attention, apply the right technique, and activate your perseverance and grit. Contract your muscles at the right moments, so you are able to pass through the barriers created by people in your path or running toward you. The basic posture for an expected collision is your body bladed (turned to become narrower), and your front forearm perpendicular to the ground with your elbow low and forward. Your rear arm is tight to your body, your chin is low, your shoulders are high, while your weight is shifted and your body is tilted forward. Figures A1 and A2 show the correct posture.

Front view of the posture during impact. The front is an arrow shape for better penetration between people. For the sake of safe training, keep your elbows low and chin down.

Side view of the posture just prior to impact. The body is bladed, leaning forward, with the front forearm perpendicular to the ground and the elbow pressed forward.

The collision occurs with the front forearm first. You should keep your elbows low to avoid hurting your training partners. Pay attention to that, as there is a tendency to lift the elbows. After the collision that enabled you to penetrate among the first line or two of participants, continue to push strongly forward while you move your body a bit to the left and right, in a snake- or fish-like motion. When you manage to get free from the crowd, maintain your balance and move to your next mission.

The mental effect of the expected collision is visible on the actions of the trainees. Those that are afraid slow down or even stop their advance to avoid the impact. Learning and practicing the drill improves trainee courage, determination, and will to execute demanding missions. The optimal mental state is to decide to be the first one through, and to be decisive and firm with your decisions and actions.

To avoid injuries, the intensity and speed prior to impact should be suitable for the group and each trainee. For beginners, the distance before starting to move should be about 1.5–2 meters (5–7 feet). Trainees should wear a mouthguard and groin protection. It is highly advised to have protection on the forearms and elbows, as there is a risk that the passing trainee may raise his elbows and hit other trainees. Headgear is recommended when trainees are working at high speed.

Those who need to aggressively, and maybe even destructively, pass through a crowd outside of a training scenario should refer to Figures A and B below.

Passing through Two Lines of Resisting Trainees

Passing through two lines of resisting trainees is similar to passing through a crowd, but now a group opposes one trainee at a time. The trainee should pass through a group of eight to ten practitioners, arranged in two lines, one in front of the other. Each pair presses together, shoulder to shoulder, to create resistance for the passing practitioner. The first two trainees in each line must each hold a kick shield. Other subsequent pairs of trainees may also hold kick shields.

In a real, non-training scenario, operators can use this technique. Position the elbow and arm horizontally, bent in a V shape to penetrate between people. This position better protects the operator's head. Penetrate with your elbow at the height of the opponents' shoulders. You may hurt the opponents using this technique.

Aggressive and destructive penetration using the "elbow strike against a crowd" technique is another option for real-life scenarios. Operators can use forearms, fists, and elbows to hit two to four people on the head. Practitioners can train for this drill by marking strikes, or by equipping training partners with helmets or kick shields.

Figure 5-1. Passing through two lines of resisting trainees.

When it is your turn to pass, start from a distance of two meters (7 feet) or less. On the instructor's command, run into the two lines. Toughen your forearm, arm, shoulder, and body before impact. Keep your body tilted forward a bit. Your chin should be low and your core muscles should be tight. Do not hit the barrier with your head, neck, or shoulder. After the collision, continue to penetrate between the two lines of resisting partners. Simulate the motions of a snake or a fish to advance. You can move your arms and elbows a bit, but keep them low.

When you are a person that weighs around 80 kilograms (176 pounds), trying to pass through a group of eight people is difficult. Assuming each person averages a similar weight, you are facing 640 kilograms (over 1,400 pounds) of resistance. The resisting group should apply reasonable pressure to keep the passing trainee inside the lines for about fifteen to twenty seconds. When you have managed to pass them, regain your balance and continue to the next phase.

The next phase of this drill offers several options. Trainees may return to the line of the passing trainees to go through another round. Trainees may go to the rear of the resisting lines to take the place of a practitioner who goes to the line of passers. Trainees may pass through the lines and then execute a Krav Maga technique, such as a series of attacks on a pair of Thai pads held by a waiting partner, or a defense against a knife attack by a waiting partner.

The following figures show this drill from an overhead view.

Preparing to pass through two lines of resisting trainees.

Making contact with the first two resisting trainees.

Penetrating the two lines of resisting trainees.

Inside the lines of resisting trainees. The trainee should spend fifteen to twenty seconds inside the lines.

Preparing to exit the two lines.

After passing the two lines, and fulfilling another mission.

The following figures show this drill from alternative views.

The first two practitioners hold kick shields for safe training.

Side view of the trainee when making contact with the first two practitioners.

Overhead view of the trainee making contact with the first two practitioners.

Overhead view of the trainee working to pass through the middle of the group.

Passing through a Circle of People

In this drill, all practitioners pass through the middle of a circle. Divide the trainees into groups of eight to ten people, ideally of similar heights and weights. Position them in a circle of about two meters (7 feet) in diameter. The starting position is the same as described in Figures A1 and A2. On the instructor's command, all practitioners try to be the first person to pass through the center of the circle to reach the other side. After reaching the other side, participants should turn back toward the center, reform the circle, and be ready to start again.

Collisions happen close to the center and impacts may come from various directions. Be careful not to raise your elbows so as not to hit other trainees.

A variation of this drill involves placing two to four trainees in the center of the circle. On the instructor's command, those in the center move to the edge and those at the edge move to the other side. Those moving outward have the sensation of being pressed mentally and physically, and they need to overcome their anxiety.

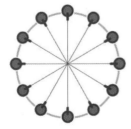

Figure 5-2. Passing through a circle of people.

Figure 5-3. Passing through a circle of people, when several trainees begin in the center.

The following figures show these drills from an overhead view.

Trainees form a circle and are ready to pass.

The trainees try to pass through the center of the circle.

Each trainee tries to be the first to pass through the middle and reach the other side.

The group has passed through the center of the circle.

Three trainees begin in the circle's center.

On the instructor's command, the trainees in the center try to reach the edge, while those on the edge try to pass through the center.

Passing through a Rotating Circle of People

This drill is similar to the previous one, except the trainees jog while forming a circle. On the instructor's command, the trainees turn, face the center, and pass through the middle to reach the other side. After reaching the other side, trainees should reform the circle and jog again.

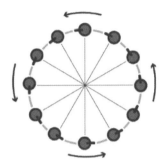

Figure 5-4. Passing through a rotating circle of people.

A variation of this drill involves placing a few trainees inside the rotating circle. Those trainees jog in the opposite direction. As before, on the instructor's command, all trainees turn to their left, those in the center move to the edge, and those at the edge move to the other side. Those moving from the inside outward, even while jogging, have a sensation of being pressed and oppressed mentally and physically and need to overcome their rising anxiety.

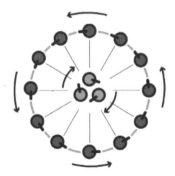

Figure 5-5. Passing through a rotating circle of people when three trainees begin in the center.

The following figures show these drills from an overhead view.

The circle jogs counterclockwise. In this example, the instructor monitors the group from inside the circle.

The instructor gives a command and exits the circle.

The group collides in the center.

The group members pass through the center.

Three trainees jog inside the rotating circle.

On the instructor's command, those in the center move to the edge and those at the edge move to the other side.

Passing through a "Door"

Another variation related to passing through a crowd involves moving quickly through a narrow passage, or a "door." Simulate a narrow opening using a couple of focus mitts or kick shields placed on the ground. You can also use the gap between two hanging heavy bags. All trainees form one line, about 2-3 meters (7–10 feet) away from the opening. Some are closer and some farther away from the "opening," which is narrower than the line of participants.

On the instructor's command, everyone should pass to the other side of the "door." Upon reaching the other side, the trainees should turn around immediately, form a line, and prepare for another command to pass through to the other side. In the beginning, the "door" can be about two-thirds of the length of the line of participants. As the training session progresses, the instructor can narrow the "door."

It may be difficult to maintain balance and not fall due to becoming entangled with the legs of other trainees. If you do fall, try to roll away. If you cannot roll, pull your hands and legs to you as soon as possible, so that others don't step or fall on them.

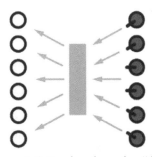

Figure 5-6. Passing through a "door."

The following figures show this drill from an overhead view.

Trainees create a line 1-2 meters (3-7 feet) away from the "door" formed by two kick shields.

On the instructor's command, each trainee strives to be the first to pass through the "door" without touching it.

Passing through a "Door" from Two Directions

In this variation of higher intensity, the group is divided in two, with each half forming a line on either side of the "door." When the command to pass is heard, each trainee tries to be the first one to pass through the opening. We recommend that trainees wear protective gear.

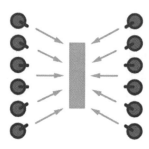

Figure 5-7. Passing through a "door" from two directions.

The following figures show this drill from an overhead view.

The trainees form two lines about a meter away from the "door" formed by two kick shields.

On the instructor's command, each trainee strives to be the first to pass through the "door."

Passing through a Crowd from Four Corners

Divide the trainees into four groups. From four corners of an imaginary square, the groups face the center. On the instructor's command, the first four trainees, one from each group, move forward to pass through the center to the opposite side. Each should try to be the first one to pass. After passing, each should proceed to the end of the opposite line. Initially, trainees should walk through the center. Later, trainees should burst through, increasing their speed and intensity of collision.

Trainees' posture during impact and the technique to pass through the crowd are the same as in the previous drills.

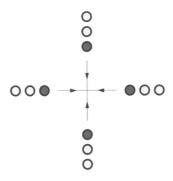

Figure 5-8. Passing through a crowd, from four corners.

The following figures show this drill from an overhead view.

Divided into four small groups, all trainees are waiting in four lines, approximately 2 meters (7 feet) from each other.

On the instructor's command, the first four trainees, one from each group, move forward to pass through the center to the opposite side.

After passing, each practitioner should proceed to the end of the opposite line.

Passing through a Crowd from Four Corners in Teams

In this variation of the previous drill, two people from each line pass through the center. Partners should start with their left arms and legs forward. The left hand and forearm of the second person should be placed on the first person's back, diagonally downward from the right trapezius muscle to the area under the left shoulder blade. After the collision, the person at the back should push the person in the front to assist in passing through the crowd. The first person should think, "I am clearing the way for my VIP," while the second person thinks, "I am supporting my friend." Both should try to be the first pair to pass through the center. After passing, the team should proceed to the end of the opposite line and change roles, so that the person that was first to collide is now the second person in the pair.

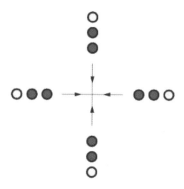

Figure 5-9. Passing in teams through a crowd from four corners.

The following figures show this drill from an overhead view.

Divided into four small groups, partners wait in four lines, approximately 2 meters (7 feet) from each other.

The first two from each line (eight people in total) lunge forward to be the first ones to pass through the center.

The partner in the rear pushes the partner in front.

The teams pass through the crowd and then go to the back of the opposite line.

Passing through Two Lines: A Corridor of Attackers

In this drill, trainees enter a "trap." In reality, you should avoid such a situation, but this is a drill to practice your techniques, make decisions under stressful conditions, and strengthen your mental, physical, technical, and tactical abilities. Select one or a few trainees, and then divide the remainder of the group into two lines. Those in the lines act as attackers. The trainee that passes is the defender. According to the level and experience of the trainees, the attackers can use unarmed techniques, such as a strike, kick, choke, headlock, wrist grab, bear hug, and so on. Attackers can be armed with dummy knives, firearms, sticks, or stones. Attackers can present a target for the defender to strike, such as a focus mitt or a kick shield. Attackers can also stand still, but in these cases the defender should ignore them and move to the next attacker. In fact this drill can be presented to trainees even after several hours of training, as long as the attacks are very basic ones that the defender has already learned how to defend against. The first iterations of this drill should involve a single attack against the defender at a time. Later variations can involve multiple attackers and simultaneous attacks against the defender at a time. Once the defender makes his way through the whole corridor of attackers, he should join the end of the line of attackers on one side. The attacker at the head of the line on that side leaves his position and joins the group of defenders, or just becomes the new defender.

Appropriate protection gear is highly recommended here, especially when training more realistically.

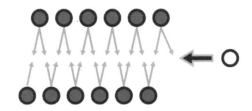

Figure 5-10. Passing through two lines: a corridor of attackers.

The following figures show this drill from an overhead view.

The defender (in white shirt) starts at the beginning of the corridor of attackers.

Attackers may act from the front, side, and diagonally from the rear.

The defender counters a knife attack from the side while identifying a problem from the other side.

The defender hits a target held by one of the attackers.

Breaking through a Circle of People Holding Pads

In this drill, a trainee stands at the center of a circle of five to eight people holding kick shields. On the instructor's command, the group starts pushing, pressing, or striking the person in the middle, using the kick shields. On the instructor's command, the person in the center must break through the circle. The technique of passing through a crowd used until now, or the elbow against a group (an arrow-like action), are both suitable solutions. Once outside the circle, the trainee should fulfill another mission, such as striking a target held by another trainee. A variation of this drill involves making the trainee at the center responsible for selecting the proper time to initiate a breakout.

The following figures show this drill from an overhead view.

The trainee at the center is surrounded.

The attackers forming the circle press and lightly strike the trapped trainee.

On the instructor's command, the trainee begins to escape the circle.

Once outside the circle, the escaped trainee accomplishes a secondary mission, such as defending against a knife attack. Here he is using a preemptive kick.

While on the Ground, Breaking through a Circle of People

In this variation, the trainee in the center of the circle starts on his back. Attackers strike or kick lightly with their pads and legs. The defender defends or absorbs the strikes until commanded by the instructor to break out. The defender strikes at the attackers' pads until he is able to stand up and escape.

The following figures show this drill from an overhead view.

Attackers circle a trainee on the ground.

Attackers strike or lightly kick with their pads and legs, while the defender blocks the attacks or covers the attacked areas.

When commanded to escape, the defender strikes at the attackers' pads until he is able to stand up and escape.

The defender rises, and bursts through the circle of attackers.

Reaching a Target While Blocked by a Circle of People

This drill combines chasing with group movement. Five to eight trainees form a circle and hold hands. One of the trainees forming the circle is selected to be the target. A lone trainee is positioned outside the circle, as the "attacker." The attacker's goal is to touch or tag the target trainee. The circle rotates, either clockwise or counterclockwise, to avoid having the target be touched.

Another variation of this drill requires the trainees on either side of the target to hold a kick shield between the target and the attacker. Again, both the attacker and the circle rotate, but the attacker must now try to strike the kick shield.

A final variation requires the attacker to penetrate the circle and reach the target from the inside. Those forming the circle must block the attacker with their bodies.

Instructors can allow the circle and attackers to change the direction in which they are running, either when teamed together or independently.

The following figures demonstrate the concepts behind these drills.

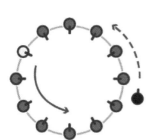 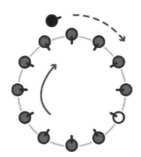 

A1. A circle of trainees, with the target marked with a white circle. The attacker is outside the circle and runs to reach the target.

A2. The attacker changes direction and runs to reach the target. The people forming the circle should immediately change direction, too.

A3. The attacker reaches the target.

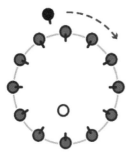 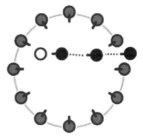

B1. In this variation, the attacker must break through the circle to reach the target.

B2. The attacker breaks into the circle and reaches the target.

Other Considerations for Passing through Crowds

This final section offers a few tips for those who have to pass through crowds in tactical and real-life situations.

If you see a tightly packed group of people approaching, you may not be able to pass through them. It may be helpful to place yourself near a wall. Press along the wall, moving people with your forearm and knee. Assist your movement by strongly pushing with your rear hand, but keep your elbows low.

A soldier, a police officer, or a bodyguard may need to move through a crowd while holding a handgun, assault rifle, or submachine gun. You must prevent the crowd from deliberately or accidentally taking the weapon. Keep your handgun secure in its holster while pressing your elbow backward. If you have already drawn your handgun, hold it in two hands, with one hand holding the handle and the other the slide or drum. The barrel should point diagonally downward (to the front or rear, depending on which shoulder is in front). Your shoulder, upper arm, and elbow should be the arrow to penetrate through the crowd moving against you. In case you carry an assault rifle, one option is to move it backward and pin it to your back with one hand. The barrel should be pointing diagonally downward and backward away from you.

When a very tight group is either moving slowly or is stopped, the best solution may be to climb and crawl over the crowd. Put your hands and legs on their shoulders and heads. This is an emergency maneuver that the operator takes in order to save lives.

Similarly, another dangerous situation involves two large groups pressing against each other, or a single large group pressing against an immovable object like a wall or single doorway. This deadly type of event has happened at football games, at big music concerts, and in overcrowded religious gatherings. People can suffocate to death as they are pressed from behind and from the front by huge crowds.

If you identify that such an event is developing, it may be too late to start going in any direction but up. Jumping or climbing up to bring your chest and stomach area above people's shoulders is an effective way to continue breathing. Ideally, making your way through the crowd using the techniques described earlier is a preferred solution.

CONCLUSION

The essence of combat mindset includes character qualities such as courage, determination, perseverance, and grit. In this chapter, we described different families of training methods, drills, and techniques that elevate and tighten these qualities of the mind and spirit.

Chapter 6

The First Integration of Mental and Technical Training

KMG Training Principles

We teach Krav Maga Global trainees of all kinds, whether instructors, corporate executives, military officers, civilian students, or special forces fighters, to function under stressful conditions. One purpose of the training is to improve your decision making when stressed, reduce your reaction time to the minimum needed to make efficient and effective responses, and recruit logical thinking when violence is not an immediate threat. We apply the following general principles to our training.

Usually, at least three individuals are involved in exercising KMG self-defense techniques: an instructor and two trainees. The instructor provides expertise and feedback. The trainees take turns in the roles of defender and attacker. In cases where only an instructor and trainee are available, the instructor can take the role of attacker while the trainee acts as defender, and vice versa. As the number of trainees in a session increases, they select partners and all learn from the instructor.

Training begins with the instructor offering clear explanation and demonstration of the specific problem the trainee is learning to handle. The instructor also explains the family of related problems, the actions and the mentality of the attacker, his (or her) intuitive behavior while attacking, and the attacker's natural responses to the defender's actions. The instructor offers the best solution for the specific problem.

The instructor encourages the trainee to sense the problem at hand. For example, the trainee might look at a punch or kick toward his (or her) body, or feel an attacker's grabbing motion, or observe a stick swung toward his head. The role of the attacker is played by a training partner, who delivers the attack in a slow but realistic and controlled manner to avoid injuring the trainee. The initial training environment is calm, to give the trainee a chance to understand the problem and solution without suppressing the natural fighting response.

Trainees begin learning to deal with the problem through "dry drills." These are motions in the air, taken in a slow and controlled manner, typically by the trainee alone against a simulated attack. Over the course of several repetitions, the trainee gradually increases the speed and explosiveness of the technique. The instructor helps the trainee "ramp" the motion, that is, the instructor begins with the first motion, which the trainee imitates, and then the instructor adds other motions until the trainee executes the entire technique. After dry drills and ramping, the trainee begins practicing the self-defense technique with a partner.

After the trainee understands how to execute the primary technique and grasps its principles, the instructor may introduce variations on the initial attack, and counters to those variations. Variations can include changes in the angle of the attack, or the attacking limb, the position of the attacker, or the behavior of the attacker. The instructor also begins elevating the intensity of the practice, thus introducing a likely stress response in the trainee. The simulated aggressor applies stronger, faster, and more complex attacks, perhaps grabbing the defender prior to the primary attack. The aggressor may shout at the defender, or order him to take certain actions, or swear at him. The instructor may tell the defender to close his eyes and only open them when told or signaled, or when the defender feels the attack start. The defender may have to react within a confined space, or against a wall, or he may need to confront multiple opponents.

When more preparation is possible, the instructor may choose to vary the physical environment in which the training session takes place. The instructor may conduct a session with the trainee sitting or lying down, or in a small room, a staircase, a corridor, sitting in a vehicle, or walking or standing on a rocky or slippery surface. The trainee might wear different footwear, such as boots or, for woman trainees, high heels, or the trainee might be barefoot.

Clothing might also vary from light summer outfits to a heavy winter coat, or an evening dress and high heels, usually worn by women but rarely by men (see page 204).

Practicing under these conditions gives the trainee a chance to improve decision making and function under adverse conditions, to solve new problems under stress, to increase determination, controlled aggression, and to acquire and demonstrate persistence and courage. The drills give the trainee a chance to widen his or her attention and to sense an opponent's intentions. Ideally the trainee applies calming and self-control techniques by focusing the mind and body while minimizing internal dialogue. Finally, the trainee learns to seek a balance between arousal and calm, or between position, tension, and relaxation.

Sample KMG Training Sequences

In the following figures, we visually demonstrate training sequences that incorporate the principles we just explained. Don't worry about learning the specific techniques demonstrated in this section. The purpose here is to show the gradual escalation in complexity and stress-inducing components. In later sections we share more details on attacks and defenses to create the environment needed to develop a combat mindset.

"Dry drilling," an early part of the learning process. The trainee becomes acquainted with the moves of the technique. The trainee executes a 360-degree outside defense with a counterattack.

Working with a partner. The simulated attacker slowly delivers an overhand circular strike to simulate a slap, punch, or knife attack. The trainee executes the same 360-degree outside defense with a counterattack as shown in Figure A.

The simulated attacker strikes with a rubber knife. The stress level increases when a dummy weapon appears. The defender executes the same defense as shown in Figures A and B.

The simulated attacker strikes with a wooden knife. The stress level increases again when a different dummy weapon appears. The trainee executes a variation of his previous defense, executes a counterattack, and then grabs and controls the arm holding the knife.

The simulated attacker strikes with a dummy metal knife. The stress level increases once again due to the realistic appearance of the fake weapon. The defender executes a forearm defense against a straight knife stab the attacker sends toward his chest.

The simulated attacker strikes with a real though blunt metal knife. The attacker and defender should move carefully. This is a stressful situation for both parties.

The simulated attacker can add to the complexity and stress of the drill by varying his initial position. Here, attacking from the side, he sends the knife to the abdomen area.

Stress rises considerably when defending against several attackers. The trainee must move, attack, defend, counter, and take the initiative. The trainee positions himself such that one aggressor is blocking the way of the other(s). The group should train with less dangerous tools, e.g., rubber knives.

To increase your sense of self-efficacy, you have to practice in all kinds of environments and start from all possible positions, especially those in which the defender has a limited ability to move. Here the aggressor approaches from the side.

The aggressor attacks from the side. The trainee defends while standing up to achieve a range suitable for countering with kicks.

In this variation, the trainee starts with his eyes closed. Once he feels the contact of the attacker's empty hand or leg, or the first thrust of the knife, or when he hears a sound or verbal command, the defender responds.

The defender opens his eyes as early as possible and responds with the appropriate defense and counterattack.

The attacker first delivers a kick and immediately follows with a knife stab. This is a more complex scenario requiring the trainee to identify the aggressor's actions and divide his resources to counter them.

After defending against the kick, the trainee addresses the knife attack. This requires better decision making, skill, and training.

The previous figures demonstrate how trainers can tailor exercises to suit the needs and capabilities of the trainees. Beginners can practice the dry drilling, open hand, and dummy rubber knife exercises in Figures A to C. Intermediate practitioners can add the exercises involving wooden, metal, and blunt knives in Figures D to F. Intermediate students can also incorporate the different angles and multiple opponent variations in Figures G and H. More advanced students can add the changes in environment and responses in Figures I1 to K2.

Becoming a Proficient Attacker

Most people in the civilized world learn very early in life not to use violence to solve problems. We are instructed to talk politely, not to shout, and not to point at other people. Although violence is part of nature, it is regularly and strongly suppressed. This is the right way to educate a young person; it is excellent until he needs to fight. When you have to defend yourself or your friend, family member, or colleague, well-directed violence may be the only answer.

Unfortunately, most of us are neither trained nor ready to deal with such a situation. This is true when the government drafts a young man or woman to serve in the military or police force, or when we accept a child, teenager, or an adult into a Krav Maga program. There is an immediate conflict between what people have been taught up to that moment and what they are instructed to do in a military boot camp, police course, or Krav Maga program.

Becoming an attacker is an important aspect of developing a combat mindset for two reasons. First, in a self-defense situation, the defender must be able to protect and act physically. Achieving this goal relies on defense and counterattack, which are impact actions that result in some sort of damage. If a person cannot activate an attacker mindset, then he or she cannot fully defend and counterattack. Second, the practice of developing self-defense skills requires trainees who can assume the role of defender and attacker. This means that every person engaging in self-defense must face a realistic, albeit simulated, attacker. This attacker, acting as a realistic training partner, must exhibit the postures, actions, and verbal and physical behaviors a defensive trainee may encounter in reality. Without realistic attackers, defenders do not feel the required stress levels to engage the necessary parts of their brains to develop efficient and effective physical and mental responses. The bare truth is that without a realistic attacker, the defender never manages to really learn, sense, and internalize the practiced material.

A trainee is responsible for improving the abilities of his (or her) partner. More importantly, the attacker has to simulate a real problem. If the attack is too dangerous, too complex, too fast, or too strong, a novice defender fails and may get hurt. If the attack uses unrealistic moves, is at an inappropriate range, or otherwise fails to simulate the proper attacker and proper actions, the novice defender does not learn realistic reactions. The designated attack must activate, even if only partially, the natural response, the intuitive defensive reaction against that sort of "dangerous" move. Therefore, when beginning to practice self-defense, we recommend starting relatively light and slow and always maintaining control.

Basic Strikes to the Front

The following figures illustrate basic hand strikes and kicks. The practitioners deliver them to imaginary targets "in the air." We call this "shadow striking" or "shadow fighting." It represents the first level of training, with the goal of familiarizing the student with the elementary aspects of the technique. These motions can be chained into a series, combining different attacks in a specific and designated rhythm (and there are different kinds of rhythms). The following motions change from long range to short range, ending with what we call "finishing mode," or visually scanning the environment and looking to meet the next challenge.

Front kick, a long-range attack.

Straight strike, a medium-range attack.

Hook strike and the following are short-range attacks.

Elbow strike.

Grab and headbutt.

Knee kick to the groin.

Hammer strike downward to the back of the head.

"Finishing mode:" Move away and scan the area. Look for other dangers, as well as companions you should take care off, an exit, or valuables you may have dropped. Stay in a combat mindset.

Basic Strikes to the Rear

The following sequences demonstrate shadow striking and kicking backward, sideways, and forward, while efficiently transitioning between different angles, directions, and ranges. You close and open the distance from your imaginary target, change your position and strike combination, all as you plan or see fit, and then end with "finishing mode."

Starting position.

Defensive rear kick, straight kick backward.

Return the kicking leg to the ground while turning toward the target.

Side kick. Long range is still maintained.

Sideways hammer strike at medium range, while closing the gap to the imaginary target.

Straight strike with the rear hand.

Uppercut to the chin, at short range.

Forward hammer strike and the following figures demonstrate short-range attacks.

Grab and knee kick to the groin.

Downward elbow strike.

Knee kick to the head.

Kick while moving diagonally away, back to long range.

Move away and scan the area in "finishing mode." Look for other dangers, or your companions, or even common objects to use as weapons, and for an exit. Stay in a combat mindset.

Training with a Partner Holding Pads

Once you are comfortable delivering strikes to the air, consider training with a partner holding pads. You begin to learn how to regulate your body and mind while delivering an impact to an object. Partners can hold focus mitts, Thai pads, or kick shields. If you do not have a partner or the necessary hand pads, you may be able to strike a hanging heavy bag. The way of holding the target, reacting, and meeting the attack is a skill to be learned by the trainee who holds the target. The following figures show strikes to a partner holding Thai pads.

Start from a proper stance and position, in this case the "general outlet" or fighting stance.

Close the distance by stepping forward with the right leg, then kick with the left leg.

Straight left strike, before the kicking leg has returned to the ground. This technique includes a so-called "broken rhythm" because of this timing.

Straight right palm heel strike.

Grab with one hand, and prepare to deliver a hammer strike with the other.

Pull with left hand, and deliver a hammer strike with the right.

The trainee grabs behind his partner's neck. His palms overlap and his forearms squeeze the sides of his partner's neck.

Knee kicks to the groin or solar plexus.

In the following sequence, the trainee starts in different postures and orientations to the training partner.

The partner is at the trainee's side, at medium range.

Respond with a horizontal hammer strike.

Straight strike with the rear hand.

Elbow strike is delivered while closing the distance. Conclude with "finishing mode," which is not shown here.

Training with a Partner Holding a Kick Shield

You can deliver more power and impact when your partner protects himself with a larger pad. Start in a general ready stance or a passive stance, simulating a non-ready scenario. Execute a series of attacks at different ranges, directions, and positions. Fluidity, aggression, determination, and innovation are characteristic of this line of training. Start lightly and progress in speed, power, impact, and energy. The partner holding the target must be familiar with the way of reacting to the different strikes. The following figures show strikes to a partner holding a kick shield.

The trainee begins in an outlet stance. She is too far from the pad holder to execute a normal standing kick.

The trainee delivers a sliding kick with her rear, right, leg. As she kicks with the right leg, she slides the left leg forward to close the distance.

The kick makes contact with the pad.

Landing forward and delivering a straight strike with the right hand.

Follow with a straight strike with the left, rear, hand, also called a "cross."

Advance and deliver a horizontal elbow strike with the right elbow.

Delivering a hammer strike with left fist.

Double-hand grab of the target, followed by a knee kick.

Follow with another hammer strike to the target that you pulled downward.

Move away and scan the area in "finishing mode." Look for other dangers, your companions, or even objects you may have dropped, and for an exit. Stay in a combat mindset.

Training in a Group with one Pad Holder

In the following example, a group of trainees strike a partner holding a pad. Observe how the trainee links a series of techniques together to create a striking combination.

All participants begin in a passive stance.

The first person launches a series of attacks, from long to short range, beginning with a front kick.

Straight strike with the front, right hand.

Straight punch with the rear, left hand.

After closing the gap to the target, deliver a horizontal elbow strike.

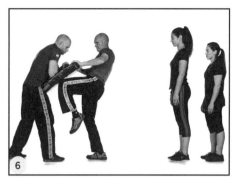

Grab, pull, and deliver a knee kick to the solar plexus area.

The first trainee moves away in "finishing mode." The second trainee begins her kick.

The second trainee connects with a kick. The trainees continue in turn to deliver series of attacks, with the same or different sequences of strikes.

Marking Attacks on a Partner

After striking the air and targets, it is time to aim attacks at a real person. We must attune the mind to the idea of hitting and causing injury to a human being, something that is against the way most people were raised. Each attack should be executed in the correct manner. All components of the technique should be formed and integrated appropriately. The only difference is that the attacks should stop and recoil a few centimeters before making contact. We call this training method **marking attacks**. Attacks should be done slowly, to avoid triggering your partner's fighting response. Thus, these drills do not suppress your partner's natural and very important reaction of responding, defending, and countering.

Begin with a single attack, such as one kick or one strike, delivered at low speed. As you get comfortable with the process of marking, and your partner becomes comfortable with looking at attacks, switch to delivering a short series of attacks, such as a kick to the groin followed by two straight strikes with the left and right hands. At the early phase, repeat each series several times. Later, combinations can be longer and more varied. For example, you can start with your side or your back to your partner (the target). You can execute a series of attacks by first attacking backward, then sideways, followed by turning and attacking to the front, then continuing with changing the distance and the angle to the partner (as demonstrated earlier in this chapter with attacks in the air). At a later stage, you can practice delivering series of attacks to multiple opponents.

This practice elevates the level of aggression and normalizes the idea of inflicting damage on another person. This concept infiltrates and gets accepted by the mind. More aggressive marking includes taking your partner to the ground, executing kicks and other attacks while your opponent is lying down, and then stopping and moving away. These drills include mental switches from being calm to becoming very aggressive and back to being calm. Your level of personal control is enhanced and you develop the mental skill to accept inflicting pain on others. Remember that these attacks are intended to be components of a self-defense scenario, where you are protecting yourself, or others, from a dangerous aggressor.

In the following figures, we demonstrate marking a series of attacks.

Two trainees face each other. One assumes an outlet stance.

Advancing with the rear leg in preparation for a front kick with the front leg.

A front kick to the groin. Notice that the trainee can reach but does not make contact with the target here or in the subsequent stages of the series.

A straight strike with the left (front) hand that recoils before hitting.

Straight strike with the right (rear) hand is marked to the chin.

Closing the gap and marking a hook strike.

Elbow strike to the jaw, stops short.

Uppercut with the rear hand that recoils a few centimeters before making contact.

Grab one shoulder and mark a rear-leg knee kick to the groin. Notice that the trainee makes contact with his partner's shoulder, but not with his knee.

Downward hammer strike.

Push the partner away. The trainee makes contact with his partner to deliver the push.

Move away and scan the area in "finishing mode." Look around for other dangers, or companions, locate fallen objects such as your keys or phone, and search for an exit. Stay in a combat mindset.

The marking attack methodology is an effective training method. It helps overcome natural barriers to striking another person, while helping the trainee develop a sense of distance and body awareness for himself and his opponent.

CONCLUSION

In order to develop a combat mindset, or fighting spirit, the initial phase should focus on the ability to attack. In several phases we have shown how to change the state of mind and embedded education of the typical student who, from childhood, constantly got the message not to attack, to erase his own aggression, and to be submissive. This chapter also describes how we elevate load, difficulties, and progress in training of defenses against any kind of attack and aggressor.

Chapter 7

Strength and Power Drills

The drills we describe in this chapter improve your power, strength, and other components of your physical fitness. When you integrate and incorporate them and also develop mental resources and practice Krav Maga techniques using these drills, you reach a completely different level of performance.

The following drills are divided into two main sections. The first is exercising (mainly) alone while combining exercises like sit-ups, push-ups, squats, bridging, and chin-ups with striking in the air or against pads. The second is strength and power drills with a partner, where the benefits are more on the mental and social sides. These drills create trust and confidence, friendship and cooperation. The result of the approach is that you learn to work like a fighter, not an exerciser.

Always use your best technique and start with light impact and slower strikes. As you develop your skills and abilities you can increase your speed and impact.

Individual Drills

The following figures demonstrate a power drill to strike the floor.

Start from the top position of the push-up. Shift your weight to one hand.

Lift the other arm, bringing your fist close to your temple, in preparation to deliver a hammer strike.

Move down and hit the floor with a hammer strike. Bend your base elbow and lower your chest. Then push up to return to a higher position and repeat.

Alternatively, move down and hit the floor with an elbow strike.

To increase the difficulty of each variation, lift your leg on the same side as the striking hand to improve core muscle strength.

The following figures demonstrate a power drill to strike the air.

From a push-up action, rise up and strike backward with an elbow strike.

Similarly, from a push-up action, rise up and strike backward with a hammer strike.

The following figures demonstrate a power drill with a strike or a defense that creates impact with a target.

From a push-up action, rise up, turn your body, and strike backward against a pad with an elbow or a hammer strike. The partner holding the pad can react lightly by pressing back.

Not only attacks but also defenses can be incorporated into strength drills. From a push-up position, perform an outside defense by hitting a pad with your forearm.

The following figures demonstrate a power drill to strike a target while doing sit-ups. Although these are presented here with a partner, they could also be done in the air or striking a hanging bag.

Prepare to perform a sit-up. Your partner holds focus mitts and pins your legs, to make the sit-ups easier.

Sit up while hitting the target diagonally upward.

Strike with the other hand while still sitting upward, and then lie down.

In this variation, you sit up while striking a target and defending a hook-like attack. It is possible for both trainees to perform this drill by alternating sit-ups.

The following figures demonstrate another power drill to strike a target while doing sit-ups.

Place two focus mitts next to you, about head level. Crunch forward in a sit-up position.

As you lean back, deliver hammer strikes to each target as you approach the floor. Be sure that the strike is above shoulder level, to simulate a strike to head level when you are standing.

In this variation, lean backward and deliver elbow strikes to each target as you approach the floor.

The following figures demonstrate a power drill and a squat integrated with striking a target.

Squat while a partner holds Thai pads.

Rise and kick.

Squat in front of your partner.

Rise and strike the two targets. Perform a defense with one forearm against a circular strike and counterstrike the other pad with your punch.

The following figures demonstrate a power drill integrated with a hand strike or a kick while bridging.

Bridge upward and diagonally sideways.

Hit the target with your far hand. The strike is similar to a hook; the elbow is above the target and your fingers point away from you.

Bridge upward and diagonally.

Turn your body and start to kick. Balance yourself with your far hand.

Turn your body and hit the target vertically downward. The striking surface is the ball of your foot.

The following figures demonstrate a power drill to strike while kicking upward.

Lie on your back, knees bent, holding your hands by the sides of your face.

Bring your knees above your shoulders and your feet over your chest or head.

Kick upward with both legs at the same time. You can train by yourself and kick in the air, or with a partner holding a target.

It is also possible to deliver a combination of several kicks, one after the other. The most relevant here is a series of stomping kicks.

Perform a set of chin-ups or pull-ups while kicking. Kick when you are not moving, or kick once or twice every time you rise up. Alternatively, you can perform a chin-up or pull-up while kicking in a different direction. It is optional to practice with a partner, for example, to perform a block defense with the shin against a roundhouse kick as you rise up. Counterattack with the other leg.

Drills with a Partner

Power drills with a partner develop courage and trust, friendship and unity. Trainees may begin by feeling worry, anxiety, and uncertainty. By performing these drills, they become stronger mentally and physically.

These drills that we created require coordination and synchronization between the trainees; they need to support each other in order to succeed. Without the correct moves and attention to each other's performance, the practice fails and the goals are not achieved. Thus, these drills also assist in developing better relations among trainees, mutual care and respect, bonding and unity.

The following figures demonstrate a partner power drill for pushing.

Start with straight arms, leaning on each other. The more you lean forward, the more weight and load you have on your hands.

Simultaneously, perform push-ups while moving your heads to the left and right.

The following figures demonstrate another partner power drill for pushing.

Start with straight arms, right to right or left to left. With your bodies straight, tilt and lean on each other. The more you tilt, the more weight you have on your hands.

Perform a one-hand push-up and come closer, shoulder to shoulder, then push away to the positions shown in Figures B2 and B1. Alternate hands at the top of each push-up.

The following figures demonstrate another partner power drill for pulling.

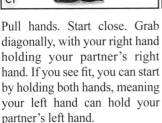

Pull hands. Start close. Grab diagonally, with your right hand holding your partner's right hand. If you see fit, you can start by holding both hands, meaning your left hand can hold your partner's left hand.

Decrease tension slowly and lean away until your elbows are straight. Pull back to a close position (C1) and then change hands. Repeat the lean, pull, and switch.

The following figures demonstrate a partner power drill for push-ups. This drill is more demanding than a regular push-up on the floor or a standing push-up with a partner. To get the participants acquainted with the drill, we suggest a progressive learning process.

One person lies down, palms up, elbows straight. The other stands in a push-up position from above, with elbows straight.

Initially, only the upper person does the push-up (in incremental distances) while the lower person acts as the base. The trust between partners influences performance.

Starting position.

Here, the lower person does the push-up (in incremental distances) while the upper person keeps his arms straight.

From the starting position as in D1, both partners start bending in incremental distances.

Both partners bend their elbows, bringing their chests closer together, and perform a push-up.

If a partner is not strong enough, you can minimize the weight on the lower person by advancing your feet forward and bending the knees.

If the partner is much stronger, he can lift two training partners. In this case, the push-up must be performed gradually.

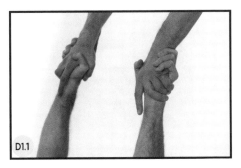

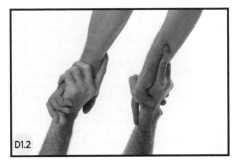

This is a close-up of the recommended hand grip. The palm and heel of the hands lean on each other. The index finger is positioned on the middle of the partner's forearm, like holding a pistol.

The following figures demonstrate a partner power drill for sit-ups.

Interlace your legs, knees bent, lying on your back, with your head up. Both trainees, defender and attacker, should sit up at the same time.

Sit up and block a circular attack, using an outside defense. Attacks should vary with direction, height, and angle.

The defender may also perform a simultaneous counterattack with an outside defense.

In this variation, the defender sits up and counters a knife attack.

The following figures demonstrate a partner power drill for sit-ups with defenses against straight attacks.

In this variation, while sitting up the defender performs an inside defense against a straight strike.

In this final variation, while sitting up the defender performs both a hand defense and a body defense with a simultaneous counterattack against a straight strike.

The following figures demonstrate another partner power drill for sit-ups, where one person absorbs strikes on a pad that he is holding.

One trainee lies back, holding a kick shield, then starts to sit up. His partner prepares to deliver a straight or hammer strike.

The partner sits up, absorbing strikes to the shield (or directly to his body, if not holding a shield). The person sitting up should resist the strike as his torso rises.

Strength Drills with a Partner that That Develop Trust

The following drills integrate power training with trust. If the partners do not trust each other, they cannot perform or safely complete these exercises. The idea in the following training method is to repeat the techniques several times with each hand and each position, according to the capabilities of the trainees. When one hand cannot support the partner, the trainees should join both hands. If the falling partner is not strong enough to have his weight supported by a hand to the head, the rear partner can place his palm on the lower part of his partner's neck. Repetitions can be done with alternating hands and positions each time, or several repetitions with one hand and then with the other.

The rear partner imitates a straight strike with his rear hand. The palm rests on the back of the falling partner's head.

The falling partner lifts his chin a bit. The rear partner recoils his arm, bending and lowering his elbow, supporting his partner.

The falling partner is at the lowest point. If the rear partner requires it, he can help hold the falling partner with both hands.

The rear partner pushes the falling partner forward, practically performing the motion of a slow rear-hand strike.

In this variation, the rear partner holds the falling partner with his front hand.

The rear partner recoils his arm, bending and lowering his elbow, supporting the falling partner.

The following power drill involves falling forward, rather than backward as in the previous drill. Practice slowly and pay special attention to the change of direction from down to up, where there is a great burden on the neck muscles.

The supporting partner holds the falling partner by the forehead. The falling partner can reduce the load on his neck by holding his partner's arm.

The supporting partner lowers the falling partner forward.

The supporting trainee pushes his partner up.

The partners return to the initial position.

In this variation, the falling partner is strong, experienced, and confident enough to rely on his neck muscles while tilting forward.

The supporting partner lowers the falling partner and then pushes him again to the initial position.

The following power drill involves falling sideways, rather than forward as in the previous drill. Initially, the falling partner can repeat the drill with one side to the supporting partner. At a later stage, the falling partner can switch positions and fall toward the supporting partner every time with another side—right, left, front, and rear.

The supporting partner holds the falling partner by the side of the head. The falling partner can reduce the load on his neck by pressing the opposite side of his head.

The supporting partner lowers the falling partner sideways and then pushes him back to the standing position.

In this variation, the falling partner relies on his neck muscles while tilting sideways.

The supporting partner lowers the falling partner.

In the drills described in Figures C1 to F2, we showed the supporting partner exercising power drills while performing a strike-like motion with his rear hand. The same drills can also be performed with the front hand.

Strength Games with a Partner

The last two power partner drills presented in this chapter are competitions. The following figures show partners that start from the plank position, then push each other while walking on all fours and keeping their torsos parallel to the ground.

The partners assume the push-up position, with the tops of their left shoulders touching each other.

When told to start, the partners push each other. Be careful with the level of pressure to avoid injury. The winner is the one who moves his partner beyond a certain point.

The following figures show partners pushing each other while sitting back to back.

The partners sit back to back, knees bent, palms resting on the ground.

When told to start, the partners push each other. Be careful with the level of pressure to avoid injury. The winner is the one who moves his partner beyond a certain point.

CONCLUSION

In this chapter, we described a bundle of power exercises and drills, performed either alone or with a partner to create trust and bonding between trainees, elevate fitness level, and enhance technical capabilities, attacking, and defending concepts and mental focus. The different drills are logically and naturally divided into several sectors according to their nature and the ways that the trainees function.

Chapter 8

Functional Games

Functional games are fun, but we have witnessed many other benefits for trainees. They prepare trainees to learn new techniques and tactics. They simulate conditions trainees may encounter outside the gym. Occasionally the functional games make the participants more aware and capable in certain components related to the technical, tactical, or physical aspect of what lies ahead. We so often use a functional game to set up and elevate certain mental aspects that we see as necessary, and the goal of the game is to be both fun and efficient for the learning process.

Trainees gain experience and enhance their abilities while avoiding much of the usual stress.

Like animals in nature—wolves and big cats, or their domesticated counterparts, dogs and cats—we see that playing prepares them to be what they are designed to be. They play with their siblings or parents, with other members of the pack, or with weakened prey. What are military drills and war games but the same approach by human beings? Training simulations or the real-life fighting of combat pilots are even called "dog fights." This can relate even more to those animals that are fighting and hunting where it is practically a three-dimensional environment, in sea or air. For example, look at the games that hawks, eagles, dolphins, and orca whales play.

These games prepare us for reality in a fun, less stressful, less dangerous, and non-damaging setting. We put ourselves in an atmosphere where we can learn easily, where the mind is much freer to absorb information and achieve our goals.

When we apply KMG to the task of training corporate directors, managers, and team leaders, we create analogies to clarify the principles, relations, ingredients, and aspects that are common between physical and nonphysical conflicts, arguments, and stress-induced events, incidents, and relations. The participants in KMG Executive Program and workshops experience relevant functional drills, games, and situations of physical threat modified for them, and the use of different tactics to handle these situations. This helps the workshop participants to identify, through their physical conduct, their ability to control and handle themselves and their counterparts, to manage others and cope with stressors. Concepts, principles, tactics, and techniques taken from the KMG milieu and an array of games are translated and applied to the world of management, including decision making under stress, team building, improving communication, neutralization of destructive emotions, change of negative self-talk (internal monologue and thoughts), and more.

Families can also benefit from playing functional games. The bond between parents and children can become stronger. Cuddling and light wrestling and grappling games entail a lot of physical contact; the skin, which is our largest organ, is constantly stimulated. This stimulus results in new contacts among synapses in the brain. Minds are connected, and fun and laughter are characteristic to these games. Functional games improve cognitive as well as physical abilities. Balance, power, and stamina develop side by side with self-control, determination, and perseverance. Children learn how to face failure, accept defeat, overcome frustration, and deal with obstacles and disappointments. Children develop discipline and self-restraint. Sometimes you need to adapt a game to address differences in size, power, emotional state, mental level, and resources, but the benefits are apparent.

Push-Pull Games

This "area control" game involves two partners pushing each other until one is moved outside a marked area, or across a designated line. This resembles a sumo competition. For untrained people, we only allow pushing or pulling to achieve victory though avoid throws that might prove harmful.

One modification is to have other participants standing around, observing the two partners. The moment there is a winner, the first person who jumps in and touches the winner is the next one to compete against that winner. The idea in this case is both to have as many wins, and to participate in as many games, as possible.

A variation involves having one partner control and defend an area, or an object, while the other tries to push the protector away. In both games, trainees need to be focused, alert, and decisive. They must follow instructions, control their level of aggression, and monitor emotions such as frustration and anger.

The following figures demonstrate push-pull games.

The two participants are inside the marked area. On the instructor's command, they start trying to push each other out.

The person who steps out or touches the ground with any body part other than the feet loses.

In this variation, partners are pulling into or out from an area. The pair opposes each other from two sides of a border.

The winner is the person who takes his partner over to his side.

In this game, one partner protects an object ("the target") that is on the floor, or hanging from above, or put on the wall. One person is controlling the approach to that object and protecting it.

The other person tries to switch places and "jobs" with the protector and become the protector.

The attacker manages to achieve the goal of dominating the area and object, by pulling, pushing, and turning the protector.

The attacker manages to win here by pushing the protector backward and taking his place. These games develop a strong spirit, but also gain the ability to accept a loss.

Push-Pull Games with a Tool or Weapon

We can augment push-pull games by adding an object to the competition. Trainees can hold a stick, soldiers can hold a rifle or a rope, and managers can use items found in the office and are safe to use, such as a thick old coat or a solid book. One interesting and fun variation for most sectors involves occupying a chair. In a sense, the person who controls the chair has asserted his position in the leadership or managerial hierarchy. These games excite the participants' mental states, triggering their perceptions of dominance and what they feel they deserve. Instructors might also increase the difficulty level by including two-against-one or two-against-two scenarios.

The following figures demonstrate push-pull games with a tool or other object.

Two partners hold a stick. Each tries to push his partner away from his own area.

Two partners hold a stick. Each tries to pull the partner to his own area.

A rope-pulling competition, using a thick rope, strong belt, or stick.

Military or law enforcement trainees may use an assault rifle or extendable baton. Goals for these drills include developing weapon retention, balance, stamina, determination, aggression, and self-control.

The following figures demonstrate push-pull games with a weapon.

Trainees use a training assault rifle to push or pull. This is very relevant to the subject of weapon retention, keeping your own firearm when an attacker tries to take it. This is a preparation drill, and less of an accurate technical solution.

Pushing and pulling a weapon can be a power drill.

The following figures demonstrate push-pull games where a chair is the object of interest.

Trainees compete over who sits on the chair.

Trainees may push or pull each other in order to dominate the area.

One participant manages to overcome his partner's resistance, and sits on the chair.

Controlling an Object or Area and Applying KMG Techniques

In the previous drills, trainees use general physical motions such as pushing and pulling to accomplish a goal. They control an object or area using basic body mechanics. The following drills demonstrate controlling an object or area, followed by applying KMG techniques. Trainees learn to transition their mindset from one of competition to one of attack and self-defense.

Trainees drill in a defined area, with a tool on the ground. The goal of each of them is to dominate the tool, or the weapon, but not to grab it yet.

On the instructor's command, each partner tries to grab the dummy knife.

The trainee who grabs the knife attacks his partner, who executes the appropriate defenses and counterattacks. Changing the mindset is the essence of this drill, from a game or a competition to a lifesaving technique.

Sticky Hands Drills

In this game, the two participants stand in a relaxed manner, with knees bent. Both are trying to slowly push each other off balance by shifting the weight and pressure on the partner's arm, chest, abdomen, or hip area. The actions are soft and relaxed, with very light pressure between the hands. The aim is to cause the partner to move a leg because of loss of balance. Each is trying to sense the intentions and actions of the partner, to anticipate and act as early as possible. If you overcommit and try to push too hard and your partner avoids the push, you may find yourself off balance.

This game demands self-control, practices emotional restraint and thus improves the participant's ability to stay relaxed, maintain a calm and focused mind, overcome frustration and desire, and deal with minor stress. The game suppresses the ego. You lose concentration and reduce performance the moment you focus on the result, or care about how your image as a trainee, fighter, or instructor is perceived by others. The moment you maintain a calm mind, when you do not care about the result, when you are focused on the moment and minimize your internal monologue, your performances improves. The wrong mindset is to become stressed due to your performance, or anxious because you are going to lose a point, or proud that you momentarily gained a point.

The following figures demonstrate the one-handed "**sticky hands**" drill.

Two partners face each other, in a calm, low posture, with the same hand and leg forward. Start with the wrists touching.

Each tries to slowly push to a point that can move his partner off balance. Resistance and contact should be minor. The body moves forward and backward, turning and pivoting so that the pressure slides away.

Each tries to deflect his partner's "attacks," but maintains light contact. You must not resist or press strongly against your partner, but flow and redirect his motion (which is perceived as an attack).

One partner lost his balance. If you "win a point," do not care about it. If you lose for a moment, ignore it. Focus on doing and improving; stay focused on the action.

There are many variations within this family of drills. You can do it with one hand each, while standing in the same place, bending your knees and resting on your pelvis (as shown in Figures A1 to A4), or be dynamic, moving and stepping in any suitable direction. You can practice with two hands, requiring improved attention span, focus, and concentration. Another variation involves trying to grab your partner's wrist while avoiding being grabbed. If you are grabbed, use a KMG release. A byproduct of this game is improving your ability to grab and to hold on to what you grabbed. This is analogical to grabs done during defenses against handgun, rifle, or knife threats, or while performing techniques against knife attacks or other armed or empty-handed strikes, defenses, and controls.

The following figures demonstrate the two-handed **"sticky hands"** drill.

The two partners stand, one in front of the other, with the same leg forward. Start with the wrists of the two hands touching, one on the inside and the other on the outside.

Each tries to slowly push to a point that can move his partner off balance. Resistance and contact should be minor. Each hand attacks and defends.

Each tries to deflect his partner's "attacks," but maintains light contact. You must not resist or press against your partner, but flow and redirect his motion.

The body moves forward and backward, turning so that the pressure slides away. Search for targets and openings. When you find one, push lightly to unbalance your partner.

Rooster Games

The "**rooster**" family of games requires balance, invoking attacks and defenses mainly done with the body while jumping on one leg. By bumping your partner's body with your shoulder, chest, or upper arm, you put him off balance while keeping your balance. Both partners should stay on one leg at all times. You "win" by causing your partner to touch the ground with both legs. While jumping or standing on one leg only, you keep or regain balance, advance and retreat, defend and attack.

Variations include pushing or pulling your partner with one hand, or even with the floating leg.

In this set of games, we drill and elevate the desire to win. We create excitement, enthusiasm, interest, and fun. We offer opportunities to innovate new moves, solutions, and problems. This family of games forces the trainee to deal with failure, as well as to develop courage and perseverance, control aggression, and overcome frustration and criticism.

The following figures demonstrate "**rooster**" games.

Partners fold their arms on their chests, with their elbows pressed against the ribs. While keeping your balance, attack and defend while standing or jumping on one leg.

Bump your partner with your shoulder and upper arm area. Keep your elbows near your body.

In this variation, partners grab their ankles with their opposite hands. They hold their other hands to their chests. A variation is to use the free hand to push or pull the partner.

The partners make contact with their upper bodies. The goal is to get your partner off balance, causing him to touch the ground with both legs.

In this game, partners squat, shoving and pushing their partner's hands, shoulders, or knees to get him off balance.

Trainees can deflect or stop their partner's hands. These are active defenses. Trainees can also push their partner's knees, hands, or shoulders. These are active attacks.

King of the Hill

The goal of the next family of games is to push others away from a marked area or pull them into it. Some of the games are played by individuals, while others are group games.

The following figures demonstrate "**king of the hill**" games.

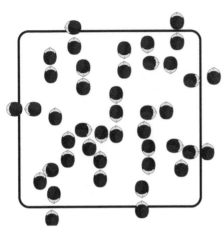

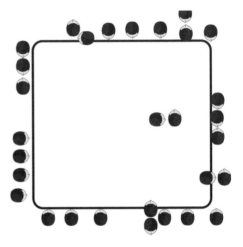

A1. In the "last man standing" variation, participants start inside the marked area. On the instructor's command, they push one another, individually or in a small team, to send others out of the marked area.

A2. You lose when you step out of the area or touch the ground with any body part other than your feet. The winner is the last person to stay in the marked area.

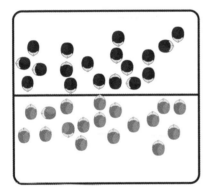

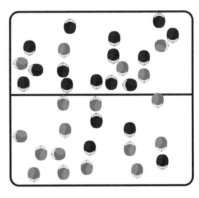

B1. In the group version, two groups start inside their marked area. On the instructor's command, they pull one another's members into their territory. In this variation, a player pulled out of his home area is a "prisoner" and does not assist his new "team."

B2. The winning group is the one that has more members in its area when the bell rings.

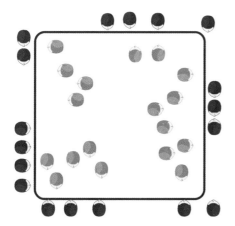 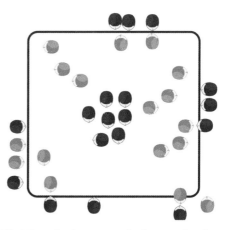

C1. Another group version: one group starts inside the designated area while the other starts outside the area. On the instructor's command, they pull one another to their areas. In this variation, a pulled trainee becomes a member of the group that "got him." A player changes teams when both of his feet have left his home area.

C2. The winning group is the one that has more members in its area when the bell rings.

Touching Games

The following games play a very important role in mental preparation because they resemble a fight. The rules and actions may be defined, such that trainees can perform only a small number of moves. Rules and actions can also be set, such that trainees have freedom to choose what kind of attacks, defenses, and actions they can utilize.

These games improve reaction time, determination, dealing with failure, self-control, and ignition of aggression, skills to overcome frustration, and the ability to focus and concentrate. This family of games has a strong relation and relevance to KMG techniques. We use these games as analogies and fun ways to improve techniques, such as inside and outside hand defenses, body defenses and evasions, timing in defenses and counterattacks, enhancing attacking skills, minimizing your preliminary actions that usually show your intentions, and improving your physical fitness and mental capacities as a fighter.

Although the following figures show empty-hand techniques, partners could also use dummy training knives or other training tools.

The following figures demonstrate touching games.

Both participants are in a ready position, usually moving around, planning to touch and ready to defend.

On the instructor's command, both try to touch their partner and also defend the target area named by the instructor. In this example, the top of the head is the target.

Be careful not to hit or scratch your partner's eyes or face.

When the instructor calls out another part of the body (e.g., the knee), partners compete to touch and defend that area.

The following figures demonstrate other touching games.

In this variation, two compete against one. Each is trying to touch and defend the target area that was called.

In this variation, all participants are trying to defend while attacking. We call it the "no friend game."

Fencing Games

Fencing games resemble classical fencing. Usually we play these games empty-handed. Partners try to touch each other in the chest and abdomen area while defending those areas. Initially, both trainees use only one hand, the one that "holds" the weapon. The palm is clenched as if holding a screwdriver, with the thumb and second joint of the index finger pointing forward. With the forearm, you should perform inside and outside defenses to prevent your partner's hand from touching you.

Many variations are possible. For example, the partners can use both hands, defending and attacking with the "weapon" hand, while the other hand is used only for defense. You can stand with the attacking hand at the front or at the rear.

We can add different missions and options. For example, a partner can attack the weapon hand (as if to hurt and disarm it), or attack other parts of the body, such as the legs or even the head and neck, given appropriate protection. Trainees can add kicks to the drills. If we wish to create more impact, it is possible to put a glove on the attacking hand. The higher levels of this game resemble fighting with a knife in your hand against an armed or unarmed opponent.

Both participants are in a ready position, usually moving around, planning to touch and ready to defend while using only the front hand.

The partner on the right performs an inside defense with the forearm, against a high stab. He also moves his body out of the line of attack as an evasive maneuver.

The trainee on the left performs a low outside defense with the forearm, defending against a low stab. He also moves his body out of the line of attack.

The partner on the right performs an outside defense with the forearm against a high stab. As soon as possible, he moves his body out of the line of the attack.

Tapping and Touching Feet and Related Games

This family of games works on reaction time, and on body motion for avoiding attacks and changing distances. These games also improve accuracy and speed of action with the legs, and improve protecting parts of the body, such as the groin area.

The following figures demonstrate tapping and touching feet games.

Partners are ready and moving in the area.

The trainee on the left tries to touch his partner's instep with his foot. The partner moves or lifts his foot.

To enhance the drill, now there are two kinds of targets, at two heights: the instep and the groin area. Defend the groin by moving the shin inward or outward. Evasive actions are also necessary.

Catching, Snatching, and Grabbing: Reaction Games

The following games develop readiness, focus, attention, accuracy of movement, and shorten response time. At a higher level when we integrate KMG techniques into the games, and in order to be successful, you need to quickly transform from a playful, fun, and competitive mental state to a fighter's state of mind, to deal with knife attacks, or to turn into an attacker with a knife in your hand.

In the following figures, one partner tries to catch an object dropped by his partner.

Partners stand facing each other. One is ready to drop a small stick held by its two ends, positioned at the level of his upper stomach or chest. The trainee's hand, ready to grab, is around 25 centimeters (10 inches) above the stick.

The partner drops the stick without any warning. The trainee catches the stick as high as possible.

In this variation, the trainee starts with his hands behind his head. You can start by gazing at the object, but later we recommend using your peripheral vision.

In this variation, the trainee starts with his hands behind his back. Continue to grab the stick from above, as seen in the previous drills.

In the following figures, one partner tries to catch an object held in his partner's hand.

The aim is to grab and take the object that is resting on your partner's open palm. The "attacker" practices accuracy in motion and not telegraphing his intentions. His action is similar to a straight strike.

The trainee on the left starts in a semi-passive stance. The partner on the right holds a dummy training knife in his open palm.

The trainee reaches for the knife and grabs it before the partner closes his hand.

The following figures demonstrate variations where follow-up activities take place after the previous games. Here we integrate Krav Maga techniques with the reaction game.

In this variation, the trainee on the left manages to grab the knife from his partner. The trainee simulates a stabbing action. The partner performs a defense and counterattack.

Here, the trainee on the right manages to keep control of the knife and simulates a stabbing action. His partner performs a defense and counterattack.

The following figures demonstrate variations of the grabbing games.

Both trainees are ready, waiting for a sign, positioned equidistant from the object.

When the instructor gives a signal, both partners burst forward and try to grab the object (a training knife, in this case).

One manages to grab the knife.

He then simulates a stabbing action. The partner performs a defense and counterattack.

The following figures demonstrate more variations of the grabbing games.

Both trainees are ready, waiting for a signal, positioned equidistant from the object and facing away from each other.

When the instructor gives a signal, both partners reach backward and try to grab the object (a training knife, in this case).

Later, after grabbing the object, other missions can be added, such as attack and defend.

Tails

In this game, we try to grab an object attached to the partner's body, e.g., piece of cloth, a sock, or even a rubber knife that is tucked into his waistband. It can also be the training shirt tucked into the pants. The aim is to take the object or pull the training shirt out. The object can be located in different locations, usually around the waist or belt level.

The following figures demonstrate the "**tails**" games.

Partners are ready, moving, and planning.

One manages to trap his partner's arm, turn him, and grab the training tool.

One managed to take the object. Then next mission could be to change roles, or attack and defend, or the one who lost the object does a burpee (full-body exercise used in strength training and as an aerobic exercise).

Coordination Drills

These drills improve coordination, patterns in the brain, and learning capabilities. Coordination drills can include technical aspects. Practicing in a group can help minimize and control the ego by making trainees feel ridiculous when failing to perform the challenging drills. Laughing at your own moves is a common effect, which also serves to reduce ego and makes you more aware of your own limitations.

The following are sample coordination drills.

- Step jumping while raising and lowering the arms to the sides (to shoulder level).
- Spread jumping while raising and lowering the arms forward and backward (to shoulder level).
- Spread jumping, opening the legs sideways, while raising and lowering the arms at 90 degrees (to shoulder level), one arm raised forward and the other to the side. Alternate sides with every jump. The same drill may include 360-degree defenses and counterattacks.
- Spread jumping while raising and lowering the arms (to shoulder level), arms at 90 degrees lifted in opposite phase to the leg motion. When closing the legs, lift the arms. You can do the same drill with a 360-degree defense and attack (see Figures B1 to B4).
- Walking/running/kicking in place and circling the arms (same or different directions, alternating directions every few circles).
- Walking/running/kicking in place while circling the head.

The following figures demonstrate complex coordination drills.

The trainee tilts his body forward, arms spread out, with one forward and the other backward.

The trainee performs a defensive (straight) rear kick, alternating his left and right legs, while circling the arms, each in a different direction. After three or four circles, change the direction in which each arm moves.

A3

The trainee kicks left and right, one after the other, while keeping good balance. He cycles his arms at the opposite sides.

The following figures demonstrate coordination drills that incorporate KMG techniques.

B1

Start with your legs spread and your hands down. In some manner the drill resembles the popular "jumping jacks."

B2

Jump and bring your legs tightly together. Simultaneously perform a high outside defense with one hand while countering with the other. One hand is open while the striking hand is clenched.

B3

Simultaneously recoil your hands and jump back to the starting position.

B4

Jump and bring your legs tightly together. Simultaneously perform a strike with a defense to the other side. Another more challenging option is to perform a low outside defense with one hand while bending low and forward at the waist.

CONCLUSION

We continue building mental resilience and powers, harnessing drills and "games" that use competition and aggression to elevate mental capacities and powers, while others are slow and relaxed in order to neutralize the ego, disturbing thoughts, and problematic internal monologues. Some other methods in this chapter focus on improving coordination, reaction, and response time while minimizing the exposure of intentions and desires, resulting in improving self-control and conduct.

Chapter 9

Krav Maga for Government, Law Enforcement Agencies, Special Forces, and Security Personnel

Although the Israel Defense Force (IDF) had already begun practicing Krav Maga in the 1950s, the system is deeply rooted in the knowledge and experience of its founder, Imi (Emrich) Sde-Or (Lichtenfeld) (1910-1998). Grandmaster Imi integrated lessons from his days as a highly accomplished wrestler and boxer in Bratislava, then Czechoslovakia, in the 1920s and 1930s, and as a fighter resisting fascist thugs in the late 1930s. Later in the 1940s, he was an instructor of the special commando unit of the Haganah paramilitary organization, which, after Israel declared independence in 1948, became the core of the IDF. He instructed fighters in the Palyam, which was the predecessor to the Israeli Navy, and then he became the IDF's chief instructor of physical education and hand-to-hand combat in the 1950s and 1960s.

As head of the Professional Committee and the founder's most distinguished successor, Eyal Yanilov saw the progress and changes in the system since the mid-1970s. With Grandmaster's Imi's blessing, Yanilov led this process of change starting in the mid-1980s to develop Krav Maga into an integrated technical and then tactical system. For the last few decades, Yanilov and his students have trained individuals, instructors, elite units, undercover agents, law enforcement personnel, and homeland and security officers from around the globe. We hope this chapter augments the training we have provided to these communities.

Investing in Human Resources

We frequently ask if well-equipped special forces, protection, security, or law enforcement personnel are also trained to deal with different levels of conflict, to distinguish between lower and higher risks, and whether they are capable of correct decision making during high-stress and violent events. Are they able to function well in close protection missions (guarding executives or VIPs)? Can they adequately react when executing low-danger peacekeeping or peace enforcement tasks? The same questions apply to counterterrorism and rescue operations, as well as close combat or urban raids in the heart of hostile populations, or at the center of densely populated cities.

We seek to develop determined and aggressive "agents-officers-fighters" who are also considerate and levelheaded, capable of fulfilling demanding and dangerous tasks, as well as capable of maintaining high moral standards and superior physical and mental resistance and stamina. Aspects of their daily routines may be boring, but they need to be ready to respond appropriately to different challenges in a fraction of a second in an intuitive and decisive manner.

Modern defense, security, and law enforcement organizations need the proper methods and tools to guide policemen, officers, undercover agents, and members of elite units in the development of essential technical, tactical, mental, and physical capabilities. Study and training in self-defense, third party protection (protecting another person, fellow officer, or VIP), defensive tactics, and hand-to-hand and close combat (with or without a weapon in hand) are key parts of that education.

The KMG approach takes all types of training to a higher level and creates operators, fighters, and warriors with proven results. We deliberately avoid instructional methods that train officers to become boxers and kickers, who get good results in the ring, or mere operators of equipment—technicians who only know how to use batons, firearms, or other "tools" that make holes in paper targets.

KMG Training Goals for Government Units

We pursue the following goals through KMG training for government units. We use the term "government units" as shorthand for the sorts of teams discussed previously.

- We raise members and officers of any unit to the highest level possible—mentally, technically, tactically, and physically. We create determined, effective, efficient, considerate, and empathic fighters and officers.
- We include specific material for armed officers or security personnel to function appropriately with any kind of personal firearm when it cannot

or should not be discharged, when it is useless at close range, when it may be too dangerous to shoot, when it is illegal to fire, when they are capable of solving the problem without using lethal force, thereby saving lives and avoiding killing people outside of a war environment.
- We train systematic thinking and efficient operators in different units and task forces within any kind of modern defense forces, law enforcement, or close-protection environments.
- We elevate all trainees to high levels of proficiency, capability, and efficiency using modern, effective, innovative, and unique training methods. We practice correct decision making processes, so that officers become adept at resolving problems under high-stress situations and in all relevant environments.
- We educate high-level and proficient instructors (in an array of courses) who are capable of teaching Krav Maga to different units, according to their assigned missions, risk analysis, and issued weapons and equipment.

For some government units, we divide the KMG curriculum into six levels. We define three "Fighter" levels and, above that, three "Warrior" levels, to create relevant professional grades. Officers must pass tests and complete specific requirements to advance from one level to another. The curriculum is partly generic and partly specific, tailored to each unit according to its job description and needs.

To customize a course for each unit, we collate and analyze information about the problems, dangers, and risks to officers, civilians, and dignitaries in a variety of environments. We collect data from the unit's commanders about the equipment and weapons that they use. We consider the relevant section of the KMG system, techniques, training methods, and tactics, as well as the mental and physical preparation needed. We offer top-notch education based on the distillation of our accumulated knowledge in order to advance trainees' progress in a short period of time.

Government Unit Training Curriculum

Non-civilians need specific techniques, training methods, and material in order to function on the battlefield and in other dangerous environments. For these government units, we focus on the following topics:

1. Attack principles and techniques, and ways to counter them.
2. Prevention and releases from grabs and defenses against strikes and kicks.
3. Defense against various armed attacks and threats, such as with sharp objects, blunt and stick-like objects, and threats with long or short firearms and hand-grenades.
4. Proper mental approaches and decision making.
5. Close Quarter Battle (CQB) and fighting in urban terrain, open terrain, and other locations, under varying conditions and with different kinds of equipment.
6. Dealing with sudden assaults at close range, when weapons cannot be immediately operated.
7. Handling and using a firearm to defend against armed or unarmed attacks and releases from different grabs.
8. Handling and using a firearm when the violent confrontation goes down to the ground and the need arises to defend against armed or unarmed attacks whether the assailant is standing or grappling on the ground with the defender.
9. Using a firearm as an impact weapon in the following scenarios:
    *   The weapon cannot shoot, due to stoppages or lack of ammunition.
    *   It is too dangerous to shoot due to the risk posed to other people, or other conditions make shooting too dangerous (e.g., the presence of explosives, gas or fuel in the area).
    *   It is illegal to shoot due to regulations, laws, or rules of engagement.
    *   The soldier or officer is trained and confident enough to solve the problem without applying lethal force.
    *   The soldier has orders not to shoot.
    *   Shooting does not solve the problem or does not halt the assailant. In many cases, when an assailant is under the influence of drugs, the impact of one or more bullets does not stop him from continuing his devastating attack or from using a weapon. A strong strike with the firearm often manages to eliminate the assailant's ability to continue.
    *   Shooting is against the natural response, due to sudden attack against the soldier or officer that triggers a non-shooting natural reaction.
10. Weapon retention, when an aggressor tries to take the weapon and use it against the officer or soldier or others, or handling the weapon when releasing from different kinds of grabs.
11. Handling suspects, criminals, prisoners of war, and other individuals such that pain compliance, takedown, "come-along," and handcuffing or immobilizing techniques are required.

For government units, we also address peacekeeping or peace-enforcing missions, operating among civilian populations, and proper conduct when in off-duty and civil environments, such as when on vacation. We cover protection duties, such as acting as a guard or peace officer. We also address the unique requirements of special operations teams.

We integrate here core mental components, such as courage, fighting spirit, determination, aggression, focus, concentration, and functioning under stress. We develop physical capabilities, such as power, force, stamina, mobility, flexibility, agility, and capacity to absorb strikes and impact. We refine technical and tactical skills by teaching defined and varied techniques using simulation and drills, with aggressive and defensive considerations in pre- and post-fight scenarios.

Using a Firearm as an Impact Weapon

The following figures demonstrate one element of training for government units. Here we show how to use a firearm as an impact weapon. The fighter responds by "shooting" when the target is up, advancing when the target is down, and by striking (with his hands, firearm, and legs) when "shooting" is no longer possible.

The trainee, holding a dummy firearm, is prepared, 5–8 meters (16–25 feet) from his partner.

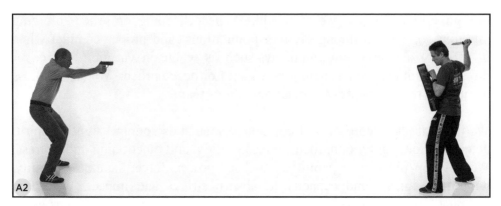

The partner simulates an active aggressor. The trainee responds by "shooting" the target.

The partner simulates an idle aggressor, the trainee responds, checks his weapon and advances.

The partner again simulates an active aggressor. The trainee stops running, aims, and shoots. At close range, the trainee holds the weapon in one hand.

The trainee gets a signal that his weapon is jammed or he has run out of ammunition. As his opponent is close, the trainee has no time to clear the weapon or reload.

The trainee advances and attacks at the appropriate range, starting with a kick.

The trainee continues by striking the target with the firearm as an impact weapon.

The trainee delivers additional strikes with the weapon, his legs, or his free hand.

The trainee delivers additional attacks as needed, then switches to the next mission, such as moving away, scanning for possible danger, clearing or reloading his weapon, or assisting others.

The following figures depict other uses of a firearm as an impact weapon versus an attacker armed with a knife. This solution is the appropriate one when the officer is confident of overcoming the danger without discharging his firearm, or he has to strike because the weapon cannot shoot.

At close range, the attacker strikes with a straight knife stab. The officer defends with his empty hand, as it is closer to the attacker.

The officer counterattacks with his firearm. He may be able to shoot, but here he has to, or decides to, deliver a straight strike with the barrel, as he traps the assailant's hand to limit his ability to act with the knife again.

The following figures depict other uses of a firearm as an impact weapon against an attacker armed with a handgun. Here it is too dangerous to shoot. If the defender tries to move and aim his gun toward the aggressor, the latter will certainly shoot. Using the hand closest to the weapon to deflect and grab the weapon allows the defender to respond efficiently and minimize the chances of getting shot.

The officer suddenly detects a handgun threat from the side.

The officer uses his empty hand to deflect and grab the weapon, as he moves away from the line of fire and line of attack. At this moment, the first counterattack may be a shot.

The officer chooses to or has to counter-attack by thrusting with his firearm to the attacker's throat. Next, he should disarm and apply the appropriate post-fight tactics.

The following figures depict other uses of a firearm as an impact weapon versus an attacker with a rifle. In a similar situation, when it is too dangerous to aim and shoot, or if shooting is not possible, the defending officer deflects the threat with his hand that is closest to the weapon (this time it is the hand holding the handgun).

The attacker suddenly aims with a rifle.

The officer deflects the threat by using the forearm of his hand holding the handgun, or with the weapon itself.

The officer turns and uses his free hand to control the rifle. He can choose to strike or shoot with his firearm.

Using a Rifle as an Impact Weapon

A rifle is held in two hands, which requires most defenses and attacks to keep both hands on the weapon. We present techniques for confrontation at close range, when it is not possible, desirable, or legal to shoot.

The following figures depict using the assault rifle as an impact weapon, for defense and counterattacks, against a bladed weapon.

The officer defends against a circular knife attack with an outside defensive, blocking motion. He simultaneously counterattacks with a strong kick.

The officer defends against a straight knife attack with an inside defensive, deflecting motion. He simultaneously moves out from the line of attack.

The officer defends against the attacker swinging a machete by using an upward blocking defense. He simultaneously counterattacks with a strong kick.

In this variation, the attacker is at very close range. The defending officer performs an inside defense with his rifle (low barrel), deflecting a low straight stab with a knife. He steps diagonally forward, moving his body away from the line of attack.

The officer immediately counterattacks with a straight strike of his assault rifle, a stab-like action. He continues with counterattacks or by firing his weapon.

The following figures depict using a rifle as an impact weapon against a handgun. In the following cases, the attempt to aim the rifle and shoot (if shooting is at all possible) takes more time then deflecting the threat.

The attacker surprises the officer at close range with a handgun threat, or an attempt to shoot.

The officer deflects the handgun with the barrel of his rifle.

The officer counterattacks by shooting or striking the attacker.

In this variation, the officer chooses to release one hand from his rifle to deflect and gain control of the handgun. The options to continue are either to shoot, if possible, or to strike with the rifle's barrel.

In this scenario, the attacker tries to stab the officer on the ground. The officer is unable to fire his weapon early enough and deflects the stab with his rifle.

As he moves his body away from the line of the descending machete, the officer also delivers kicks to the attacker and shoots his rifle, if possible.

Weapon Retention

Maintaining control of a weapon is a critical skill for all government operators, as well as for a civilian carrying a licensed firearm. The following figures depict several weapon retention scenarios.

The assailant grabs the officer's rifle to limit his actions, striking with a knife toward his neck.

The officer removes one hand from his weapon and defends against the knife attack. He counterattacks first with a headbutt or a knee to the groin and continues with additional counterattacks.

As the aggressor tries to snatch the weapon, the agent advances and counterattacks, starting here with a knee to the groin. The agent proceeds with further counterattacks and rotates his weapon to free it.

As the aggressor pulls and lowers the weapon, the agent advances, diverts it and kicks. Here too, if needed, the agent rotates his weapon to free it.

A Real-Life Story: High-Ranking Officers on High Heels

During Operation Spring of Youth in April 1973, as part of Israel's response to the massacre of its athletes at the 1972 Summer Olympics in Munich, Israeli army special forces attacked senior PLO terrorist leaders in Beirut, Lebanon. Some fighters of the elite commando unit Sayeret Matkal—with Ehud Barak, their commander at that time—also practiced cross-dressing and walking around as romantic lovers (Barak himself was disguised as an attractive brunette woman in a fancy dress). General Barak, Israel's most highly decorated soldier, was later promoted to IDF chief of staff and served as Israel's prime minister and minister of defense.

Practicing under these conditions gives the trainee a chance to improve decision making and function under adverse conditions, to solve new problems under stress, to increase determination, controlled aggression, and to acquire and demonstrate persistence and courage. The drills give the trainee a chance to widen his or her attention and to sense an opponent's intentions. Ideally the trainee applies calming and self-control techniques by focusing the mind and body while minimizing internal dialogue. Finally, the trainee learns to seek a balance between arousal and calm, or between position, tension, and relaxation.

CONCLUSION

Krav Maga emerged from the Israel Defense Forces, then it was transformed to meet the needs of law enforcement officers and other government units, and civilians of various ages and genders. In this chapter we described several methods that are characteristic to the training of law enforcement agencies, elite units and special forces, which are particularly needed when it is not possible, legal, or desirable to use a firearm as a lethal weapon.

Part Three
Growing Your Mental Strength

The whole world is a very narrow bridge,
and the main thing is to have no fear at all.

Nachman of Breslov, a renowned Hasidic Rabbi (1772-1810)

Success is not final, failure is not fatal:
it is the courage to continue that counts.

Courage is rightly esteemed the first of human qualities...
because it is the quality which guarantees all others.

Sir Winston Churchill (1874-1965)

Chapter 10

Visualization and Anchoring

Visualization is one of the best tools available to enhance your performance. You use mental images to influence bodily processes or to control pain, to influence or change your mental state, or to prepare for a corporate executive meeting, an athletic competition, or a performance. A mental image influences you in the same way that a real image does. This chapter explains how to make visualization work for you to develop a combat mindset and to manage stressful situations.

Creating a Picture in Your Mind

In some sports, prior to the competition, it is common to see athletes with their eyes closed, moving their hands and feet in specific patterns. High jumpers, for example, go through a sequence of steps and motions, transferring their weight and checking their timing. They visualize the upcoming jump so that every little detail is perfectly executed.

A Real-Life Story: Creating a Picture in Your Mind when Shooting in a Basketball Game

Zvi had enjoyed playing basketball since he was twelve, and, although not a professional player, he became quite a good shooter and was on his school's team.

After several decades of playing basketball, he discussed it one day with Krav Maga founder Imi Sde-Or, who excelled as a professional wrestler and boxer as well as an accomplished athlete, though he was not familiar with basketball.

Grandmaster Imi told Zvi, "When delivering an accurate long-range shot, you must visualize yourself—as the ball—flying through the air directly into the basket."

Zvi was astonished. "How did you know?" he asked him, as this was indeed the mental process that Zvi had experienced.

Imagine speaking in front of a large crowd. Are you nervous? If the answer is yes, you have two choices. You can try to give many speeches, and expect that your nerves may improve over time, or run a simulation before your speech in front of a supporting crowd. Alternatively, you can visualize your performance, and take advantage of the fact that your brain cannot effectively differentiate reality from fantasy. In other words, you can trick your brain into experiencing public speaking many times, without needing an audience or stage.

There are three different ways to visualize. First, you can imagine yourself from the outside, as if you are watching a "neutral" movie of yourself performing. Second, you can imagine the experience as seen through your own eyes. The first method is called dissociation, and the second is called association. Third, you can imagine the experience from the point of view of another person, directly focusing on you.

When you first start to practice visualization, you should be in a quiet place. The fewer sounds and smells you experience, the easier it is to begin. The more experienced you get, the easier it is to visualize when there are things going on around you. You can visualize while you are sitting, standing, lying down, or moving slowly. You should experiment to find out what works best for you.

The more senses you engage during the visualization exercise, the more real your brain thinks it is. Imagine what it might be like before you deliver a speech. What does the audience look like? Fill in the details; you see someone laughing, someone who looks tired, someone talking to another person, and someone stressed out because he arrived late. What clothes are they wearing? What do you hear, smell, and sense with your body? Are the people attentive? Do you feel confident?

Take these specific steps to maximize the visualization process:

1. Be in a quiet place.
2. Find a comfortable position.
3. Close your eyes (later you can visualize with your eyes open).
4. Start to imagine a specific situation.
5. Add as many details as possible.
6. Incorporate details from all of your senses.
7. Imagine how you should act in order to perform well.

You may find that when you try to visualize, you do not see anything, or you see just a dark shadow. Perhaps you hear more when you close your eyes to visualize. If you are a more kinesthetic person (learning through movement to process new and difficult information), you may need to move a bit in order to visualize.

Enhancing Visualization

Try the following technique if you have trouble visualizing. Perhaps you are trying to imagine a person attacking you from the front with a knife in his hand, to prepare for a self-defense situation. Ask a friend or training partner to hold a knife in front of you for a few seconds, in a threatening posture. Look at the knife, look at the person, look at the face, and then close your eyes and see the same image. You have primed your brain with details to use for visualization. Open your eyes, look again, then close your eyes again and visualize. You may also want to make movements related to knife defense while doing this exercise. Repeat this process several times and notice how dramatically your ability to visualize improves.

The scenarios you visualize should engage as many of your senses as possible. The scenarios can be **visual**, such as images and pictures, **auditory**, such as hearing someone shouting at you, or **kinesthetic**, such as sensing how your body feels and moves. The purpose is to create as many impressions as possible inside your mind, in preparation for a real event. When stressed, the brain searches its inner library for similar situations. You want your brain to react by saying, "I know this, I have been here before, I can handle this." By storing efficient and effective reactions in your brain, you decrease reaction time and improve the probability of responding in the best way possible.

A Real-Life Story: Visualizing Bouncer Brawls

Once while working as a bouncer in a bar, Chris, a high level KMG instructor, observed five men drinking together. The more they drank, the louder they became. One of the bartenders asked Chris to tell the group to quiet down, which he did. After a few minutes of compliance, they became louder than ever. Sensing trouble, Chris began visualizing possible scenarios, ranging from simple discussion to throwing all five out of the bar.

After two hours, the group had become too disruptive to let them remain in the bar. During that time, Chris had continued visualizing how to handle a variety of situations, down to the smallest detail. Chris felt very calm, returned to the men's table, and demanded that they quiet down. They responded by sizing Chris up, looking at each other, and then again at Chris.

Once again, the group lowered their voices, but eventually they became so loud that the bartender asked Chris to remove them from the premises. Chris returned to their table and told them to leave. All five men stood up and moved toward him in a very aggressive manner. Chris backed away a few steps and positioned himself in front of a wall, such that no one could attack him from behind. The five men spread out in a half-circle in front of him. One of them, probably the "leader" in the middle, moved his right hand back, shifted his weight, and made a fist.

Before he managed to punch him, Chris stepped forward with his left foot and kicked the man in the groin with his right leg. Without setting his foot down, Chris followed up with a roundhouse kick to the man's lowered head. Chris then grabbed the man by his shirt, spinning him around, and held him in a headlock with his right arm, so that his face was to Chris's left.

Chris retreated so that his back was against the wall again, and then hit the man several times in the face with his left hand while watching the other four men. They simply froze. Chris dropped the man and pushed him away, and said "come on" in an angry but controlled voice. They backed away, saying that Chris was crazy and that they would be back later. They grabbed their friend on the floor and retreated from the bar. Chris kept looking at them and scanning the bar for others who might decide to interfere. The men never returned.

Awareness, preparation, self-control, and visualization shortened Chris's decision making process and reaction time, and enabled him to prevail against formidable odds.

Conditioning and Pavlov

In reality, when dealing with an enemy, aggressor, attacker, whatever we name the person who wishes to harm us, it is about winning the confrontation.

Sometimes winning will be without any physical confrontation, sometimes the event will have a very hard and devastating outcome, for all sides, even death.

In KMG it is very clear that self-defense is about not getting hurt. As Imi Sde-Or (Lichtenfeld), the founder of Krav Maga, used to say, "The first rule is don't get hurt." So, the ideal outcome is that nothing happens. Not to you and also not to the opponent or attacker; no physical action occurs, no one attacks anyone, and no one suffers any injuries. If we can prevent, avoid, de-escalate, or defuse the confrontation, this is the best action. Best is to win without a battle, as the Chinese strategy philosopher Sun Tzu said. You know how you start the violent confrontation, but you do not know how it will end, so you should prefer to avoid it altogether.

In combat, however, we are talking about defeating the opponent. How do you defeat him? The end result is that the opponent is unable, either physically or mentally, to continue. Physical defeat means that his body or structure is broken, or his nervous system is not functioning (such as if he is knocked out). In self-defense and third-party protection, physical defeat may also mean that the attacker cannot reach you due to distance, such as if you remove yourself (and the VIP) away from the danger zone. Mental defeat means that his spirit is broken and that the opponent or assailant has no desire or will to continue. He practically surrenders.

Whether it is self-defense, combat, or protection, winning the confrontation without fighting—by breaking the aggressor's spirit such that he gives up without a fight or an attack—is a great achievement. Sometimes you can achieve this, usually by inflicting a high level of threat and intimidation.

In training, however, there are ample opportunities to improve; the main goal is to achieve a win-win situation and session. What does it mean to win during training? It means that you have learned and improved. How do you improve? By trying, repeating, making mistakes, failing, overcoming those problems and failures, and so eventually correcting the mistakes and improving yourself. For this you need to have a good partner who doesn't cause you harm, but is still performing as a "good attacker." The moment the attacker/partner manages to "hit" you, i.e., is able to execute a punch or a kick that makes contact, grabs you, holds you, throws you, etc., you have the chance to exercise your solutions, to practice your defenses, releases, break-fall, and so on.

All this is true for the practice of self-defense as well as for fighting, combat, and VIP protection drills, techniques, and scenario training.

All this is also correct for the practice of business skills, and of management of self under stress in nonviolent conditions, as well as any kind of interaction or conflict with other people, such as family, friends, colleagues, and competitors.

In the "mental preparations" presented in this book and also offered by KMG, we have specific drills to improve your own mental strength, courage, and how you deal with stress and fears. You should be focused, courageous, able to recruit all mental resources to fulfill the mission and win the conflict, whether you are a fighter in the ring going for a world title, a manager at a large corporation in front of the board, a member of a special unit before a hostage rescue operation, or a houseperson facing numerous missions every day.

This preparation includes, among other steps, the understanding, accepting, and even visualization of failure and defeat. You should get acquainted and friendly with failure, because we are not afraid of friends. We elaborate on this later in this book. You should "enjoy" and use failure, because doing so takes you to the next level, and that is really the goal.

Think about the different possibilities for a conclusion of a violent incident. Imagine a specific incident where an assailant attacks you. Try to visualize maximum details in this incident—the area, the attacker, the weapon used, the environment, and even visualize sounds, smells, and as many other details as possible. Since the brain does not know the difference between an imaginary situation and a real situation, it stores the information you get from visualizing so that you can retrieve it later when you find yourself in a similar real situation. You see, if you have visualized a situation before, your brain thinks you have experienced it before. Therefore, your level of stress should be less when facing that real situation than if you had not visualized the situation before.

Indeed, one of the modern, post-Freudian theories about the role of our dreams is that they serve to prepare us for possibly challenging scenarios.

Krav Maga, as a realistic, tactical, and technical system, is faced with the classic question of how to train a person to deal with life-and-death situations.

Needless to say, we don't have the privilege or the option to deal with truly real problems, get seriously injured if we fail, or even die, and then miraculously return to the previous uninjured condition in order to repeat the exercise and correct any mistakes, like in some Hollywood movies…

The real challenge is to create a realistic, true-to-life training format that raises problems and causes stress for the defender without creating the actual situation or exposing the defender to a real life-threatening condition.

The solution to this need is the use of basic and advanced technical, tactical, and simulation training, all under relatively safe conditions and in a reasonably controlled environment. It is clear that all the "regular" practices, physical self-defense, fighting, and protection of others also improve your skills and prepare you mentally for a confrontation. This mental preparation happens mainly due to the fact that while we are training physically, our mind is being exercised too.

However, in addition to our "regular" physical, technical, and tactical training and in order to further improve, there is a great need for special mental training. One of our central mental training methods using visualization is called "**Accept Defeat**," which takes you from the worst possible scenario (bad defeat) to the greatest possible success.

A Real-Life Story: The "Best Fighter" Was Hiding until the Storm Was Over

This event was the first incident on our watch, where a terrorist attacked one of the security officers from our undercover anti-terror unit, and ended with the killing of that terrorist.

The attack happened on an Egyptian bus that was crossing the border between Israel and Egypt. The security officer was checking the bus and saw a suspicious person. He asked him to approach and sit in the front; the big man complied, advanced, sat down, and then stood up holding a long knife with a 40-centimeter (15-inch) blade in his hand, and started stabbing the officer. The officer, who was equipped with a firearm that was not loaded (the regulations of most such units), defended himself with his empty hand, pushed the attacker away, and then loaded his weapon and shot the terrorist.

Another interesting thing happened: The moment the shots were heard, the other security officers started the emergency procedure—all except one, who hid behind a lamppost and waited until the incident was over. Ironically, the security officer that was attacked was at an average level in his performances on different tests. On the other hand, the officer who hid was the best at all the tests. This shows that you can't be sure of the performance of a trained person until a real incident happens, and even then, you can never be hundred percent sure what his response to the next incident will be.

How the Visualized State Changes You

Your mental state changes because of the person you are with, the location you are at, and the situation you are in. The mental picture that you created in your mind changes your mental state. This picture can be of a person, place, or situation.

If you visualize yourself with a beloved person, e.g., when your child was three or four years old, immediately your heart becomes full of love and joy. Think about another situation where you visualize yourself in a conflict with the most frightening teacher you ever had when you were a student. Immediately this mental image makes you feel anxiety and discomfort.

Most young people experience "wet dreams;" this shows that a mental image definitely changes the mental and the physical state of the dreamer.

Visualization is a powerful tool for training the brain to handle challenges. Often, however, stress is a conditioned response to a threatening situation. The concept and practice of anchoring is another tool to train your brain to respond more quickly and more efficiently when confronting danger.

Conditioning has negative as well as positive connotations. The full name of one of the co-authors of this book is Ole Christian Boe, but you will not see this elsewhere in the book. Why? When Ole was a kid and his grandmother wanted to correct his behavior, she would look at him say, "Ole Christian." That was all she would say and do. Ole learned to associate his stupid behavior with his grandmother's use of his first name and middle name. It bothers him to this day to hear someone say his first name and middle name together.

You may be familiar with Ivan Pavlov, a Russian scientist who experimented with conditioning. Pavlov entered his lab and fed his dogs, which acted as an unconditioned stimulus. The dogs salivated, which Pavlov called an unconditioned response. However, the bell over the laboratory's door sounded as Pavlov entered. This noise, called a conditioned stimulus, eventually caused the dogs to salivate. The bell became the conditioned stimulus that caused the dogs' conditioned response of salivation (some doubt whether Pavlov really used a bell in his experiments, but this is irrelevant as Pavlov used a variety of stimuli). Pavlov's work with classical conditioning influences how people perceive themselves, their behavior, and their learning processes. His studies continue to be central in modern behavior therapy.

When you experience a threatening situation, you can condition yourself to become stressed. You perceive a threat (the unconditioned stimulus) that elicits anxiety (the unconditioned response). Without training, this scenario repeats itself. However, if you handle the challenge successfully, you instill confidence and desensitize yourself to anxiety. This process is called **reverse conditioning**. Police officers and soldiers train behavioral patterns through drills to benefit from this phenomenon. Reverse conditioning creates self-efficacy—your belief influences your ability to handle challenges and stressful situations.

Anchoring

Would it not be incredible to change your mental state in an instant? When confronting danger, such a skill could mean the difference between life and death. Anchoring is a subtle tool that can help you make this rapid switch. "Anchoring" refers to cementing a connection between the mind and body. It is a type of conditioning that you can use to your tactical advantage.

Perhaps you want to be able to act more decisively in the future. The anchoring process begins by recalling a situation where you were decisive. Think, visualize, and then feel what this situation was like. When you experience the strongest emotions, anchor this feeling in your body by taking a specific physical action. For instance, close your fist in a specific way. This physical action should not be a common motion! Strengthen the anchor by visualizing the relevant image in your mind. Repeat the process many times, until you feel the same emotion and decisiveness arise when you take your distinct physical action.

Congratulations, you have created a link between your thought and feeling of being decisive and the physical action of closing your fist. Later, when you need to be in a decisive mindset, close your fist and immediately you can resume the anchored mindset of being decisive. Consider creating other anchors for an aggressive, winning or dominant mindset, a relaxed mindset, a focused mindset, and a happy mindset. Every mindset should be anchored in a different manner or in another place in your body.

Now that you understand this technique, consider times when you may have inadvertently anchored other sensations and motions. For example, you may have unknowingly anchored a feeling of aggressive driving with the motion of tightly gripping the steering wheel! Simply be aware of these situations and consider "reprogramming" yourself to act in the best manner possible.

A Real-Life Story: Physical State Changed by an Anchor

Some years ago, Eyal Yanilov suffered a long series of colds and fevers, a sort of angina. That relatively light sickness was always accompanied by a very sore throat and high fever. This recurred over several months. Some months later, during a training session, Eyal was hit in the throat, in the larynx, during training. Although it was a rather light impact, Eyal felt pain and less than half an hour later he had a high fever and felt sick, a condition that he had no sign of earlier. Eyal has realized that his throat ache was anchored to sickness. Over time he was able to overcome this conditioning, such that pressure (like in a choke) or impact (as in strike) to the throat did not result in feeling sick.

CONCLUSION

In this chapter, visualization and anchoring as methods for improving your performance have been described. You should practice how to create a picture in your mind and how to enhance your visualization process. You now know which processes are involved in conditioning and what reverse conditioning is. Visualization and anchoring are very powerful tools, and we encourage you to use these tools on a regular basis to alter your state of mind and create the desired outcomes you want in life. Some additional teaching on the subjects can be found in the next chapters.

Chapter 11

Focus and Attention Span

Navy SEAL Machowicz defines focus as "when clarity, concentration, and action converge to create a specific result in the present." Machowicz looks at focus as a laser beam. If you change your focus or what you are focusing on a little, the laser beam misses. Machowicz sees second-guessing, hesitation, the unknown, stress, pain, and fear as obstacles that diminish the quality of your focus. Confucius stated that "he who conquers himself is the mightiest warrior." An ancient Hebrew saying asks, "Who is the hero? The one who conquers his desire." Developing your combat mindset builds laser-like focus and self-control.

Defining Focus and Concentration

The famous psychologist William James wrote, "Everyone knows what attention is. It is the taking possession by the mind, in clear and vivid form, of one out of what seem several simultaneously possible objects or trains of thought. Focalization, concentration of consciousness are of its essence. It implies withdrawal from some things in order to deal effectively with others."

A very basic feature of visual information processing is the ability to select and reject information. Early studies reveal the more time you have for selection of information, the more efficient your rejection of incompatible stimuli. It is as if attention begins in a diffuse state and contracts to a focused state. People with little ability to control attention—that is, those with low working memory spans—require more time to adjust their attentional allocation than people with greater ability to control attention—those with high working memory spans. Working memory can be seen as the set of cognitive structures that are important, so that you can carry out basic cognitive operations. One reason to practice the focusing techniques in this book is to increase your working memory span and, thereby, become able to process information faster than people who do not practice to expand their working memory span. The ability to notice that we are getting anxious, and to take steps to bring our focus back to where it was, rests on our self-awareness.

The Need for Focus and Concentration

A well-known study of college athletes reveals that the athletes differed as to whether they would let anxiety disrupt their concentration. Those more easily disrupted by anxiety would perform worse in the upcoming season. If you are not able to stay focused, you start to feel anxiety, which affects your performance. Staying focused also means disregarding emotional distraction.

Attention can be divided into several types. In this chapter, we will describe two different types. The first is called selective attention. This type diverts your attention toward one specific target while you ignore everything else. This trait has a clear survival value; in a dangerous situation, selective attention helps you focus on what is most dangerous, and then find the best ways to deal with it. The second is called open attention, also known as divided attention. This type allows you to absorb information around and inside you, and to pick up subtle cues you would otherwise miss.

Today many people find themselves in a mental state that one might refer to as a "frazzle." This is a mental state where you experience constant stress, leading to an overloaded nervous system. In this mental state, the body is flushed with stress hormones such as cortisol and adrenaline. People in this state have glued their focus on things that they are worrying about, instead of maintaining focus on the tasks ahead. In the extreme, this may lead to burnout due to constant emotional exhaustion.

Warriors, whether in the boardroom or on the battlefield, must be able to identify which opponent is the most dangerous, and then deal with that threat first. In order to be able to do this, you have to focus on the threat as quickly as possible and with intent. When the threat is dealt with, focus quickly shifts to the next possible danger. The ability to shift focus is the key skill. Combat definitely sharpens this skill, as it forces you to focus in a way unlike anything else you might face.

A warrior must be able to control the mind under any conditions. In no time, the warrior can move from a relaxed state of mind and body to being totally focused on the task or threat he is facing.

A Real-Life Story: A Lawyer Who Could Not Stand before the Judge

One of our friends, a lawyer, always felt great stress when appearing in court before a judge. Ordinarily, he would not mind being in the spotlight, lecturing to groups of various sizes, conducting business meetings, or even acting in his local amateur theater group. Pleading cases in front of a judge, however, made him shiver and sweat. He would lose focus and his line of thought. A flood of destructive emotions would overwhelm him and the result was an inability to function, to the detriment of his clients.

Our friend sought our assistance, and we gave him several basic drills to master.

The first was to focus on his breathing process. Like a SWAT officer, he had to breathe slowly, count, and **pay attention to the breathing**, especially when the air changed its direction of flow.

The second was a focusing and concentration technique, like the TRATAK (see page 223). He had to breathe slowly while focusing his eyes on a black dot on the wall, at eye level, about 3 meters (10 feet) away.

The third, called "**accepting defeat**," whereby he imagined a worst-case scenario, then incrementally better situations until visualizing complete success.

After three months of exercising the first two drills about thirty minutes per day and occasionally practicing the third drill of accepting defeat, our friend practically could not recognize himself in court. He was no longer under any kind of stress in front of a judge!

Focusing Body, Speech, and Mind

When we compare the physical training of lifting weights to mental training, we can say that we train with weights to be stronger, healthier, and more attractive in the eyes of others. We also conduct mental training and practice for practical reasons: to be more able and efficient, to develop capacities and resources to deal with the daily tasks and stress of the twenty-first century, or to cope with dangerous and violent situations, such as confronting a criminal or an enemy on the battlefield.

Mental training changes the brain, a phenomenon that is a result of neuro-plasticity. **Neuroplasticity** describes the ability of the brain to change in response to experiences. Certain sections and parts of the brain grow and thicken as a response to mental training. For instance, long-term practitioners of meditation have been found to change the structure and function of their brains. Furthermore, participation in **mindfulness-based stress reduction** (MBSR) creates changes in the concentration of gray matter in brain regions that are involved in learning and memory processes, in emotion regulation, and in perspective-taking.

On the other hand, stress, **post-traumatic stress disorder** (PTSD), and chronic pain for more than half a year cause autoimmune disorders such as rheumatoid arthritis, and risky behavior such as dangerous alcohol or drug use, driving while intoxicated, gambling, and aggression. The negative effects of chronic stress cause an inflammatory state that wears out portions of the brain circuitry. As a consequence, some parts of the brain shrink.

Focusing happens on three levels: body, speech, and mind. Focusing the body means to do only certain slow, repeated, specific moves, or to not move at all. In the next section you can see an example of doing a slow-motion defense and counterattack. The moves can be different and may be done in a sitting or standing position, either while moving or staying still.

Focusing the speech is a minimization activity trying to stop the internal monologue, internal dialogue, and self-talk that buzzes in our minds. To focus the speech, we concentrate on the breathing process: on the inhale and exhale, on the points when the air stops flowing and then starts again in the opposite direction, from inhalation to exhalation, and vice versa. We describe many breathing drills later in the book.

Focusing the mind is best achieved by focusing the eyes. The eyes supply a huge amount of data to be processed by the brain. Focusing the eyes on a certain point minimizes that amount of data and the processing of it, so the mind becomes calmer.

The majority of the drills to focus the body, speech, and mind include controlling as many of our resources as possible. The essence of the following methods is to concentrate attention and resources on the actions or non-actions of the body, on breathing, and focusing the gaze on a specific point about 3 meters (approximately 10 feet) away. You can start by practicing these drills for three to four minutes. Slowly climb to five, ten, and even twenty minutes. Sometimes you may experience headaches after practicing for longer than a certain number of minutes. It is then important to return back to doing the drill for around five minutes or less.

Slow-Motion KMG Technique

Start by standing relaxed, breathing slowly, and focusing your eyes on a point approximately 3 meters (10 feet) away. Pay attention to your body and try to relax. Observe slow and controlled breathing. Slowly move your limbs and body according to the pattern of the chosen technique. Redirect your actions as the technique requires. Move very slowly while focusing on breathing and keeping your eyes on a point. When a thought comes to your mind, acknowledge it and then ignore it. Go back to the three subjects of your focus. Do the whole technique. Tense your muscles at the point of imaginary contact.

When you are familiar with the basic idea of this drill, start the next phase. Drill the technique with a contracted and tight body. Keep your body tight, with your main muscles contracted all the time, except the muscles in your face and the muscles doing abdominal breathing. Contract the muscles in your legs, pelvis, glutes, upper torso, shoulders, and arms. At a later stage, you can also contract the abdomen area and breathe with the tight muscles of the abdominal wall and lower back, as if breathing behind a shield or a wall.

Start with a five-minute drill. When your capacities are enhanced, you should stretch the training time. Advanced practitioners may take thirty minutes to complete the drill.

The following figures demonstrate performing a slow-motion KMG technique.

You can choose different techniques when performing this focus and concentration exercise. For example, you may try an inside defense against a straight strike with simultaneous counterattack, a defense against an overhead stick attack, different defenses against knife attacks, defenses against kicks, or even releases from different grabs.

The trainee stands ready to slowly perform a 360-degree outside defense with simultaneous counterattack. He starts from this standing position.

The trainee slowly lifts his arms. His body is tight, his breathing is slow and relaxed, and his eyes are fixed on a point 3 meters (10 feet) away.

The trainee continues to move very slowly.

The technique extends to the points of defending and countering. From here the trainee begins the recoiling process (Fig. 4.1 is taken from the front).

The trainee recoils his arms. His body is still tight, his breathing is slow and relaxed, and his eyes are fixed on a point.

The trainee returns to the starting position and repeats the technique using the other side of his body. Beginners should take five minutes to complete the cycle. Advanced practitioners can take thirty minutes to complete the cycle.

This drill does not work well with techniques that include bursting or fast stepping forward. If you choose a technique with an advancing motion, be sure that you advance correctly and do not mistakenly take a slow step that bends the base leg.

Focus on a Point (TRATAK)

This drill called TRATAK also focuses the body, speech, and mind. This highly effective practice is common in the Bhrigu branch of Raja Yoga. Assume a calm and comfortable posture, usually sitting or standing. Fix your gaze, breathing slowly with attention. Keep still. When a thought comes to your mind, acknowledge it, ignore it, and then refocus. It is difficult to stay focused in such a manner for more than a few seconds. Advanced practitioners may be able to keep their minds still for twelve or so seconds.

During such drills, the practitioner usually finds that after a few seconds, a thought comes to mind, an internal monologue starts, or the body suddenly moves in another way than initially decided. A need to scratch, blink, cough, or swallow may also arise. Acknowledge the thought and drop it, returning to the breathing to focus body, speech, and mind. Maintain control, be focused, and minimize the desire to move. Eventually you should not be disturbed and you can quietly work the drill.

The following figures demonstrate focusing on a point or on a candle.

Find a wall, a door, or any surface painted in a visually calming color. Attach a sticker to the vertical surface. On the sticker, color a black dot, approximately 2.5 cm (one inch) in diameter. Position the dot at eye level.

Fix your eyes on the dot, minimizing your eye movements and blinking. Pay attention to your breathing, which is slow and relaxed.

Another option is to gaze at the light of a candle, as seen in the figure above. Fix your gaze on the center of the steady flame, which is usually black.

Sit comfortably about 2–3 meters (7-10 feet) away from the black dot. Your back should be straight, and your hands resting comfortably on your thighs or one on the other.

Quieting Self-Talk and Controlling the Ego

In the following drill, you work on your ability to focus and concentrate, as well as how to relax, respond, and minimize internal monologue and self-talk. When you do not care about results and circumstances, you quiet your mind and thus perform better, respond earlier, and become more efficient. Conversely, when your mind is busy, judgmental, and constantly expecting, guessing or worrying about something that you have no control over, your performance degrades.

This drill requires the assistance of a partner. The partner should stand at a relatively close distance, from where he can push you. The partner places his two palms on your body. From the front, it is the upper chest and shoulder area; from behind, it is the shoulder blades.

The partner randomly pushes you with his right or left hand. Your partner's push must be light, fluid, about one foot (30 cm) deep or long, without signaling or telegraphing its intention. You may move by turning your body, but do not take a step. You have to add your own action to the push that created the body turn. The turn that you add is joined to the turn that your partner initiated, making it stronger.

The moment you plan, hesitate, or try to guess your partner's move, you create resistance that is easily felt by both participants. Many times, you may also lose your balance and take a step forward due to that resistance, so your lack of concentration and absence of a clear mind is more evident.

The following figures demonstrate the partner pushing drill.

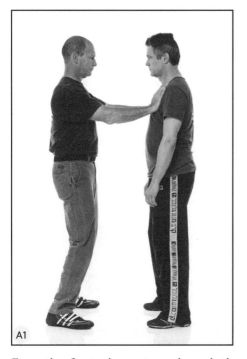

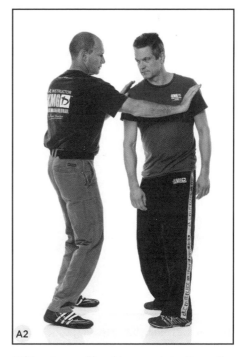

From the front, the partner places both hands on the trainee's upper chest and shoulder area. Both trainees are relaxed and ready, with clear minds.

Without revealing his own intentions, the partner pushes the trainee with one hand. Intuitively, without thought, resistance, or hesitation, the trainee adds his own turn to his partner's push.

  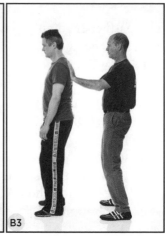

In this variation, the partner stands behind the trainee and places two hands on his shoulder blades. Both try to relax and minimize their self-talk and expectations.

With a light push, without preliminary moves or showing his intention, the partner pushes the trainee with his left or right hand. The trainee adds his own action to this movement to enhance it.

In this variation, the partner pushes from behind, while from the front, another partner holds a target. The trainee stands in a semi-passive stance and responds with a strike to the pad. The timing and impact show how focused and quiet the trainee's mind is. With time the strike becomes stronger and more fluid, and the trainee feels quiet and humble.

Another option is to strike with a hook. The body turn is very important. The trainee shifts his weight in the direction of the target. It is possible to use a heavy bag or another suitable target.

Minimizing Ego by Thanking Others

Each and every one of us managed to get where we are because of the teaching and help of others. We got our knowledge from our parents, grandparents, and nannies, through our friends, teachers, lecturers, religious leaders, and also from our bosses and other role models. We also learned from works, books, clips, and movies that other people created. As the celebrated scientist Isaac Newton commented: "If I have seen further than others, it is by standing upon the shoulders of giants."

Top achievers, high-level business people, and entrepreneurs say that they worked a lot and had great ideas, but they also point to the fact that they were in the right place at the right time to grasp an opportunity. Some may call it luck, karma, or *mazal*. Some say divine powers assisted them, as an act of God or celestial blessing. However, many people work hard, have good ideas, and still do not go as far as others.

We must be thankful to all those who taught us, to the partners with whom we trained and practiced in life, and whose interactions gave us the experiences we acquired. We should even thank our rivals and enemies who forced us to improve and achieve more. We got to where we are because of the teaching and assistance of others and also the hurdles that were put in our way.

We recommend that each day, in your mind, in your self-talk, thank all those people. Thank your parents who brought you into this world and supplied your needs for many years. Thank all the teachers and instructors who gave you your knowledge. Thank your rivals and competitors whose acts or mere existence pushed you further. People of faith may also wish to start or end the session by thanking God, who brought them to where they are, and to ask for help and assistance for the future.

You are who you are because of others and their efforts. We are all alike, we have similar needs, and just like you were given, you should give to others too, to improve their lives. Other people are like you and thus should be treated with compassion and humility.

Attention Span

If you are not able to pay attention to what is going on around you, chances are high that you can miss some important details. If you do not recognize a threat, you are not able to deal with the situation. Imagine walking along on the sidewalk. You decide to cross the road to the other side. You are not aware of your surroundings; you are thinking of something else, or looking at your phone. You step out into the street, and a fraction of a second later you sense a car coming toward you. Too late! Could you have avoided the incident? The answer is yes—if you had paid attention to your surroundings.

You also need the ability to focus your attention for longer periods of time. For a manager in a directors' meeting, it is important to pay attention to what is being said and presented, as crucial decisions may be needed. The pressure may be decreased by the ability to fix mistakes after the meeting. Military and other first responder personnel may not have this luxury. They must avoid mistakes in real time, staying alert until the mission is finished, as life and death may depend on actions taken in a fraction of a second.

Attention span is the time you can stay focused on a specific task without becoming distracted. If you manage to read through this paragraph without thinking of something else, congratulations on focusing your attention! There is also a growing consensus that the ability to focus attention on a task is crucial to achieve various goals. Attention span works similar to muscles; if you exercise your attention span, it grows.

Research from the last twenty years has demonstrated an association between a person's working memory span and his (or her) executive attention capability. Your working memory capacity is the amount of information that you can keep active in your brain at a specific time. The more information you are able to use efficiently, the better you function. Your executive attention capability refers to your ability to focus, and to remain focused, even when something interferes, either from inside you or from the outside. These interferences may be thoughts or emotions that you have created. If you let yourself become distracted by thoughts and emotions that are not relevant to the situation (e.g., thinking of a bill that you forgot to pay while you are in the middle of a verbal confrontation with someone), you simply cannot use all your resources to cope efficiently with the situation at hand. It is thus important to train to improve your attention span and your executive attention so that you are better able to handle difficult situations.

People with high working memory capacity can better adjust their attentional window to task-relevant information compared to people with low working memory capacity. Individuals that have a high working memory capacity also find it easier to overcome the influence of irrelevant information, compared to individuals with low working memory capacity. With an improved working memory capacity you can become better at distinguishing between relevant and irrelevant information in a stressful situation.

Open or Divided Attention

Imagine that you need to successfully fulfill two or more demands and execute two or more actions or missions at a time, while paying attention to one or more channels of information. When you need to perform parallel tasks, you must divide your attention among those missions. That usually weakens your performances. Imagine a few situations:

- Two people talk with you simultaneously, while you wish to answer them.
- A KMG trainee faces two attackers, one who tries to grab him while the other tries to assault him with a training knife.
- A personal assistant writes what the boss dictates while watching a presentation projected on a screen.
- A SWAT team member divides his attention between the commands he is getting, the criminal he is chasing, and the information he is delivering to his fellow officers.

In order to perform at the highest possible level, you need to practice and train by opening your attention and dividing it among several missions. Most of the time you can shift your attention and resources very rapidly between the different missions. However, it is also possible to do what looks like parallel processing.

Improving Attention

All the focusing and concentration drills in this book are very suitable for the task of improving your attention span and staying focused and attentive to the action or non-action you must take. Focusing on breathing, on the change of direction of the air flow; on a point positioned some distance away; on a slow move; on your body posture; or on a sound, are ingredients of different drills with which we develop attention span.

We have developed several integrated drills to focus on two missions or more, and to obtain and process information arriving from more than one resource. These drills enhance your ability to divide your attention, control it, use it, and manage it.

A simple drill that influences decision making is **slow fighting**. We use it as a component in some of the training to better our capacity for divided attention. As the name implies, it is fighting slowly, trying to perform defenses more slowly than the attacks that the partner is aiming at us, and using even slower counterattacks. In this training method, we try to touch the partner with every relevant attack, but impact is very light, almost nonexistent. To the slow fighting we add additional tasks to create the following drills of open attention.

Slow fight while listening to a story told by a third party, such as an instructor, who is not taking part in the slow fighting. Then answer questions about what you heard and did in the slow fight. Record the drill using a video camera to provide feedback to trainees.

Slow fight while telling a story to your partner. One trainee tells a story while the other listens and remembers. At the end of the drill, confer to discover what was understood and how many details are remembered.

A more challenging drill involves slow fighting while listening to two people, each telling a different story, or slow fighting while conversing about a certain subject. After that, each trainee asks questions, repeats part of a story, or comes up with relevant data or details that were given earlier.

The following drill incorporates self-defense practices. Stand still while a partner, defined as an attacker, circles you. From time to time, the partner attacks in a way that is not known beforehand. The attack may be a strike, kick, stab with a training knife, or swing with a stick. The defender should perform the relevant defensive actions and counterattacks, and then return to his place. Perform these actions while a third party tells a story, or while the defender has to write a text message on his phone, or while he writes about a subject on a piece of paper.

You may also drill by **identifying aggressive postures and gestures** while telling a story. In this exercise, one person tells a story while pointing at people who perform aggressive gestures toward him. The aggressors are 2–3 meters (7–10 feet) away and may make any of the following gestures: wave a fist; threaten with an open hand, as if to slap; make aggressive facial movements and move lips as in silent cursing; show a finger (flip the bird); show a palm in front of the face (*hamsa*, talk to the hand); make a move as if drawing a weapon; move a finger from one side of the neck to the other to describe cutting of the throat; and similar motions. Certain gestures may depend on the culture of the participants.

CONCLUSION

The second pillar of our mental training is focus and concentration, whether it is done on internal or external points, elements or processes. In this chapter we present innovative drills that practice how to focus and concentrate, but also how to open and divide our attention in order to achieve powers that tremendously elevate our abilities to manage conflicts, deal with an overwhelming number of missions, as well as confront multiple aggressors in violent encounters.

Chapter 12

Relaxation and Breathing

Staying relaxed is one way to reduce stress. Relaxation is a vital skill, but it is not a substitute for other mental or physical training. This chapter includes two techniques that can help you: human conditioning through cue words and progressive muscle relaxation.

Human Conditioning through Cue Words

Earlier in the book we discussed conditioning in the context of Pavlov's findings. The process of contracting and relaxing muscles while exhaling can act as a "bell." You can add a cue word or a command before or during muscle movements to enhance the relaxation effect.

Begin by lifting and tensing your shoulders. This introduces a small amount of stress. When you lower and relax your shoulders, you release the stress. Next, give yourself a command, such as "tense, relax." Repeat the motion of lifting and lowering your shoulders. Repeat this process several times. Finally, try stating the command "tense, relax," but do not move your shoulders. Try to observe whether you feel a relaxation process occur. If you do, you have conditioned yourself to relax. If not, repeat the process. If necessary, try tensing and relaxing other body parts. You could make a fist and release it, for example. Remember to include a cue word with the physical motion.

Progressive Muscle Relaxation

To relax the mind, you should focus on the muscles: the face and neck, shoulders, arms and hands, stomach, and legs. Systematically contracting and relaxing muscles is called progressive muscle relaxation. After you regulate yourself in this method you are able to mentally de-stress yourself in only few seconds.

Try the following progressive muscle relaxation. The first phase involves these actions: contract and relax your left foot and ankle, right foot and ankle, left calf, right calf, left knee and thigh, right knee and thigh, whole left leg and glutes, and whole right leg and glutes. In the second phase, continue to the torso: contract and relax the back and abdomen, the chest and lats, left hand, right hand, left forearm, right forearm, left upper arm and shoulder, and right upper arm and shoulder. For the third phase, contract and relax the neck, the jaw, and the facial muscles.

Most trainees feel best if they inhale and then, as they contract a certain area, stop breathing, maintain contracted muscles, and then exhale and relax muscles and mind. After the first scan of the body, scan again, but contract and relax bigger areas. For example, contract and relax the right leg, then the left leg, the right and then left arm, the whole torso and shoulders, the neck, and face. Contract and relax each area one or more times.

When relaxing your muscles, pay attention to the exhaling process. You can then contract and relax even bigger areas like the lower part of body, the upper part of the body, and lastly the face and neck. Finish the drill with the same process on the whole body: inhale, stop the airflow, contract the whole body, and then exhale while relaxing the muscles. After you practice this method and become accustomed to it, you can relax your body and mind in a second or two. Contract and relax the muscles of the face, neck, and shoulders, and perhaps the palms. Remember to breathe correctly.

Introduction to Breathing

The breathing mechanism is automatic, but it can also be monitored and controlled. Normally, you draw about eighteen breaths per minute. When you are sitting, your breathing rate should be about thirteen breaths per minute. Men usually breathe a little more slowly, twelve to fourteen breaths per minutes, and women usually breathe a little faster, fourteen to fifteen breaths per minute. Some people have a tendency to hyperventilate when breathing. This means that they breathe quickly regardless of what they are doing. In the long run, this is not healthy, and it is useful for these people to modify their breathing patterns.

Warning: Before starting any intensive breathing exercises, you should first consult a professional physician.

A Real-Life Story: A Breathing Technique That Changed the Life of a SWAT Officer

One of our European KMG instructors has worked as a SWAT officer for many years, performing VIP protection, anti-terror, and air marshal duties. His job is very stressful, but the wait prior to raiding a house to free hostages, for example, was especially demanding. He asked us for a drill to help neutralize his stress.

We taught him a simple drill of inhaling for four seconds, and then exhaling for four seconds. We asked him to pay special attention to the times that the airflow changes direction, from inhale to exhale, and vice versa. Our officer practiced this routine when off duty and when waiting to perform various missions. After several months, this experienced officer told us, "This drill changed my life."

There is a saying in yoga that "when you can control your breath, you can control everything." Through conscious control of your breathing, you can influence your nervous system, bodily functions, and mental states. Your autonomic nervous system regulates involuntary functions and is divided into two parts. One is the parasympathetic nervous system, also known as the "rest and digest" part of your nervous system. The other is the sympathetic nervous system, which prepares you for fight-or-flight responses. The sympathetic and the parasympathetic nervous systems can both control breathing. When you breathe out for longer than you breathe in, you activate the parasympathetic nervous system, and you start to feel more relaxed.

Abdominal Breathing

In the following sections, we describe several types of breathing. Inhaling and exhaling can be done through the nose or the mouth. In most of the breathing techniques that we use for our mental training, breathing in and out is done through the nose.

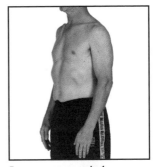

Lungs are emptied.

The first type of breathing is called abdominal breathing. Air enters the lungs when the diaphragm becomes flattened and tighter, causing the abdomen area push outward. Air flows into your lungs, especially the lower parts. Exhalation involves relaxing your diaphragm and tightening your abdominal muscles, pushing the air out. When doing abdominal breathing, your chest should stay flat and your ribs should stay low.

When learning to perform abdominal breathing, put your palms on your stomach area and feel how your belly moves out and in. Put your hands on your ribs

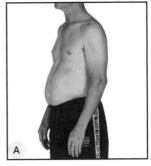

Abdominal breathing.

and chest and feel that they stay low, hardly moving during the inhale and exhale cycles. Initially, you can also monitor your performance by looking down at your abdomen and chest area. When you feel that you have learned the technique, stop looking down at your abdomen.

Midsection or "Rib" Breathing

When performing midsection breathing, your ribs move sideways and up, while your chest and abdomen area stay flat. The movements of the ribs pull the lungs, and air flows in. Keep your chest low. To exhale, press your ribs back. It is relatively more difficult for most people to inhale and exhale a significant amount of air. With training, you can certainly improve.

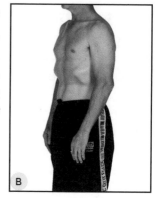

When learning to perform midsection breathing, lightly contract your abdomen and chest area while putting your palms on your ribs. Keep your elbows pulled to the rear. You should feel your rib cage widen and shrink as the ribs distance themselves from the center and return back to a low position. Initially, you can also monitor your performance by looking down at your abdomen and chest area.

Midsection breathing.

High, "Chest," or "Clavicle" Breathing

When performing high breathing, your clavicular area, upper chest, and higher parts of your ribcage come up and widen. Air flows into the upper part of the lungs. As you inhale and exhale using the upper chest and clavicle area, keep your abdomen and midsection a bit tight.

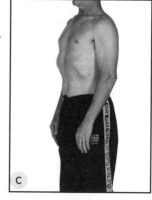

When learning to perform high breathing, put your fingers on your collarbones and let your arms hang. You can feel and see your chest elevate when you inhale, and sink when you exhale.

High breathing.

Full Breathing

The full breathing process incorporates all three types of breathing. Begin by inhaling through the nose, using the diaphragm and low abdominal breathing. Breathe slowly, with control. Continue to inhale to the midsection, activating the sides of the ribcage, and then activate the upper chest and clavicle area. Do the whole process in a fluid manner. The exhaling process is done is the same order: press your abdomen inward, then the ribs, and finally the chest.

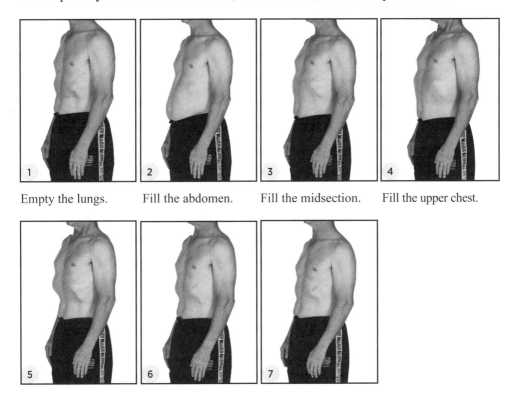

Empty the lungs.   Fill the abdomen.   Fill the midsection.   Fill the upper chest.

Exhale and empty   Empty the midsection   Empty the upper chest.
the lower abdomen.

Breathing Rhythms and Counts

You can improve control of your mind by regulating your breathing. Try the following breathing rhythm and count drills. Inhale for four seconds, then stop breathing for four seconds while the air is held in your lungs, and then exhale for four seconds. Take a slight pause, then repeat the process. Pay special attention to the moments when the air is changing direction, from inhale to stop, from stop to exhale, from exhale to pause, and from pause to inhale.

A variation of this drill involves **"full breathing**:" fill your abdomen for four seconds, your midsection for two seconds, and your upper chest for two seconds. Stop breathing for eight seconds, holding the air inside the lungs, with light contraction of the breathing muscles. Exhale in the same order: abdomen, midsection, and upper chest, with the same four-two-two count. When you have more experience, try a six-four-four count, and so on.

A third variation uses an X-4X-2X count. For example, inhale for four seconds, stop for sixteen seconds, and exhale for eight seconds. A seasoned breathing practitioner can use a ten-forty-twenty count, sustained for twenty to thirty minutes, but **do not be too ambitious and overdo it** to avoid unpleasant and even dangerous results, such as dizziness and weakness!

Breathing techniques can be done in standing position, sitting on a chair, sitting with crossed legs on the ground, and even while sitting in a lotus position, as in yoga. Start with five-minute breathing drills, and add time as the weeks pass. Consider adding a focusing component, such as staring at a dot as described in the TRATAK drill in chapter 11. When thoughts enter your mind, acknowledge them and then ignore them. Return to your breathing. When confronting a physical or mental challenge, these breathing techniques can help you stay relaxed and focused.

CONCLUSION

The third pillar of our mental buildup is relaxation and control of destructive emotions. This chapter features breathing processes and methods and body relaxation techniques. As all three pillars of mental preparation are integrated, we have many drills that are composed from several components, and breathing is a cornerstone of many of them.

Chapter 13

Body Language

Can you tell if somebody is confident or dominant? Do you know what to look for? Do you want to look and feel the same? Most of us are able to spot different mental states in other people. You can probably tell if someone is sad, happy, or angry. It may be a bit more difficult to find out who is confident and who is not. What about dominance and submission—can you spot these? What about power?

Power Poses

Harvard University professor Amy Cuddy and her research associates Dana R. Carney and Andy J. Yap from Columbia University have conducted research on so-called "power poses," and how these poses affect a person's hormone levels. Prof. Cuddy states that both humans and other animals express power physically, through open and expansive postures. Humans and other animals also express powerlessness through closed and contractive postures. We can easily see this in the animal kingdom, in primates, predators of the dog and cat families, birds, snakes, and other creatures.

Cuddy and her associates researched whether **these postures actually cause power**. She had previously noted that male students often used more space in the classroom when seated and raised their hands more often to ask questions than women did. Women, on the other hand, sat in a more contracted way and used less space when seated in the classroom.

Researchers have found that power leads to higher levels of control over one's own body and mind. Power also produces positive feelings, and is linked to the stress hormone cortisol. When you start feeling stressed, your adrenal gland produces more cortisol. Cortisol also affects the number of cells in the body that work. Powerful people have lower cortisol levels and lower cortisol reactivity to stressors than powerless people. Cortisol levels drop as power is achieved.

Testosterone levels are also closely linked to adaptive responses to challenges. Your testosterone levels reflect but also reinforce your status and dominance. Both internal and external stimuli may cause your testosterone level to rise. This leads to an increase in dominant behaviors, and these behaviors can elevate your testosterone level even further.

Researchers have found that chronically elevated cortisol levels in low-power individuals are associated with negative health consequences. These individuals get sick more often because of an impaired immune system. They may also suffer hypertension (high blood pressure) and memory loss.

Carney, Cuddy, and Yap hypothesized that high-power poses, as compared to low-power poses, cause individuals to experience elevated testosterone, decreased cortisol, increased feelings of power, and higher risk tolerance. They conducted experiments to test their hypothesis on a group of subjects. Half of the participants held high-power poses (with open limbs) for two minutes, and the other half held low-power poses (with closed limbs) for two minutes. Then, researchers measured their propensity to take risk by playing a gambling game.

Following the poses, the researchers measured various aspects of the subjects' physical and mental states. The researchers measured feelings of power with a questionnaire. To test cortisol and testosterone levels, researches collected saliva samples. They gathered these samples before and approximately 17 minutes after the participants spent their two minutes in either high-power or low-power poses.

The researchers reported the following: "Our results show that posing in high-power displays (as opposed to low-power displays) causes physiological, psychological, and behavioral changes consistent with the literature on the effects of power on power holders—elevation of the dominance hormone testosterone, reduction of the stress hormone cortisol, and increases in behaviorally demonstrated risk tolerance and feelings of power." In short, holding high-power poses for two minutes makes you look and feel powerful and dominant.

Postures and Perception

Carney, Cuddy, and Yap show that it is possible to improve your confidence and performance in situations such as a job interview, or speaking in public, just by changing your body posture. You may also seek to increase your power via posture changes when confronting your boss or when you are participating in a stressful or risky engagement.

Postures play an important role when viewed by criminals. Predators prefer "soft targets"—people who look intimidated, submissive, and afraid. When on the street, in the potential view of a criminal, it is better to be a "hard target," or someone who walks confidently and is well aware of one's surroundings. A criminal who perceives you to be a hard target is likely to wait for a soft target to come by rather than approach you.

A word of caution is necessary here. There is a difference between being confident and presenting a challenge. If you are a male and you look at another male for too long, in some situations and cultures, you can effectively challenge him. Your gaze should not last more than 1.5 seconds. If it lasts longer, it may be perceived as a challenge.

Sometimes pretending to be a soft target is the proper approach. If you are kidnapped, for instance, you may choose to pretend to be in a submissive mental state as a survival mechanism. When you perceive the correct time to attempt an escape, you exhibit all of the aggression required to free yourself and your fellow prisoners, if possible.

Strong Body Postures

We present several postures to engage different mental states. When you integrate visualization and self-talk, you will have a very powerful tool for changing your mindset, emotional state, and body awareness.

The following figures demonstrate postures that encourage a feeling of power while not necessarily threatening other people.

The "winning and achieving posture" is either a V or a Y shape, standing with your legs open, arms raised over the head, elbows locked, and chin raised. Push your chest forward and expand it with air. Clench your fists, although some may use open palms. Visualize success and tell yourself, "I made it. I won. I reached my goal."

The above-portrayed "dominating posture" involves a straight body, open legs, hands on your hips, elevated chin, and expanded chest. Tell yourself, "I am on top. Listen to me. Do what I tell you."

In this variation of the dominating posture, stand with a straight body, open legs, arms crossed on the chest, and elevated chin.

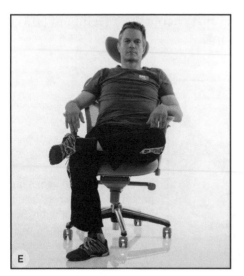

In the "relaxed, dominating, and feeling-good posture," sit with your knee to the side, with your base foot pointing partly sideways. Your chest is open, leaning backward. Tell yourself, "Everything is under control. People are following my guidance. I am open to ideas." Note that in some cultures, putting the sole of the shoe toward a person is perceived as humiliating and impolite among friends or colleagues.

The following figures demonstrate poses that encourage power while adopting a more domineering approach.

The "bossing and commanding while sitting posture" involves sitting with open legs and a straight body, leaning back. Your fingers are interlaced behind the head, not the neck. Your elbows are sideways and your chest is forward. Tell yourself, "I feel great. I am the boss. I own everything around me. Listen to me."

The "commanding and admonishing posture" involves pointing your finger toward another person (or imagined person). Put your head forward, with your other hand in your pocket or on your hip.

This posture involves making fists and holding them toward another person. It is an aggressive pose that puts your mind in a controlling and winning mode while having the side effect of suppressing or punishing another person.

For the best results, integrate your posture, internal monologue, and visualization. Tighten your muscles a bit. Activate the appropriate facial expression, and inhale to the upper chest. Add positive self-talk to the posture. You might speak loudly, shout, growl, or even whisper. Visualize where you are and the people near you. Imagine how they react and treat you.

You can manipulate the imagery for enhanced effects. For example, visualize yourself with a larger body, standing on an elevated platform, while other people are smaller and lower. You may even perceive them in gray colors or black and white. Be aware that these drills may boost your ego and elevate your sense of aggression and domination over others. Calibrate your practice to enhance your positive feelings, and avoid creating conflicts with other people.

Weak Body Postures

At the other end of the spectrum, we find body postures that create a mental state of submission and of being a victim. This may be appropriate in some situations, such as to diffuse a conflict. However, in most cases, it is beneficial to be aware of your own posture or the postures of your loved ones. Identifying weak body postures and changing them can improve a person's mindset.

In this submissive stance, your legs and hands are crossed. One palm is near the groin, with your chest sunken. Your shoulders are bent forward as if to cover the chest. Your back is rounded, your head is tilted down, and your eyes are mostly lowered. You may hear self-talk related to fear of what may be coming next, and you may expect loss and failure. You may visualize other people as threatening and physically larger than you.

In this submissive stance, your hands are crossed, your chest is sunken, and your shoulders are curved to cover your chest. Your back is rounded, your head is tilted down, and one hand is behind your neck. Your eyes look down.

These are submissive and worried sitting postures in a chair. You may be telling yourself, "I am not in the place I wish to be." Your legs are tightened together or crossed. One hand is crossed, resting on your other leg or inserted between your legs. Your other hand is behind your neck, or resting on your first hand. Your body is bent forward, with your chest sunken. Your shoulders and back are rounded as if to cover and protect your front. Your head is tilted down and your eyes are lowered. In this submissive sitting posture in a chair, your legs are crossed and your hands are between your legs. Your chest is sunken, and your back and shoulders are rounded. Your head is tilted down and your eyes are lowered.

It is important to be able to recognize these postures. You may need to alter your interactions with a person in a submissive or weak pose. You may want to help a person change his or her mindset by changing the posture. You should also recognize these postures and patterns of behavior in yourself—for instance, by taking pictures or short videos—and change them as soon as possible.

Partner Posture Drills

Partner posture drills help you experience the mental and physical aspects of assuming strong and weak poses. We recommend a three-phase approach to partner posture drills. First, partners should engage in ten to fifteen seconds of sparring. If the partners are civilian trainees without martial experience, encourage them to engage in a pushing or chasing drill. Second, partners take turns assuming strong and weak postures, holding each for two to three minutes. The person in the strong pose may enhance the experience by saying, "You will do what I tell you," or, "Shut up," or, "Stay here and don't move," or, "I am going to fire you unless you finish this job now." More aggressive options include "Next time I will punch you," or, "You deserve a beating for what you did," or, "You are good for nothing," and so on. Third, partners spar again for ten to fifteen seconds, or practice a pushing or chasing drill. Before and after each phase, pay attention to the level of aggression, confidence, perseverance, fear, anxiety, uncertainty, and stress felt by each partner. After a three-phase cycle, partners should change roles and repeat the cycle. Encourage a conversation about the experience after the second cycle concludes.

The following figures demonstrate partner posture drills.

The first phase involves partners sparring or engaging in a pushing or chasing drill for a few seconds.

Next, we put one trainee in a dominating or even aggressive posture and the other in a submissive, compliant posture, similar to complete surrender.

The trainee may switch postures during the drill.

Finally, partners spar again. After ten to fifteen seconds, stop and monitor each person's feelings and sensations and reflect on how each trainee functioned before and during the "fight."

CONCLUSION

Among the factors that change your mental state are your postures and body motions and movements, which also create and activate classical conditioning. The influence is both on the performer and the people that are with that person. Powerful or submissive postures create corresponding mindsets within all people present.

Chapter 14

Destructive Emotions, Self-Talk, and Accepting Defeat

This chapter describes techniques to address what we refer to as destructive emotions, suppressive internal dialogue or "self-talk," and feelings of anxiety and worry. We incorporate mental and physical drills to help you identify, diagnose, and mitigate conditions that challenge your mental state.

Destructive Emotions

We define a destructive emotion as a mental factor that disrupts your mind and prevents it from observing reality in a correct way. There is a discrepancy between the way things appear to your brain and the way they really are. You may feel envy, anger, hate, frustration, guilt, or regret. You may lie to protect yourself or others. You may have unmet cravings, you may blame others, and you may delay things.

You may also make social comparisons, comparing your life to the lives of others. It is natural to do this from time to time, but people who do this frequently may suffer from low self-respect, or may lack a stable sense of self-worth. Some people suffering destructive emotions are insecure, or their sense of self depends on the results of their comparisons with other people. Some people simply learn to make frequent social comparisons and then become dependent on them.

Naming and Scaling

Extended periods of destructive emotions may lead to physical and mental illness due to the stress they impose. One of the best ways to reduce the impact and influence of destructive emotions is to remove yourself from the situation. One of the easier ways to mentally distance yourself is to look at the situation from the outside. The **"naming and scaling"** technique can help. Focus on the emotion, feel it, name it, and then score it on a scale. For example, imagine that you are having a heated argument with a family member. You feel angry. Pay attention to the feeling, name it "anger," and assign it a value of one to ten, with the higher value meaning a more intense emotion. This act helps separate you from the feeling, increasing your ability to manage the destructive emotion. Consider combining the breathing and visualization techniques discussed in the book with the process of naming and scaling to enhance your emotional experience.

Another example is that you are walking along a dark street. The area is not considered dangerous, but the fact that it is dark causes you to feel fear. In addition, a dog barks, or an alley cat meows, and that intensifies your fear. There is no danger, but you are very disturbed and distracted by the fear you feel. Here, too, look inward, name the emotion, and scale it to reduce fear and continue on your way with ease and much less stress.

Naturally, when there is a need for a fast, defensive response or an aggressive reaction, introspection like naming and scaling probably isn't possible to do due to the lack of time, but if there is no emergency or danger, this method is both efficient and easy to do.

Self-Talk

Your internal dialogue, self-talk, or internal monologue is the conversation you have with yourself, or what you are thinking and telling yourself in different situations.

Researchers Rogelberg and colleagues found that constructive self-talk is positively related to effective leadership of others, and to creativity and originality as evaluated by subordinates and superiors. They also found that dysfunctional self-talk is negatively related to creativity and originality.

Imagine that you find yourself in a situation where somebody is about to attack you. Your opponent is pulling his clenched right fist backward. You feel a jolt of electricity through your body and you tell yourself, "He is going to hit me! It is going to hurt! Last time this happened, I broke my nose!" This sort of self-talk doesn't help you deal with the situation—quite the opposite, in most cases, as it enhances anxiety and stress.

Try this instead: The moment your soon-to-be attacker winds up the punch, say to yourself, "He is going to strike me. I need to take him out before he hits me." Which approach do you prefer? The one where you are afraid and just wait for the pain to arrive, or the one where you are decisive and act? Most people prefer to choose the second approach. Are you trained and ready to take the initiative, apply the correct self-talk, and use the correct physical and technical solution? The second approach puts you in the driver's seat and engages a combat mindset. The quality and quantity of your internal dialogue is a determining factor in how you handle similar confrontations.

Destructive thoughts are inserted into our minds by the messages from most companies' advertisements that try to sell us their products. It can be a car, a watch, jewelry, perfume or aftershave, a dress, a shirt or a pair of shoes. It can also be a fitness program, a drink, a smoke, some food supplement, or anything else. The message is that after you buy these products, you will be much better off, much more attractive, successful, powerful, or healthy. You will definitely smell better or different if you put on a certain scent; the problem is that these messages are much more than that. They are turning you into someone who does not believe in himself, suppressing self-confidence, and lowering your self-image. Messages are also coming from parents, who were brought up the same way, from teachers, managers and others around you. Many of the people that are doing this are close to you and have no bad intentions or destructive agenda, they believe—often because they themselves were educated this way—that this is the best way to educate you and bring you up to be a successful and happy adult. But in fact, it is about selling, controlling, and uniformity.

Changing Self-Talk

Be aware of what you say to yourself. You can change what you tell yourself; Navy SEAL Machowicz refers to this as "verbal-influence conditioning." What you say to yourself influences your mind and the result is a conditioning of your actions. The mental image is doing the same thing and having them both empowers you or disempowers you doubly. It is simple: If you say to yourself, "I will never be able to do this"—whatever "this" might be, what is the probability that you even try to do it? The words you say influence your thoughts. Your thoughts influence your feelings. Your feelings change your decisions. Your decisions guide your actions. Repeated actions become habits. Habits change your character. Changing your character changes your life.

Since it is clear that self-talk changes your subconscious, mood, and general functioning, the first and most important thing is to monitor your own thoughts that make up your internal monologue, your self-talk. The moment you find yourself speaking destructive sentences, immediately exchange them for better, positive, empowering thoughts and sentences. It is easy. Instead of thinking one sentence, change it with another self-talk, with another sentence. Avoid negative words like won't, don't, am not, and so on. Give yourself positive commands, because your subconscious cannot understand negative commands. If you say to yourself, "I must not eat this candy," your subconscious hears, "I must eat this candy."

Collect positive, empowering, and motivating phrases. Make a list and add one sentence every week, or even every day. Refer to this list every day. Put several such sentences in key places at home, at work, in your car, and elsewhere. These can counteract your environment, which constantly delivers depleting and suppressive messages that say you are not enough—not attractive enough, not powerful enough, not successful enough, not healthy enough, and much more. Consider using an application on your phone to send you reminders.

Like we wash ourselves, brush our teeth, put on perfume or aftershave and deodorant every day, we should also practice swapping the destructive sentences with the constructive ones.

Accepting Defeat

A violent conflict in reality is a win-lose situation. At its extreme, losing means dying. You may die, or your partner, a family member, a colleague, or even a bystander may die. Thus, we cannot afford to lose or to make a mistake, because we do not know the outcome of a violent confrontation. In nonviolent conflicts, we are likely to suffer less drastic consequences. However, we can still fear negative outcomes. Such fear can be paralyzing and drastically damage our decision making.

In training, however, both you and your partner should win, get better, improve, and come out from the session more efficient, knowledgeable, and experienced.

In most of our daily activities, we can make mistakes, get feedback, and get better. People are worried about mistakes and terrified of failure. They should not be. Most failures only bring you to a better place and improve and fine-tune you. If you do not try, you do not fail. What should you do? Do nothing, achieve nothing, and get nowhere in life? This is not an option. Making mistakes is very much a part of life, a part of growing, and an integral part of success.

One way of looking at it is that you are doing fine if you make **different mistakes** each time. Pat Riley, a famous American baskteball coach, said, "Great players crave instruction on their weaknesses."

Any problem, hurdle, difficulty, or obstacle should be converted into a ladder that you use to climb to higher grounds.

Thomas J. Watson, 1874–1956, chairman of IBM, wrote, "Would you like me to give you a formula for success? It's quite simple, really. Double your rate of failure. You're thinking of failure as the enemy of success. But it isn't at all... You can be discouraged by failure—or you can learn from it. So go ahead and make mistakes. Make all you can. Because, remember that's where you'll find success. On the far side."

No less a genius than Thomas Edison famously said, regarding the invention of the light bulb, "I have not failed. I've just found ten thousand ways that won't work."

How can we train for such situations if we are flooded with emotions due to fears of failure? Usually we are not able to prepare ourselves effectively under high stress. Fortunately, we have an answer, called "accepting failure" or "accept defeat." This training method involves acknowledging that when facing a confrontation or problem, we could lose. Such a loss could take place on the street, in the office, or on the battlefield. When we expose our minds to such a scenario using visualization, we desensitize it to the feelings and stresses associated with failure. We do not train ourselves to focus on losing, or to become conditioned to losing. Rather, we permit our minds to accept the possibility of loss, and thereby manage the anxiety and fear response that are associated with such a possibility. Just remember the common saying, "You can't win them all."

A Real-Life Story: The Medical Student Who Had a Problem with Blood

A friend was in her fourth year of medical school at Tel-Aviv University, where she and her classmates were required to draw blood for the first time from patients at the hospital. This young woman, along with dozens of other medical students, was in complete panic. She and her fellow students had all failed their first attempts to draw blood from one another the evening before they had to draw blood from real patients in the hospital. We advised her to try the "accepting defeat" drill.

She started by visualizing and "practicing" the worst-case scenario, only once. The results were awful. The patient died, she was expelled from the university, taken to court, and her father, who was a medical professor, denounced her. Then, in several stages, in each of which she was more efficient and successful, she progressed from the worst to the best and most desirable outcome.

Next, she visualized herself successfully drawing blood from three different patients. One was rather large, the second was of regular build, and the third was very skinny. Next, she visualized the best possible scenario ten times. She imagined drawing blood from ten different arms, through a curtain, so that she did not see the people involved. She physically did some basic moves in the air to assist with the visualization and feeling.

The session with the young woman took about twenty minutes. The next day, she flawlessly executed blood draws from several patients. What happened? Her mind was desensitized. Her subconscious "felt" that it has "been there and done that." She was neither stressed nor worried, and thus she functioned at her best.

Here is another example of the "accepting defeat" exercise. A manager makes a mistake that he fears will cost his company a large sum of money. His boss, the owner of the company, schedules a meeting with the manager in thirty minutes. The manager fears he will lose his job. His nervous system engages a fight-or-flight stress response. His thoughts and emotions are out of control. His heart rate and blood pressure are high, he is sweating, his stomach is irritated, and he has taken two trips to the men's room already.

The manager decides to try the "accepting defeat" drill. He starts with visualizing the worst possible meeting. The boss shouts at him, and fires him without compensation. His family is shocked; he cannot pay his mortgage, and his wife takes their two young kids and leaves to stay with her parents. Next, he visualizes several different results, one incident after the other, all progressively becoming better until he reaches the best-case scenario. There may be several directions that he can take for the best-case scenario. One can be to stay with the company, reduce his salary in order to compensate for the loss, and thus gain respect from the owner and other employees. Another may involve being fired but finding a new job or opening his own business, a dream that he has had for long time. A third may be learning that his mistake wasn't a mistake at all, but somehow a success!

A Real-Life Story: How "Accepting Defeat" Helped Eyal Yanilov Cope with a Threatening Lawsuit

Eyal had a verbal agreement with an American instructor to spread Krav Maga in the United States. Despite their understanding, the instructor later decided to pursue this goal without Eyal.

Naturally, Eyal felt betrayed, but he decided to train new American instructors and students within the framework of his international Krav Maga organization, which was based in Israel, since he believed it was important for them to learn authentic Israeli Krav Maga from its origin.

The American instructor retaliated by suing Eyal and demanded several millions of dollars in damages. Eyal was quite shocked and could not sleep for a couple of nights. At the time, he was married with two teenage children. How could he care for them if he lost the case? Fortunately, he decided to fight back.

Eyal started by using the technique of "accepting defeat." He visualized losing the case in court, having to sell his home to pay the bills, and then being forced to separate from his family. Then he imagined a series of better results. Eyal decided to ignore any possible negative outcomes and just focus on doing his best to fight the case—after the "accept defeat" drill, it was a feasible mental task.

Together with his lawyers and several loyal friends, Eyal assembled hundreds of pages of documents from Israel and abroad that explained his rights to teach Krav Maga in the United States. Although it was necessary for him to pay substantial legal fees, he ultimately prevailed when the case was thrown out of court by a federal judge, who ruled in Eyal's favor on every count.

Accepting Defeat KMG Drill

Let us return to the possibility of using the "accepting defeat" drill to manage the stress of a violent confrontation. In this variation, you should visualize that you are experiencing an attack. At the extreme, you could die if assaulted by an opponent. By accepting failure, you lessen your fear of getting hurt and significantly improve your ability to function under pressure. This drill conditions your subconscious to these stressful conditions, because it handles internal and external images the same way.

The transition from the visualized defeat to visualization of complete success should take you several steps, commonly around five or six steps.

The following figures depict a physical variation of the accepting defeat drill. The image of the attacking partner appears graphically transparent to simulate that he is a visualized opponent.

First, trainee visualizes the worst possible outcome: The attacker strikes him, and the trainee falls to the ground.

The trainee visualizes an attack.

The trainee simulates getting hurt and falling.

The trainee simulates lying helpless on the ground with his attacker looming.

The second set of visualizations, not pictured, involve imagining the victim performing ineffective defenses. He manages to fight back, but he is still hurt and falls to the ground.

The third set of visualizations depict a minimally effective defense and escape.

The trainee notices the attacker once he swings his weapon.

The trainee performs a partial defense that prevents injury.

The trainee escapes.

The last set of visualizations involve a successful reaction and defense. It includes neutralizing the assailant, perhaps disarming him, and then different possibilities like checking on the friend that accompanied you, searching for your belongings, checking yourself for injuries, calling the authorities and reporting the case, or any other desirable and relevant process.

After reaching full success, visualize yourself ten to fifteen times as the winner.

The trainee notices the attack early enough to perform an efficient defense.

The technique to counter an overhead one-handed stick attack also applies to an ax.

The trainee performs additional counter-attacks while controlling the aggressor.

The trainee visualizes "finishing mode," moving away from the danger zone.

A Real-Life Story: Ringo Star Was Lost!

In his early 30s, Zvi had a strong and loyal dog named Ringo that one day disappeared.

Naturally, he became very distressed, thinking of the worst scenarios that might have happened to his beloved dog. Zvi's mentor, Prof. A. G. Beged-Dov, who heard about it, advised him to imagine, instead, that the dog's new owner was a lovely kid who plays with Ringo and cared for it, and they were both very happy together...

Begged-Dov's wise message was that we actually live in the stories we like to tell ourselves, so let's make them good ones!

Your main point of view for the visualization should be as if you are taking part in the incident. However, it is also beneficial to visualize it from an outside point of view, as if you are looking at a TV screen, and also from the point of view of the attacker.

Do you need to practice this whole process often and against every attack? The answer is no. You should only have a taste of this training method. Overall you should not be focused on or invest much in losing; you should not be conditioned to lose, but only to be in a state of mind of accepting the possibility of loss.

From time to time, especially if you find yourself anxious, worried, or unsure about your mental strength and preparedness (maybe when having a new boss at work, a different kind of problem, or an especially difficult technique), you can use this protocol. If you are worried about an explicit attack, like an assault rifle threat that you have not seen before; an especially difficult location, like a dark parking lot; unfavorable conditions such as cold and rainy weather; or a specific kind of attacker, maybe with painted faces and bloody clothing, then it is definitely most suitable to use this method of accepting defeat.

CONCLUSION

Our thoughts are practically manifested in our internal monologue, the self-talk that is running inside our minds. These thoughts turn into actions, the actions into habits, and the habits change our characters and thus our lives. Therefore, the way to direct our lives is via our self-talk. This chapter describes how to control and change our emotions (especially the destructive ones) and self-talk and overcome fears of specific and general confrontations and violent encounters.

About the Authors

Eyal Yanilov

Eyal Yanilov learned Krav Maga since 1974 directly from its founder, Imi Sde-Or (Lichtenfeld), and served as his closest assistant and most distinguished follower for nearly twenty years, until his passing in 1998.

Since Grandmaster Imi nominated Eyal in 1987 as head of the professional committee and assigned him to develop the modern Krav Maga curriculum, Eyal has made Krav Maga into an integrated technical and tactical system.

Yanilov and Sde-Or co-authored *Krav Maga: How to Defend Yourself against Armed Assault,* published in 2001, which included forewords by Israel's Prime Minister Yitzhak Rabin and President Shimon Peres, both Nobel Peace Prize laureates. The long-awaited second volume, **Krav Maga: How to Defend Yourself against Physical Attack**, will finally be published in spring 2020.

Eyal constantly strives to share his knowledge of genuine Krav Maga with audiences all over the world as head instructor and president of Krav Maga Global (KMG). He has been teaching civilian students since 1975, civilian instructors since 1980, and international and Israeli military, law enforcement, anti-terror, undercover, and special forces since 1985. Along with his Krav Maga career, the author has also been studying and applying western and eastern mental training methods since 1980.

Yanilov, who holds a BS in electrical engineering, is the only person who has ever earned both the Founder's Diploma of Excellence and the highest Krav Maga rank awarded by Grandmaster Imi.

Ole Boe

Ole Boe has been responsible for the Norwegian Military Academy's concept of stress management, and for preparing officers mentally for combat and other stressful and challenging situations. Ole has published over 270 scientific articles and research reports on learning under stress, stress management, decision making, leadership, and leader performance under dangerous and unpredictable situations.

Ole Boe served as an operational officer in a Norwegian military special unit conducting VIP protection, hostage rescue, and close combat. He taught close combat and combat mindset training for special police units, military special forces, and similar units in many countries, from the Congo to Cambodia. From 2003 to 2016 Dr. Boe served as associate professor at the Norwegian Military Academy, where he taught leadership to army officers. In 2017 and 2018 he served as an associate professor of military leadership at the Norwegian Defence University College. He currently works as a full professor of organization and leadership at the School of Business at the University of South-Eastern Norway. He is also a professor of organizational psychology at Bjørknes University College, and serves as a part-time professor in leadership and leadership development for the Norwegian Military Academy and in military leadership for the Norwegian Defence University College.

The author is a graduate of the Norwegian Defense Command and Staff College, and holds a PhD in cognitive psychology. He became a Krav Maga instructor under Eyal Yanilov in 1998 and is an Expert Level 3 member of KMG's Global and International Teams (GIT).

Acknowledgments

The authors and publisher wish to express their gratitude and appreciation to the following persons who significantly contributed to the book's creation:

To the Norwegian Armed Forces for the use of their graphic material in this book.

To KMG instructors Rebecca O'Connor, Natasha Hirschfeld, Tommy Blom, Rune Lind, Balazs Szabo, and Matt Beecroft, as well as to Yoav Yanilov, who spent many hours taking pictures and performing tiring demonstrations in front of the camera.

To the KMG instructors who took part in the "Combat Mindset and Mental Conditioning Instructors Course" (Israel, summer 2015), repeatedly performing hard tasks and drills, so that we could have the appropriate pictures for this work.

To Rami Sinai, our photographer, who methodically and meticulously took thousands of shots that give this book its look, clarity, and supportive content.

To Giulio Venturi, the graphic designer of the book and to Sigalit Orgad-Doron for her final touch in accurately applying our numerous corrections and the cover design.

To senior lecturer Merete Ruud at the Norwegian Military Academy for her most-appreciated help with the English editing of the first version of this book.

To KMG practitioner Richard Bejtlich, who performed the initial English language edit of the book: You did a great job streamlining longer passages and clarifying their meaning.

To Katie Roman for her invaluable expert language editing of the English version of the book.

Eyal's Gratitude

My deepest gratitude is firstly conveyed to my wife Merav, for three decades of loving, assisting, supporting, and enabling me to chase my dream and fulfill the mission of changing people and the world for the better. Her advice, work, dedication, and sacrifice were an integral part of spreading the Krav Maga knowledge that led to empowering and changing the lives of tens of thousands of human beings.

To my teacher, mentor, and practically my best friend for many years, Imi Sde-Or (Lichtenfeld), the founder of Krav Maga: He was first and foremost my teacher, starting when I was a teenager. Over the years our relationship developed into a deep friendship. According to his family, Imi saw me as a son, but above all, Imi served as a role model. He was a gentleman and a fighter whose spirit and mental fortitude served as a beacon of light for hundreds of elite soldiers and KMG instructors, first in the IDF (Israel Defense Forces) and later in civilian life where he educated generations of students and instructors.

To my Raja Yoga teacher from Varanasi, India, Shiv Shankar Tripathi (Shibugi): His vast knowledge and teaching took me to a much higher level of capacity, understanding, and practicing of mental training.

To Shihan (Kyokushin Karate) Ronen Katz, my friend and yoga teacher from Israel: His enthusiasm, knowledge, caring, dedication, and assistance were a tremendous contribution to me and thus to all who learned from me.

To my students from the civilian and government units around the world, to the instructors and officers of special forces whom I have trained since the early 1980s: They challenged me, asked questions, and brought problems, needs, and requests that required thought, deep digging, decisions, and solutions, which made me a better man, practitioner, and instructor.

To those of my former students, competitors, and rivals who have brought hurdles, some annoying challenges, and even (failed) lawsuits to my doorstep: They mainly forced me to battle, innovate, and excel.

To Zvi (Zvika) Morik, our publisher and my friend for over thirty years, who started as Imi Sde-Or's student and assistant and trained under me two decades later: Zvi was the force behind the publication of the series of books on Krav Maga that Imi and I wrote. Without his unmatchable work, patience, and tolerance, that work could not have seen the light of day. Zvi's guidance and professionalism have made this project much easier to realize.

Last but not least, to Dr. Ole Boe: Thank you for being my friend and partner on the road of mental training, as well as my a student for twenty years, and for developing this project together. Side by side, we have designed and built specific seminars and courses for students and instructors, which we delivered together or separately. You have invested countless hours of writing and work, including flying to Israel and other countries, so that we could sit together and write this book.

Ole's Gratitude

My deepest gratitude goes first and foremost to my better half, Therese Magnusson, for her never-ending support in letting me work on this book. Without her support—that is, taking care of the children and all our domestic duties—I would not have been able to find the time to finish the book. Allowing me to travel both near and far to contribute to this book has been a vital part of the success of producing it. She accepted that even when I was home, I was mentally somewhere else, which has truly meant a lot to me!

To all the students and instructors of Krav Maga all over the world that I have had the pleasure to deliver knowledge to over the years: Thank you. The trust you have put in me makes me very humble. For this, I am very grateful.

To all the soldiers and officers in both the Norwegian Armed Forces and in other countries, police officers in different police units around the world, and all the cadets, past and present, at the Norwegian Military Academy: I am deeply grateful for all the hardships and good moments we have shared together. I am also thankful for everything I have learned from you over the years. Allowing me to experiment on you with "weird" exercises is something that I will appreciate forever. The amount of sweat and blood you have given up during the years is just astonishing. You are definitely true warriors in heart and in spirit.

To all my military and civilian colleagues at the Norwegian Military Academy: Thank you for all the valuable and helpful conversations we have had over the years related to the topics covered in this book. Your integrity and straight-forward feedback have been a refreshing part of my life.

To my commanders at the Norwegian Military Academy, who gave me the option of deciding for myself what to work on while being on research leave during the last few years: Finding the time to write this book would have been impossible without your support.

To fellow members of my former military special unit: Learning about what mental strength and character really are has been a life changer. Ax throwers you definitely are.

To my closest family, who created a childhood environment that produced a doer: Learning to do your best and letting others decide whether it is good enough or not has proven to be an extremely valuable tool in my life.

I would like to express my deepest gratitude to Merav Yanilov, Eyal's wife, for the hospitality and generosity she has granted me over the years. I have stayed in Eyal's and Merav's home so many times, and have felt that I have intruded so many times. I am sure that I have stolen a lot of time from her husband. Merav has always made me feel very welcome, and I am extremely grateful for this. She has been an inspiration during times of working on the book, with her constant support and encouragement to finish the work.

Finally, to my teacher and mentor both in Krav Maga and in so many other aspects of life, Eyal Yanilov: The amount of knowledge that you have shared cannot be described. Words cannot express how thankful I am for the more than twenty years that we have known each other, and for being friends. As Imi was a role model, a gentleman, and a fighter showing you and so many others which path to travel in life, you have done the same for me. For this, I am eternally grateful to you, and for being a partner in the adventure of mental training that ultimately produced this book.

Commonly Used Concepts & Terms

Accepting defeat: A training method that involves acknowledging that when facing a confrontation or problem, you could lose. The drill desensitizes the mind to the possible worst-case scenario and reduces stress.
Aggressive postures and gestures, identifying: Specific training drills aiming at teaching you to pick up on aggressive signals from other people.
Anchoring: The process of cementing a connection between mind and body.
Attacker–disturber–target (ADT): Specific drills and games that develop aggression, determination, courage, focused attention, and perseverance.
Attention span: The time you can stay focused on a specific task without becoming distracted.
Attentional rubbernecking: The process of drawing your attention to stimuli with a strong emotional aspect.
Auditory exclusion: The loss of hearing due to stressful conditions.

Body language: Conscious and unconscious movements and postures by which attitudes and feelings are communicated.
Body posture, strong: A pose that relates to commanding, winning, or even threatening or aggression, and thus produces positive feelings.
Body posture, weak: A pose that shows weakness, vulnerability, or misplacement, and thus produces negative feelings.
Breathing, abdominal: Breathing only with your diaphragm and stomach area.
Breathing, full: A full breathing process that incorporates abdominal, midsection or "rib" breathing, and high or "chest" breathing.
Breathing, high or "chest" or "clavicle": Breathing with your clavicle area and upper chest.
Breathing, midsection or "rib": Breathing only with your midsection and lower ribs.

Character strength: A psychological ingredient, process, or mechanism that defines a virtue.
Character, classifying: A classification of twenty-four universally valued character strengths within six main virtues.
Chasing game: A drill aimed at reaching and overcoming adversity and installing courage and controlled aggression.

Choke response: The feeling that you are not able to swallow or breathe.

Combat mindset: A mental attitude incorporating character qualities such as courage, determination, perseverance, mental toughness, aggression, and grit.

Concentration: The ability to focus on the task at hand and ignore distractions.

Conditioning: A form of learning in which one stimulus comes to signal the occurrence of a second stimulus.

Conditioning, classical: A form of conditioning, also known as Pavlovian conditioning, in which one stimulus comes to signal the occurrence of a second stimulus.

Conditioning through cue words: Practicing the use of a cue word or a command before or during muscle movements to enhance the relaxation effect, i.e., conditioning yourself to become relaxed instead of feeling stressed.

Controlled aggression: The ability to be aggressive but still control your level of aggression and emotions, so that it is suitable for the situation you are in.

Controlling the ego: The ability not to care about results, circumstances, your image, or your status in the eyes of yourself or others, thus allowing you to control and quiet your mind in order to perform better, respond earlier, and become more efficient.

Coordination drill: A drill incorporating different moves of the limbs, head, and body to improve coordination, patterns in the brain, and learning capabilities.

Coping theory: A model explaining how humans relate to stress. The theoretical explanations for the source of and ways of dealing with stress can be broadly categorized based on three considerations: a response-based, a stimulus-based, or a transaction-based account.

Cue word: A selected word or a command, like "relax" or "courage," that is used before or during muscle movements to enhance the relaxation effect or other states of mind, including courage and aggression.

Death grip: A response to a most stressful situation involving holding an object extremely tightly.

Destructive emotion: A mental factor that disrupts your mind and prevents it from observing reality in a correct way. A destructive emotion includes negative emotions such as anger, fear, and frustration.

Destructive emotion, defusing of: A technique aimed at reducing anger, fear, and frustration so that you can control your mental state and perform better under stress.

Determination: A part of your combat mindset in which you show firmness of purpose.

Difficult talk: A conversation with an underperforming employee.

Divided attention: Your ability to absorb information around and inside you, and to pick up subtle cues that you would otherwise miss. See **open attention**.

Enactive mastery experience: An action you have mastered before is likely to influence your ability to solve a similar task. This is one of the most effective ways to boost your confidence and increase your belief in your abilities.

Exercise-induced activation (EIA) of the nervous system: An increase in the heart rate and activation of the nervous system due to physical activity.

Fear response: The process of perceiving a situation as negative, consisting of four elements, including 1) the cognitive element, or what you are thinking about; 2) the somatic element, or what happens in your body; 3) the emotional element, or what you feel; and 4) the behavioral element, or what you do or do not do, otherwise known as the fight-or-flight response. The purpose of the fear response is to give you the option to flee or fight.

Fencing game: A game that resembles classical fencing, but using clenched fists only.

Fight–flight–freeze (FFF): A behavior that results from a stressful situation.

Fighting spirit: The ability to continue your chosen response regardless of the difficulties you meet.

Fighting stress: Techniques and drills aimed at reducing your stress level so that you can perform better.

Fight-or-flight response: Your instinctive response to a threatening situation or confrontation. See **fight–flight–freeze**.

Focus mitt: Equipment used for practicing strikes or defenses.

Focus on a point (TRATAK): A specific focusing and concentration technique in which you sit or stand, staring motionlessly, commonly at a black dot.

Focus; focusing: When clarity, concentration, and action converge to create a specific result in the present.

Focusing body, speech, and mind: A set of drills that aim to focus and concentrate your mind by breathing, staring at a specific point without moving.

Frazzle: A mental state where you experience constant stress, leading to an overloaded nervous system.

Functional game: A game that prepares you to learn new techniques and tactics or improve your related abilities. Some games also simulate conditions you may encounter outside the training area.

Grit: Emotional strength that involves the exercise of will to accomplish goals in the face of opposition, external or internal. Grit includes courage and resolve.

Hormone-induced activation (HIA) of the nervous system: An increase in heart rate and activation of the nervous system due to experiencing stress.

Human conditioning: The process of learning new behavior via the process of association.

Impact weapon: A weapon (even a firearm) that can be used to hit a target, or strike, defend, or deflect an attack (armed or unarmed).

Improving attention: Focusing and concentration drills suitable for the task of improving your attention span and staying focused and attentive to the action or non-action you must take.

Internal monologue/dialogue: The conversation you have with yourself, or what you are thinking and telling yourself in different situations. See **self-talk**.

Kinesthetic sense: The perception and understanding of how your body feels and moves.

King of the hill game: A specific game in which the goal is to push others away from a marked area or pull them into it.

Krav Maga: An integrated system of self-defense, fighting skills and tactics, and third-party protection. Krav Maga was founded by Imi Sde-Or (Lichtenfeld), then refined, developed, and initially spread throughout the world by Eyal Yanilov, Grandmaster Imi's most distinguished disciple and right hand.

Krav Maga Global (KMG): The global Krav Maga organization founded by Eyal Yanilov.

Leadership, developmental: A Swedish model aiming to provide a comprehensive picture of leadership.

Leadership, in extremis: Leadership that takes place in extreme situations.

Leadership, non-: When a leader is present but not active in leading.

Leadership, transactional: Leadership that mainly focuses on supervision, organization, and performance, and where the leader promotes compliance through both reward and punishment.

Leadership, transformational: Leadership that positively affects the achievement of results in both service-oriented and production-oriented organizations.

Marking attacks: Stopping an attack and recoiling just few centimeters (1-2 inches) before making contact, without reaching the attack's maximum range.

Mental attack plan: Choosing how, when, and where you train, and which stages and methods you use.

Mental challenge: A challenge that you may consider difficult to perform mentally, and often also physically.
Mindfulness training: Transferring awareness to the present moment, away from negative stress reactions themselves.
Mindfulness-based stress reduction (MBSR): A specific training program that incorporates mindfulness to assist with pain and a range of conditions and life issues, which were initially difficult to treat in a hospital setting.
Minimizing ego: A process of understanding that you managed to get where you are because others taught and helped you. Your thoughts are less about yourself, your place in the hierarchy, or the property and objects you own.
Monster with brakes: A soldier or fighter who has gone through the process of training aggression and aggression control in order to be aggressive when needed but still able to be in control, follow commands, and regulate his (or her) emotions and make appropriate decisions.

Naming and scaling: A specific drill in which you focus on the emotion, feel it, name it, and then score it on a scale, usually between one and ten.
Neuro-linguistic programming (NLP): The connection observed between neurological processes ("neuro"), language ("linguistic"), and your behavioral patterns learned through experience ("programming").
Neuroplasticity: The ability of the brain to change (e.g., certain areas grow or shrink) in response to experiences.

OODA loop: An acronym indicating the process of observing–orienting–deciding–acting.
Open attention: Your ability to absorb information around and inside you, and to pick up subtle cues you would otherwise miss. See **divided attention**.

Partner game: A game that includes two people.
Partner posture drill: A drill that helps you experience the mental and physical aspects of assuming strong and weak poses.
Perseverance: An emotional strength that involves the exercise of will to accomplish goals in the face of external or internal opposition.
Post-traumatic stress disorder (PTSD): A mental health condition that is triggered by a traumatic event that was either experienced or witnessed.
Posture: The position in which someone holds his or her body when standing or sitting, or a particular approach or attitude.
Posture and perception: The signals you send by a specific posture and the interpretation of this posture by others.

Power drill: A drill that is intended to strengthen your physical condition, including your speed.

Power pose: A pose that affects your hormone levels and actually causes you to feel powerful.

Progressive muscle relaxation: Techniques to systematically contract and relax muscles and, thereby, relax the mind and the whole body.

Reaction game: A game used to develop readiness, focus, attention, accuracy of movement, and shorten response time. A reaction game often involves catching, snatching, and grabbing.

Relaxation: The ability to stay relaxed as a way of reducing stress.

Relaxation and breathing: The process in which taking control over your breathing leads to relaxation.

Reverse conditioning: When you handle a challenge successfully, you instill confidence and desensitize yourself to anxiety.

Rhythm and count: Different drills used in breathing in order to improve control of your mind.

Rooster game: A funny game that requires balance by invoking attacks and defenses, mainly with the body, while jumping on one leg.

Self-control: The ability to regulate what you feel, think, and do.

Self-efficacy: What you consider attainable with the skills you possess.

Self-talk: The conversation you have with yourself, or what you are thinking and telling yourself in different situations. See **internal monologue**.

Slow fighting: Fighting much slower than your real speed, aiming to defend slower than your partner's attacks, and using even slower counterattacks while controlling your breathing and mental state.

Slow-motion technique: Performing a technique very slowly while paying attention to what goes on inside your mind and body.

Startle reflex: An involuntary reaction to a situation, in which you blink and pull your head away from something moving toward you.

Sticky hands drill: A drill in which you and your partner try to slowly defend against each other's push, or push each other off balance by shifting weight and pressure on your partner's arm, chest, abdomen, or hip area.

Stimulus: Something that triggers action or exertion or quickens actions, feelings, or thoughts.

Strategic vision: When you use mental images to influence bodily processes or to control pain, either to influence or change your mental state, or to prepare for a corporate executive meeting, an athletic competition, or a performance.

See **visualization**.

Strength drill: A drill that aims to develop your ability to resist or move weight load. See **power drill**.

Stress mindset: An approach that sees stress as an enhancement factor in which you consider challenges as solvable problems, not threats.

Stress-is-enhancing mindset: A view that the stress that you are exposed to is actually beneficial for you.

Submit: When you surrender in hope that your opponent will not begin to hit you, or that he will stop attacking or hurting you if he already started.

Survival stress reaction: A condition where a perceived threat stimulus automatically activates the sympathetic nervous system.

Tag game: A game used to develop combat mindset and controlled aggression.

Tails game: A game in which you try grabbing an object attached to your partner's body, e.g., a piece of cloth, a rubber knife, or a training pistol in a holster that is tucked into your partner's waistband or belt.

Thai pad: Equipment used to practice striking, kicking, or defending against attacks.

Touching game: A game in which participants compete in touching and defending a specific area per the trainer's instructions. Such games play a very important role in technical and mental preparation because they resemble a desirable technique or a fight.

TRATAK: A specific focusing and concentration technique (see **Focus on a point**).

Vicarious experience: Seeing others succeed, which is a factor involved in building self-efficacy.

Virtue: A core characteristic valued by moral philosophers and religious thinkers.

Visualization: See **strategic vision**.

Weapon retention: Keeping your firearm while an attacker is trying to take it.

Willpower: A mental process in which you aim to rationally control your actions.

References

Abbott, A., & Collins, D. (2004). Eliminating the dichotomy between theory and practice in talent identification and development: considering the role of psychology. *Journal of Sports Sciences, 22*(5), 395–408.

Abbott, D. H., Keverne, E. B., Bercovitch, F. B., Shively, C. A., Mendoza, S. P., Saltzman, W., Snowdon, C. T., Ziegler, T. E., Banjevic, M., Garland, T. Jr., & Sapolsky, R. M. (2003). Are subordinates always stressed? A comparative analysis of rank differences in cortisol levels among primates. *Hormones and Behavior, 43*, 67–82.

Ahmed, L., & de Fockert, J. W. (2012). Focusing on Attention: The Effects of Working Memory Capacity and Load on Selective Attention. *PLoS ONE 7(8)*, e43101.

Alexander, J., Groller, R., & Morris, J. (1990). *The Warrior's Edge*. New York: William Morrow.

Asken, M. J., Grossman, D., & Christensen, L. (2010). *Warrior Mindset*. USA: Warrior Science Publications.

Archer, J. (2006). Testosterone and human aggression: An evaluation of the challenge hypothesis. *Neuroscience & Biobehavioral Reviews, 30*, 319–345.

Aristotle. (n.d.a). *Nicomachean Ethics, book IV* (translated by Irwin, T.). Cambridge UK: Hackett Publishing Company.

Aristotle. (n.d.b). *Courage is the first of human qualities because it is the quality which guarantees the others*. Retrieved from https://www.brainyquote.com/quotes/aristotle_121141

Atkinson, R. L., Atkinson, R. C., Smith, E. E., & Bem, D. J. (1993). *Introduction to psychology* (11th ed.). Florida: Harcourt Brace Jovanovich.

Bacon, S. J. (1974). Arousal and the ranger of cue utilization. *Journal of Experimental Psychology, 102*, 81–87.

Baddeley, A. D., & Logie, R. H. (1999). Working memory: The multiple-component model. In A. Miyake & P. Shah (Eds.), *Models of working memory: Mechanisms of active maintenance and executive control* (pp. 28–61). New York: Cambridge University Press.

Baer, R. A. (2003). Mindfulness training as a clinical intervention: a conceptual and empirical review. *Clinical Psychology: Science and Practice, 10(*2), 125–143.

Bandura, A. (1997). *Self-efficacy: The exercise of control*. New York: W. H. Freeman and Company.

Bandura, A. (1995). Exercise of personal and collective efficacy in changing societies. In A. Bandura (Ed.), *Self-Efficacy in Changing Societies* (pp. 1-45). New York: Cambridge University Press.

Bandura, A. (1991). Self-efficacy mechanism in physiological activation and health-promoting behavior. In J. Madden, IV (Ed.), *Neurobiology of learning, emotion, and affect* (pp. 229–269). New York: Raven Press.

Bandura, A. (1986). *Social foundations of thought and action: A social cognitive theory*: Englewood Cliffs: Prentice-Hall, Inc.

Bandura, A. (1978). The self system in reciprocal determinism. *American Psychologist, 33*, 344–358.

Bandura, A. (1977). *Social learning theory*. Oxford, England: Prentice-Hall.

Bass, B. M., & Avolio, B. J. (1990). *Transformational leadership development: Manual for the Multifactor Leadership Questionnaire*. Palo Alto, CA: Consulting Psychologists Press.

Bass, B. M., & Riggio, R. E. (2006). *Transformational leadership. Second edition.* Mahwah, NJ: Lawrence Erlbaum Associates.

Baumeister, R. F., & Tierney, J. (2011). *Willpower: Rediscovering the greatest human strength.* New York: Penguin. Press.

Beer, J., Lombardo M., & Bhanji, J. (2010). Roles of medial prefrontal cortex and orbitofrontal cortex in self-evaluation. *Journal of Cognitive Neuroscience 22(9)*, 2108–2119.

Bianco, T. (2001). Social support and recovery from sport injury: Elite skiers share their experiences. *Research Quarterly for Exercise and Sport, 72*, 376–388.

Biswas-Diener, R., Kashdan, T. B., & Minhas, G. (2011). A dynamic approach to psychological strength development and intervention. *Journal of Positive Psychology, 6* (2), 106–118.

Bjørklund, R. A. (1997). *Politipsykologi (Police psychology)*. Nesbru: Vett & Viten.

Bjorner, J., Kristensen, T. S., Orth-Gomer, K., Tibblin, G., Sullivan, M., & Westerholm, P. (1996). *Self-rated health: A useful concept in research, prevention, and clinical medicine.* Stockholm: Swedish Council for Planning and Coordination of Research.

Bleckley, M. K., Durso, F. T., Crutchfield, J. M., Engle, R. W., & Khanna, M. M. (2003). Individual differences in working memory capacity predict visual attention allocation. *Psychonomic Bulletin & Review 10*(4), 884–889.

Boe, O. (2018).Officer Development at the Norwegian Military Academy. In S. Rawat (Ed.), *Cadet Diary Psychology of Warrior Ethos and Cadet Leadership Development* (pp. 167–184). New Delhi: Rawat Publications.

Boe, O. (2016a). *Mental toughness before and after a combat fatigue course*. Oslo: Norwegian Military Academy.

Boe, O. (2016b). Character strengths and its relevance for military officers. In S. Rawat (Ed.), *Military psychology: International perspectives* (pp.113–126). New Delhi: Rawat Publications.

Boe, O. (2015a). Developing leadership skills in Norwegian military officers: Leadership proficiencies contributing to character development and officer competency. *Procedia-Social and Behavioral Sciences Journal, 186*, 288–292.

Boe, O. (2015b). Character in military leaders, officer competency and meeting the unforeseen. *Procedia-Social and Behavioral Sciences Journal, 190*, 497–501.

Boe, O. (2015c). Does practicing close combat training improve the perceived ability to perform better in stressful conditions? *Procedia-Social and Behavioral Sciences Journal, 190*, 409–415.

Boe, O. (2014). *Prosjektbeskrivelse for KS FoU-prosjekt: Karakter hos militære offiserer (Project description for NMAs research and development project: Character in military officers)*. Research project applied for to the Norwegian Military Academy, 1–39. Oslo: Norwegian Military Academy.

Boe, O. (2013). Leadership development in Norwegian junior military officers: A conceptual framework of building mission-solving competency. *Proceedings of the 16th International Military Mental Health Conference (16IMMHC)*.

Boe, O. (2006). *Factors affecting combat efficiency in stressful conditions*. Oslo: Norwegian Military Academy.

Boe, O. (2003). *Physical and mental reactions during a threatening or dangerous situation*. Kvarn: Swedish Army Combat School.

Boe, O. (2000a). En hotfull situation-vad händer i kroppen och i hjärnan? (A threatening situation—what happens in the body and the brain?) *Fighter Magazine, 3*, 50–51.

Boe, O. (2000b). Bättre fly än illa fäkta? (Is it better to run than to fight poorly?) *Fighter Magazine, 4*, 50.

Boe, O. (2000c). Vad behöver du att tänka på innan du hamnar i en hotfull situation? (What do you need to consider before ending up in a threatening situation?). *Fighter Magazine, 5*, 50.

Boe, O., & Bang, H. (2017). The Big 12: The Most Important Character Strengths for Military Officers. *Athens Journal of Social Sciences, 4*(2), 161-174.

Boe, O., & Bang, H. (in press). Assessing the correlation between character strengths and mental toughness in military officers. *Procedia-Social and Behavioral Sciences*.

Boe, O., Bang, H., & Nilsen, F. A. (2015a). Selecting the most relevant character strengths for Norwegian Army officers: An educational tool. *Procedia-Social and Behavioral Sciences, 197*, 801–809.

Boe, O., Bang, H., & Nilsen, F. A. (2015b). The development of an observational instrument in order to measure character strengths. *Procedia-Social and Behavioral Sciences, 197*, 1126–1133.

Boe, O., Bang, H., & Nilsen, F. A. (2015c). Experienced military officer's perception of important character strengths. *Procedia-Social and Behavioral Sciences Journal, 190*, 339–345.

Boe, O., & Bergstøl, H. O. (2017). Theoretical and Practical Aspects of Self-Efficacy in Military Cadets. *International Journal of Learning, Teaching and Educational Research, 16*(7), 10–29.

Boe, O., Eldal, L., Hjortmo, H., Lilleng, H., & Kjørstad, O. (2014a). *KS Offisersutviklingskonsept (The Norwegian Military Academy's concept of officer development)*. Conceptual description for use at the Norwegian Military Academy. Oslo: Norwegian Military Academy.

Boe, O., Eldal, L., Hjortmo, H., Lilleng, H., & Kjørstad, O. (2014b). *KS Offisersutviklingskonsept (The Norwegian Military Academy's concept of officer development)*. A short one-page conceptual description for use at the Norwegian Military Academy. Oslo: Norwegian Military Academy.

Boe, O., & Hagen, K. (2015). Using mindfulness to help reducing the perception of stress in an acute stressful situation. *Procedia-Social and Behavioral Sciences, 197*, 858-868.

Boe, O., & Hegan, J. (2003). Fear response-what goes on in your brain and body when you are under threat. Retrieved from http://www.kravmagacombat.com/articles/FearResponse.pdf

Boe, O., & Holth, T. (2015a). Self-awareness in military officers who uses developmental leadership as their leadership style. *Procedia Economics and Finance, 26,* 833–841.

Boe, O., & Holth, T. (2015b). Investigating the correlations between personality traits and leadership styles in Norwegian military cadets. *Procedia Economics and Finance, 26,* 1173–1184.

Boe, O., & Holth, T. (2015c). The relationship between developmental leadership, results of leadership and personality factors. *Procedia Economics and Finance, 26,* 849–858.

Boe, O., & Ingdahl, A. (2017). Educating monsters with brakes: Teaching soldiers aggression and aggression control. *Kasmera, 45*(3), 1-30.

Boe, O., & Marthinsen, P. I. (2016). *Close combat-Can close combat training reduce stress, and is this transferable to other situations?* Oslo: Norwegian Military Academy.

Boe, O., & Olsen, C. S. (2016). *Do cadets with experience from military international operations perceive the coping with stress education given at the Norwegian Military Academy different as compared to cadets without this experience?* Oslo: Norwegian Military Academy.

Bong, M., & Clark, R. E. (1999). Comparison between self-concept and self-efficacy in academic motivation research. *Educational Psychology, 34,* 139–154.

Bong, M., & Skaalvik, E. M. (2003). Academic self-concept and self-efficacy: How different are they really? *Educational Psychology Review. 15,* 1–40.

Booth-Kewley, S., Larson, G. E., Alderton, D. L., Farmer, W. L., & Highfill-McRoy, R. (2009). Risk factors for misconduct in a navy sample. *Military Psychology, 21*(2), 252–269.

Bray, D. W., & Howard, A. (1983). The AT & T longitudinal studies of managers. In K. W. Schaie (Ed.), *Longitudinal studies of adult psychological development* (pp. 112–146). New York: Guilford.

Bremner, J, D. (2006). Traumatic stress: effects on the brain. *Dialogues in Clinical Neuroscience, 8*(4), 445–461.

Bremner, J, D. (1999). Does stress damage the brain? *Biological Psychiatry, 45*(7), 797–805.

Buch, R. Säfvenbom, R., & Boe, O. (2015). The Relationship Between Academic Self-Efficacy, Intrinsic Motivation for Military Studies, and Perceived Military Competence Among Military Academy Cadets. *Journal of Military Studies, 6(1),* 1–17.

Burman, J. T., Green, C. D., & Shanker, S. (2015). On the Meanings of Self-Regulation: Digital Humanities in Service of Conceptual Clarity. *Child Development, 86(5), 1507–1521.*

Burns. J. M. (2003). *Transforming leadership: A new pursuit of happiness.* New York: Atlantic Monthly Press.

Burns, J. M. (1978). *Leadership.* New York: Harper & Row.

Burton, L., Westen, D., & Kowalski, R. M. (2012). *Psychology: 3rd Australian and New Zealand edition.* Australia: John Wiley & Sons Australia, Ltd.

Cannon, W. B. (1932). *Wisdom of the Body.* USA: W.W. Norton & Company.

Cannon, W. B. (1926). Physiological regulation of normal states: some tentative postulates concerning biological homeostasis. In A. Pettit (Ed.), *A Charles Richet: ses amis, ses collègues, ses élèves* (in French). Paris: Les Éditions Médicales.

Carney, D. R., Cuddy, A. J. C., & Yap, A. J. (2010). Power Posing: Brief Nonverbal Displays Affect Neuroendocrine Levels and Risk Tolerance. *Psychological Science, 21*(10), 1363–1368.

Catania, C. A. (1994) Query: Did Pavlov's Research Ring a Bell?, *PSYCOLOQUY Newsletter*, Tuesday, June 7, 1994.

Chan, D. W. (2002). Stress, self-efficacy, social support, and psychological distress among prospective Chinese teachers in Hong Kong. *Educational Psychology, 22*, 557–569.

Chidester, T. R., Helmreich, R. L., Gregorich, S. E., & Geis, C. E. (1991). Pilot personality and crew coordination. *International Journal of Aviation Psychology, 1,* 25–44.

Clausewitz, C. von. (1832/1984). *On war* (translated by M. Howard & P. Paret). New Jersey: Princeton University Press.

Coe, C. L., Mendoza, S. P., & Levine, S. (1979). Social status constrains the stress response in the squirrel monkey. *Physiology & Behavior, 23*, 633–638.

Cohen, S., & Wills, T. (1985). Stress, social support, and the buffering hypothesis. *Psychological Bulletin, 98*, 310–357.

Collins, J. (2016). *Self-discipline: The ultimate guide to self-discipline like a US Navy SEAL.* San Bernardino: California.

Colzato, L. S., Spape, M., Pannebakker, M. M., & Hommel, B. (2007). Working memory and the attentional blink: blink size is predicted by individual differences in operation span. *Psychonomic Bulletin & Review 14*(6), 1051–1057.

Comer, R. (2005). *Fundamentals of abnormal psychology* (4th ed.). New York: Worth Publishers.

Cornish, D., & Dukette, D. (2009). *The Essential 20: Twenty Components of an Excellent Health Care Team.* Pittsburgh: RoseDog Books.

Cowan, N. (2001). The magical number 4 in short-term memory: A reconsideration of mental storage capacity. *Behavioral and Brain Sciences, 24,* 97–185.

Cowley, G., Murr, A., Carmicheal, M., Scelfo, J., Rosenberg, D., & Jefferson, D. (2003, February 24). Our bodies, our fears. *Newsweek, 141*, 42.

Cox, R. H. (2007). *Sport Psychology: Concepts and Applications.* New York: McGraw-Hill.

Cripe, B. (1999). *Building self-esteem.* Columbus, Ohio: The Ohio State University.

Crocker, J., & Wolfe, C. T. (2001). Contingencies of self-worth. *Psychological Review, 108*, 593–623.

Cronbach, L. J. (1951). Coefficient alpha and the internal structure of tests. *Psychometrika*, 16(3), 297–334.

Crum, A. J., Salovey, P., & Achor, S. (2013). Rethinking stress: The role of mindsets in determining the stress response. *Journal of Personality and Social psychology, 104*(4), 716–733.

Dane, E., & Brummel, B. J. (2014). Examining workplace mindfulness and its relations to job performance and turnover intention. *Human Relations, 67*(1), 105–128.

Davis, P. A., Woodman, T., & Callow, N. (2010). Better out than in: The influence of anger regulation on physical performance. *Personality and Individual Differences, 49*, 457–460.

Deci, E. L., & Ryan, R. M. (1995). Human autonomy: The basis for true self-esteem. In M. H. Kernis (Ed.), *Efficacy, agency, and self-esteem* (pp. 31–49). New York, NY: Plenum Press.

Dilts, R., Grinder, J., Delozier, J., & Bandler, R. (1980). *Neuro-Linguistic Programming: Volume I: The Study of the Structure of Subjective Experience.* Cupertino, CA: Meta Publications.

Doornbos, M. M. (1996). The strengths of families coping with serious mental illness. *Archives of Psychiatric Nursing, 10*, 214–220.

Doss, W. (2007). *Condition to Win. Dynamic techniques for performance oriented mental conditioning.* New York: Looseleaf Law Publications, Inc.

Duncan, C. P. (1949). The retroactive effect of electroshock on learning. *Journal of Comparative and Physiological Psychology, 42*, 32–44.

Easterbrook, J. A. (1959). The effects of emotion on cue-utilization and the organization of behavior. *Psychological Review, 66*(3), 183–201.

Eccles, D. W., & Feltovich, P. J. (2008). Implications of domain-general "psychological support skills" for the transfer of skill and the acquisition of expertise. *Performance Improvement Quarterly, 21*, 43–60.

Eccles, J. S., Wigfield, A., & Schiefele, U. (1998). Motivation to succeed. In W. Damon (Series Ed.) & N. Eisenberg (Vol. Ed.), *Handbook of Child Psychology. Vol. 3: Social, Emotional, and Personality Development* (5th ed.) (pp. 1017–1095). New York: Wiley.

Edison, T. A. (n.d). *I have not failed. I've just found 10,000 ways that won't work.* Retrieved from https://www.brainyquote.com/quotes/thomas_a_edison_132683.

Elsass, W. P., Fiedler, E., Skop, B., & Hill, H. (2001). Susceptibility to maladaptive responses to stress in basic military training based on variants of temperament and character. *Military Medicine, 166*, 884–888.

Endler, N. S., & Magnusson, D. (1976). Toward an interactional psychology of personality. *Psychological Bulletin, 83*, 956–979.

Ericsson, K. A., & Kintsch, W. (1995). Long-term working memory. *Psychological Review, 102*, 211–245.

Ericsson, K. A., & Smith, J. (1991). Prospects and limits of the empirical study of expertise: An introduction. In K. A. Ericsson & J. Smith (Eds.), *Towards a general theory of expertise: Prospects and limits* (pp. 1–38). New York: Cambridge University Press.

Eriksen, C. W., & Hoffman, J. E. (1973). The extent of processing of noise elements during selecting encoding from visual displays. *Perception & Psychophysics, 14*, 155–160.

Eriksen, C. W., & St. James, J. D. (1986). Visual attention within and around the field of focal attention: A zoom lens model. *Perception & Psychophysics, 40*, 225–240.

FBI. (2016). *Law Enforcement Officers Killed and Assaulted 2016.* Retrieved from https://ucr.fbi.gov/leoka/2016/federal/federal_topic_page_-2016.

FBI. (2004). *Law Enforcement Officers Killed and Assaulted 2004.* Retrieved from http://www.fbi.gov/ucr/killed/2004/downloads/LEOKA2004.pdf.

Fidje, D. S. (2011). *Krigsskolens Program for Lederutvikling—og kravene til stressmestring for ledere i strid. (The Norwegian Military Academy's program of leadership development—and the demands of coping with stress for leaders in combat)*. (Bachelor thesis in military studies; leadership and land power). Oslo: Norwegian Military Academy.

Finkel, E. J., DeWall, C. N., Slotter, E. B., Oaten, M., & Foshee, V. A. (2009). Self-regulatory failure and intimate partner violence perpetration. *Journal of Personality and Social Psychology, 97*(3), 483–499.

Fiore, S. M., Hoffman, R. R., & Salas, E. (2008). Learning and performance across disciplines: An epilogue for moving multidisciplinary research toward an interdisciplinary science of expertise. *Military Psychology, 20*, 155–170.

Fjeldheim, T. (2014). *Tenk som en kriger: Nå dine mål med mental styrketrening (Think like a warrior: Reach your goals with mental strength training)*. Oslo: J. M. Stenersen Forlag.

Flore, S. M., & Salas, E. (2008). Cognition, competition, and coordination: The "why" and the "how" of the relevance of the sport sciences to learning and performance in the military. *Military Psychology, 20* (Suppl.), S1–S9.

Florian, V., Mikulincer, M., & Taubman, O. (1995). Does hardiness contribute to mental health during a stressful real-life situation? The roles of appraisal and coping. *Journal of Personality and Social Psychology, Vol. 68,* (4), 687–695.

Forsvaret (2012). *FSJ grunnsyn på ledelse i Forsvaret (The Norwegian Armed Forces Chief of Defence basic view of leadership in the Armed Forces)*. Oslo: Norwegian Armed Forces.

Forsvarsstaben (2014). *Forsvarets fellesoperative doktrine (Norwegian Armed Forces Joint Operational Doctrine)*. Oslo: Norwegian Defence Staff.

Forsvarsstaben (2007). *Forsvarets fellesoperative doktrine (Norwegian Armed Forces Joint Operational Doctrine)*. Oslo: Norwegian Defence Staff.

Fried, R. (1990). *The Breath Connection*. New York: Plenum Press.

Garcia, R. (1989). *Field study of side handle baton techniques*. Millstadt, ll: PPCT Research Publications.

Garnett, J. (2010). *The Journey Continues: Life's Travel Guide for Teens and Young Adults*. New York: iUniverse Inc.

Gayton, S. D., & Kehoe, E. J. (2015a). A prospective study of character strengths as predictors of selection into the Australian Army Special Forces. *Military Medicine, 180*(2), 151–157.

Gayton, S. D., & Kehoe, E. J. (2015b). Character Strengths and Hardiness of Australian Army Special Forces Applicants. *Military Medicine, 180*(8), 857–862.

Gratton, G., Coles, M. G. H., Sirevaag, E. J., Eriksen, C. W., & Donchin, E. (1988). Pre- and poststimulus activation of response channels: A psychophysiological analysis. *Journal of Experimental Psychology: Human Perception and Performance, 14*, 331–344.

Goleman, D. (2013). *Focus: The hidden driver of excellence*. London: Bloomsbury Publishing Plc.

Griffith, J., & Vaitkus, M. (1999). Relating Cohesion to Stress, Strain, Disintegration, and Performance: An Organizing Framework. *Military Psychology, 11*, 27–55.

Grossman, D. (1995). *On Killing: the psychological cost of learning to kill in war and society.* New York: Back Bay Books.

Grossman, D., & Christensen, L. W. (2004). *On combat. The psychology and physiology of deadly conflict in war and peace*. PPCT Research Publications.

Grossman, D., & Siddle, B. K. (2001). Critical incident amnesia: The physiological basis and implications of memory loss during extreme survival situations. *The Firearms Instructor: The Official Journal of the International Association of Law Enforcement Firearms Instructors*, Issue 31.

Gruber, K. A., Kilcullen, R. N., & Iso-Ahola, S. E. (2009). Effects of Psychosocial Resources on Elite Soldiers' Completion of a Demanding Military Selection Program. *Military Psychology, 21*, 427–444.

Gruszka, M., Jago, T., Lea, R., & Parish, E. (2001). *Differences in level of anxiety during practice and competition*. Sydney: Australian Catholic University.

Hall, J. C. (2009). Utilizing Social Support to Conserve the Fighting Strength: Important Considerations for Military Social Workers. *Smith College Studies in Social Work, 79(3)*, 335–343.

Hammermeister, J., Pickering, M. A., McGraw, L., & Ohlson, C. (2010). Relationship between psychological skills profiles and soldier physical fitness performance. *Military Psychology, 22*, 399–411.

Harlow, R. E., & Cantor, N. (1995). To whom do people turn when things go poorly? Task orientation and functional social contacts. *Journal of Personality and Social Psychology, 69*, 329–340.

Hassmén, P., Hassmén, N., & Plate, J. (2003). *Idrottspsykologi (Sport psychology)*. Stockholm: Författarna och Bokförlaget Natur och Kultur.

Hazlett, G., & Morgan, C. A. (2003, October). *Special forces soldier: Model of high performance under stress*. Paper presented at the Peak Soldier Performance Conference, Santa Barbara, CA.

Heitz, R. P., & Engle, R. P. (2007). Focusing the Spotlight: Individual Differences in Visual Attention Control. *Journal of Experimental Psychology: General, 36*(2), 217–240.

Hockey, G. R. J. (1970). Effect of loud noise on attentional selectivity. *Quarterly Journal of Experimental Psychology, 22*, 28–36.

Holth, T., & Boe, O. (2010). *Finnes det noen sammenhenger mellom lederstilen utviklende lederskap og ulike personlighetstrekk hos kadetter på KS? (Do any correlations exist between the leadership style developmental leadership and different personality traits among Norwegian Military Academy cadets?)* Norwegian Military Academy research series no 4. Oslo: Norwegian Military Academy.

Holmes, T. H., & Rahe, R. H. (1967). The social readjustment rating scale. *Journal of Psychosomatic Research, 11*(2), 213–218.

House, J. S., Landis, K. R., & Umberson, D. (1988). Social relationships and health. *Science, 241*, 540–544.

Humara, M. (1999). The Relationship Between Anxiety and Performance: A Cognitive-Behavioral Perspective. *Athletic Insight The Online Journal of Sport Psychology, 1*(2), 1–14.

Hölzel, B. K., Carmody, J., Vangel, M., Congleton, C., Yerramsetti, S. M., Gard, T., & Lazar, S. W. (2011). Mindfulness practice leads to increases in regional brain gray matter density. *Psychiatry Research, 191*(1), 36–43.

Idler, E. L., & Benyamini, Y. (1997). Self-rated health and mortality: A review of twenty-seven community studies. *Journal of Health and Social Behavior, 38*, 21–37.

Insightstate.com. (2016). *How Do Destructive Emotions Affect Us?* Retrieved from http://www.insightstate.com/spirituality/how-do-destructive-emotions-affect-us/

James, W. (1890). *The Principles of Psychology.* Retrieved from http://infomotions.com/sandbox/great-books-redux/corpus/html/principles.html#chapter11.

Janelle, C. M., & Hatfield, B. D. (2008). Visual attention and brain processes that underlie expert performance: Implications for sport and military psychology. *Military Psychology, 20*, 39–69.

Janelle, C. M., & Hillmann, C. H. (2003). Expert performance in sport: Current perspectives and critical issues. In K. A. Ericsson & J. Starkes (Eds.), *Recent advances in research on sport expertise* (pp. 19–48). Champaign, IL: Human Kinetics.

Jetmore, L. F. (2005). *The Path of the Warrior: An Ethical Guild to Personal & Professional Development in the Field of Criminal Justice.* Flushing, New York: Looseleaf Law Publications, Inc.

Jex, S. M., Bliese, P. D., Buzzell, S., & Primeau, J. (2001). The impact of self-efficacy on stressor-strain relations: Coping style as an exploratory mechanism. *Journal of Applied Psychology, 86*, 401–409.

Jones, G., Hanton, S., & Connaughton, D. (2002). What is this thing called mental toughness? An investigation of elite sport performers. *Journal of Applied Sport Psychology, 14*, 205–218.

Jonides, J. (1983). Further towards a model of the mind's eye's movement. *Bulletin of the Psychonomic Society, 21*, 247–250.

Kabat-Zinn, J. (2003). Mindfulness-based interventions in context: Past, present, and future. *Clinical Psychology: Science and Practice, 10*, 144–156.

Kane, M. J., Conway, A. R. A., Hambrick, D. Z., & Engle, R. W. (2007). Variation in working memory capacity as variation in executive attention and control. In A. R. A. Conway, C. Jarrold, M. J. Kane, A. Miyake, & J. N. Towse (Eds.), *Variation in Working Memory* (pp. 21–48). Oxford University Press.

Kane, M. J., & Engle, R. W. (2003). Working-memory capacity and the control of attention: the contributions of goal neglect, response competition, and task set to Stroop interference. *Journal of Experimental Psychology: General 132*(1), 47–70.

Keltner, D., Gruenfeld, D. H., & Anderson, C. (2003). Power, approach, and inhibition. *Psychological Review, 110*, 265–284.

Kennedy, S., Kiecolt-Glaser, J. K., & Glaser, R. (1990). Social support, stress, and the immune system. In B. R. Sarason, I. G. Sarason, & G. R. Pierce (Eds.), *Social support: An interactive view* (pp. 253–265). New York: John Wiley & Sons.

Kernis, M. H., Paradise, A. W., Whitaker, D. J., Wheatman, S. R., & Goldman, B. N. (2000). Master of one's psychological domain? Not likely if one's self-esteem is unstable. *Personality and Social Psychology Bulletin, 26*, 1297–1305.

Kobasa, S. C. (1979). Stressful life events, personality and health: An inquiry into hardiness. *Journal of Personality and Social Psychology, 37*, 1–11.

Kolditz, T. Λ. (2010). *In Extremis Leadership: Leading As If Your Life Depended On It.* San Francisco, CA: Jossey Bass.

Kristenson, M., Olsson, A. G., & Kucinskiene, Z. (2005). Good self-rated health is related to psychosocial resources and a strong cortisol response to acute stress: The LiVicordia study of middle-aged men. *International Journal of Behavioral Medicine, 12,* 153–60.

Lally, P., van Jaarsveld, C. H. M., Potts, H. W. W. & Wardle, J. (2010), How are habits formed: Modelling habit formation in the real world. *European Journal of Social Psychology, 40,* 998–1009.

Lambertsen, C. (2016). *Navy SEALs mental toughness: A guide to developing an unbeatable mind.* San Bernardino: California.

Larsson, G. (2006). The developmental leadership questionnaire (DLQ): Some psychometric properties. *Scandinavian Journal of Psychology, 47,* 253–262.

Larsson, G. & Kallenberg, K. (2006) *Direkt ledarskap (Direct leadership).* Stockholm: Forsvarets bok- och blankett forråd, Syllabus AS: Swedish Defence College and Swedish Defence.

Lau Tzu. (n.d.). *Tao Te Ching: The Classic Book of Integrity and the Way* (translated by Mair, V. H. in 1990). New York: Bantam Books.

Lazar, S. W. (2005). Mindfulness research. In C. K. Germer, R. D. Siegel, & P. R. Fulton (Eds.), *Mindfulness and Psychotherapy* (pp.220-238)*.* New York: Guilford Press.

Lazarus, R., & Folkman, S. (1984). *Psychological stress and the coping process.* New York: Springer.

Levine, S. & Ursin, H. (1991). What is Stress? In M. R. Brown, G. F. Koob, & C. Rivier (Eds.), *Stress: Neurobiology and Neuroendocrinology* (pp. 3-21). United States of America, NY: Marcel Dekker, Inc.

Leonard, G. (1986). The Warrior: is the American soldier all that he can be? Or does this country need a few good samurai? *Esquire* (July 1986), 64–71.

Limbert, C. (2004). Psychological wellbeing and job satisfaction amongst military personnel on unaccompanied tours: The impact of perceived social support and coping strategies. *Military Psychology, 16,* 37–51.

Linnartz, K. (2013). *All about yoga.* Munchen: Gräfe und Unzer Verlag GmbH.

Lu, L. (1997). Social support, reciprocity, and well-being. *The Journal of Social Psychology, 137,* 618–628.

Lupien, S., Maheu, F., Tu, M., Fiocco, A., & Schramek, T. (2007). The effects of stress and stress hormones on human cognition: Implications for the field of brain and cognition. *Brain and Cognition, 65,* 209–236.

Lusk, J. D., Sadeh, N., Wolf, E. J., & Miller, M. W. (2017). Reckless Self-Destructive Behavior and PTSD in Veterans: The Mediating Role of New Adverse Events. *Journal of Traumatic Stress, 30*(3), 270-278.

Lyon, B. (2012). Stress, Coping and Health: A conceptual overview. In V. H. Rice (Ed.), *Handbook of stress, coping, and health: implications for nursing research, theory, and practice* (2nd ed.) (pp. 3–23). Thousand Oaks: SAGE Publications.

Machowicz, R. (2008). *Unleash the warrior within.* Philadelphia: Da Capo Press.

Mandler, G. (1982). Stress and thought processes. In L. Goldberger & S. Breznitz (Eds.), *Handbook of Stress: Theoretical and Clinical Aspects* (pp. 88-104). New York: The Free Press.

Marcus, F. M. (1991). *Mattering: Its measurement and theoretical significance for social psychology.* Paper presented at the annual meeting of the Eastern Sociological Association, Cincinnati, OH.

Markstrom, C. A. (2001). *The psychometric properties of the Psychosocial Inventory of Ego Strengths for high school students.* Unpublished manuscript. Morgantown: West Virginia University.

Markstrom, C. A., Sabino, V. M., Turner, B., & Berman, R. C. (1997). The Psychosocial Inventory of Ego Strengths: Development and assessment of a new Eriksonian measure. *Journal of Youth and Adolescence, 26*, 705–732.

Marshall, S. L. A. (1947). *Men Against Fire: The Problem of Battle Command.* Norman: University of Oklahoma Press.

Martens, R., Vealey, R. S., & Burton, D. (1990). Competitive anxiety in sport. Champaign, IL: Human Kinetics.

Maslow, A. H., Hirsh, E., Stein, M., & Honigmann, I. (1945). A clinically derived test for measuring psychological security-insecurity. *Journal of General Psychology, 33*, 21–41.

Matthews, M. D., Eid, J., Johnsen, B. H., & Boe, O. (2011). A comparison of expert ratings and self-assessments of situation awareness during a combat fatigue course. *Military Psychology*, 23(2), 125–136.

Matthews, M. D. (2008). Positive psychology: Adaptation, leadership, and performance in exceptional circumstances. In P. A. Hancock, & J. L. Szalma (Eds.), *Performance under stress* (pp. 163–180). Aldershot, England: Ashgate.

Mazur, A., & Booth, A. (1998). Testosterone and dominance in men. *Behavioral & Brain Sciences, 21*, 353–397.

McCormick, C., Mathews, I., Thomas, C., & Waters, P. (2010). Investigations of HPA function and the enduring consequences of stressors in adolescence in animal models. *Brain and Cognition, 72*, 73–85.

McCoy, B. P. (2007). *The passion of command The moral imperative of leadership.* Quantico, VA: Marine Corps Association.

McDonald, S. P. (2013). Empirically based leadership—integrating the science of psychology in building a better leadership model. *Military Review.* January–February edition 2013.

McKay, J. M., Selig, S. E., Carlson, J. S. & Morris, T. (1997). Psychophysiological Stress in Elite Golfers during Practice and Competition. *The Australian Journal of Science and Medicine in Sport, 29(2)*, 55–61.

McWhirter, N., & McWhirter, R. (1966). *Guiness Book of Records.* New York: Bantam.

Mead, N. L., Baumeister, R. F., Gino, F., Schweitzer, M. E., & Ariely, D. (2009). Too tired to tell the truth: Self-control resource depletion and dishonesty. *Journal of Experimental Social Psychology, 45*(3), 594–597.

Metcalfe, J., & Mischel, W. (1999). A hot/cool-system analysis of delay of gratification: dynamics of willpower. *Psychological Review, 106*(1), 3–19.

Milgram, N. A., Orensten, R. & Zafrir, E. (1989). Stressors, Personal Resources and Social Support in Military Performance during War. *Military Psychology, 1*, 185–199.

Mischel, W., & Grusec, J. (1967). Waiting for rewards and punishments: effects of time and probability on choice. *Journal of Personality and Social Psychology, 5*(1), 24.

Moldjord, C., Laberg, J. C., & Rundmo, T. (2015). Stressors, social support and military performance in a modern war scenario. *Journal of Military Studies, 6*(1), 1–18.

Money, K., Hillenbrand, C., & Camara, N. D. (2008). Putting positive psychology to work in organizations. *Journal of General Management, 34*(2), 21–26.

Moran, L. (1967). *The anatomy of courage.* London: Houghton Mifflin Company.

Morgan, C. A., Cho, T., Hazlett, G., Coric, V., & Morgan, J. (2002). The impact of burnout on human physiology and on operational performance: A prospective study of soldiers enrolled in the Combat Diver Qualification Course. *Yale Journal of Biology and Medicine, 75*, 199–205.

Most, S. B., Chun, M. M., Widders, D. M., & Zaid, D. H. (2005). Attentional rubbernecking: cognitive control and personality in emotion-induced blindness. *Psychonomic Bulletin Review, 12*(4), 654–61.

Mylle, J. (2014). *Opening speech at the 16th International Military Mental Health Conference,* December 2014, Brussels, Belgium.

Niemiec, R. M. (2014). *Mindfulness and character strengths: A practical guide to flourishing.* Cambridge, MA: Hogrefe.

O'Donovan, A., Cohen, B. E., Seal, K. H., Bertenthal, D., Margaretten, M,, Nishimi, K., & Neylan, T. C. (2015). Elevated risk for autoimmune disorders in Iraq and Afghanistan veterans with posttraumatic stress disorder. *Biologigical Psychiatry, 77*(4), 365–74.

Ormrod, J. E. (2006). *Educational psychology: Developing learners* (5th ed.). Upper Saddle River, NJ: Pearson/Merrill Prentice Hall.

Osinga, F (2006). *Science Strategy and War: The Strategic Theory of John Boyd.* Abingdon, UK: Routledge.

Overdale, S. & Gardner, D. (2012). Social Support and Coping Adaptability in Initial Military Training. *Military Psychology, 24*, 312–330.

Papp, M. (2010). *Yoga på djupet (Yoga in depth).* Västerås: Ica Bokförlag.

Pearlin, L. I., & LeBlanc, A. J. (2001). Bereavement and the loss of mattering. In T. J. Owens, S. Stryker, & N. Goodman (Eds.), *Extending self-esteem theory and research* (pp. 285–300). Cambridge: Cambridge University Press.

Pensgaard, A. M., & Hollingen, E. (2006). *Idrettens mentale treningslære (The mental training theory of sports).* Oslo: Gyldendal Norsk Forlag AS.

Peterson, C., Park, N., Hall, N., & Seligman, M. E. P. (2009). Zest and work. *Journal of Organizational Behavior, 30*, 161–172.

Peterson, C., & Seligman, M. E. P. (2004). *Character strengths and virtues: A handbook and classification.* New York: Oxford University Press.

Peterson, C., Stephens, J. P., Park, N., Lee, F., & Seligman, M. E. P. (2010). Strengths of character and work. In P. A. Linley, S. Harrington, & N. Page (Eds.), *Handbook of positive psychology and work* (pp. 221–231). New York: Oxford University Press.

Picano, J., & Roland, R. R. (2012). Assessing psychological suitability for high-risk military jobs. In J. H. Laurence & M. D. Matthews (Eds.), *The Oxford Handbook of Military Psychology* (pp. 148–157). New York: Oxford University Press.

Picano, J., Williams, T. J., & Roland, R. R. (2006). Assessment and selection for high risk operational personnel. In C. H. Kennedy, & E. A. Zillmer (Eds.), *Military Psychology: Clinical and Operational Applications* (pp. 335–370). New York: Guilford.

Plaud, J. J., & Wolpe, J. (1997). Pavlov's contributions to behavior therapy: The obvious and the not so obvious. *American Psychologist, 52*(9), 966–972.

Poole, B. J., & Kane, M. J. (2009). Working-memory capacity predicts the executive control of visual search among distractors: the influences of sustained and selective attention. *Quarterly Journal of Experimental Psychology, 62*(7), 1430–1454.

Redick, T. S., & Engle, R. W. (2006). Working memory capacity and attention network test performance. *Applied Cognitive Psychology, 20*(5), 713–721.

Richeson, J. A., & Trawalter, S. (2005). Why do interracial interactions impair executive function? A resource depletion account. *Journal of Personality and Social Psychology, 88*(6), 934–937.

Riley, P. (n.d.). *Great players crave instruction on their weaknesses.* Retrieved from http://www.azquotes.com/quote/686617

Riordan, C. (2010). Six elements of mental toughness. *Forbes Magazine*, September 17th.

Rogelberg, S. G., Justice, L., Braddy, P. W, Paustian-Underdahl, S. C., Heggestad, E., Shanock, L., Baran, B. E., Beck, T., Long, S., Andrew, A., Altman, D. G., & Fleenor, J. W. (2013). The executive mind: leader self-talk, effectiveness and strain. *Journal of Managerial Psychology, 28*(2), 183-201.

Rohall, D. E., & Segal, D. R. (2001). *General and specific forms of mattering affecting Russian officers: Reaction to organizational downsizing.* Unpublished manuscript.

Rosenberg, M. (1979). *Conceiving the self.* New York: Basic Books.

Rosenberg, M., & McCullough, C. (1981). Mattering: Inferred significance and mental health. *Research in Community and Mental Health, 2*, 163–182.Traumatic stress: effects on the brain

Sapolsky, R. M. (2005). The influence of social hierarchy on primate health. *Science, 308*, 648–652.

Sapolsky, R. M., Alberts, S. C., & Altmann, J. (1997). Hypercortisolism associated with social subordinance or social isolation among wild baboons. *Archives of General Psychiatry, 54*, 1137–1143.

Sarason, I. G., Pierce, G. R., & Sarason, B. R. (1994). General and specific perceptions of social support. In W. Avison & I. Gotlib (Eds.), *Stress and mental health: Contemporary issues and prospects for the future* (pp. 151–177). New York: Plenum.

Schieman, S., & Taylor, J. (2001). Statuses, roles, and the sense of mattering. *Sociological Perspectives, 44*, 469–484.

Segerstrom, S., & Miller, G. (2004). Psychological stress and the human immune system: A meta-analytic study of 30 years of inquiry. *Psychological Bulletin, 130*, 601–630.

Selye, H. (1956). *The stress of life.* New York: McGraw-Hill Book Co.

Shafer, L. F. (1947). Fear and courage in aerial combat. *Journal of Consulting Psychology, 11*, 137–143.

Siddle, B. K. (1995). *Sharpening The Warrior's Edge.* Belleville, IL: PPCT Research Publications.

Sivik, T., Delimar, D., Korenjak, P., & Delimar, N. (1997). The role of blood pressure, cortisol, and prolactin among soldiers injured in the 1991–1993 war in Croatia. *Integrative Physiological and Behavioral Science, 32*, 364–375.

Shavelson, R. J., Hubner, J. J., & Stanton, G. C. (1976). Self-concept: Validation of construct interpretations. *Review of Educational Research, 46*, 407–441.

Shoda, Y., Mischel, W., & Peake, P. K. (1990). Predicting adolescent cognitive and self-regulatory competencies from preschool delay of gratification: Identifying diagnostic conditions. *Developmental Psychology, 26*(6), 978.

Smith, R. E., Smoll, F. L., & Schutz, R. W. (1990). Measurement and correlates of sport-specific cognitive and somatic trait anxiety: The Sport Anxiety Scale. *Anxiety Research, 2*(4), 263–280.

Sosik, J. J., Gentry, W. A., & Chun, J. A. (2012). The value of virtue in the upper echelons: A multisource examination of executive character strengths and performance. *Leadership Quarterly, 23*, 367–382.

Squire, L. R. (1986). Mechanisms of memory. *Science, 232*, 1612-1619.

Steckler, T., Kalin, N. H. & Reul, J. M. H. M. (Eds.). (2005). *Handbook of Stress and the Brain. Vol.1. The Neurobiology of Stress.* Amsterdam: Elsevier B.V.

Stetz, T. A., Stetz, M. C., & Bliese, P. D. (2006). The importance of self-efficacy in the moderating effects of social support on stressor-strain relationships. *Work & Stress, 20*(1), 49–59.

Sutherland, V. J., & Cooper, C. L. (1990). *Understanding Stress: A Psychological Perspective for Health Professionals.* Great Britain: Chapman & Hall.

Sun Tzu. (490 BC). *The Art of War* (translated by Cleary, T. in 1988). Boston: Shambhala Publications, Inc.

Tang, Y. Y., Ma, Y., Wang, J., Fan, Y., Feng, S., Lu, Q., Yu, Q., Sui, D., Rothbart, M. K., Fan, M., & Posner, M. I. (2007). Short-term meditation training improves attention and self-regulation. *Proceedings of the National Academy of Sciences of the United States of America, 104*(43), 7152–17156.

Tangney, J. P., Baumeister, R. F., & Boone, A. L. (2004). High self-control predicts good adjustment, less pathology, better grades, and interpersonal success. *Journal of Personality, 72*(2), 271–324.

Taylor, J., & Turner, J. R. (2001). A longitudinal study of the role and significance of mattering to others for depressive symptoms. *Journal of Health and Social Behavior, 42*, 310–325.

Tenenbaum, G., Edmonds, W. A., & Eccles, D. W. (2008). Emotions, coping strategies, and performance: A conceptual framework for defining affect-related performance zones. *Military Psychology, 20*, 11–37.

The Quotation Page (n.d.). *Quotation #9757 from Classic Quotes*. Retrieved from http://www.quotationspage.com/quote/9757.html

Thor. (2010). Introduction. In Asken, M. J., Grossman, D., & Christensen, L. *Warrior Mindset.* USA: Warrior Science Publications.

Thoits, P. A. (1986). Social support as coping assistance. *Journal of Consulting and Clinical Psychology, 54*, 416–423.

Todes, D. P. (2002). *Pavlov's Physiology Factory.* Baltimore, MD: Johns Hopkins University Press.

Torgersen, G. E. (Ed.). (2018). *Interaction: Samhandling under Risk (SUR) – A Step Ahead of the Unforeseen.* Oslo: Cappelen Damm Akademisk.

Torgersen, G. E., Steiro, T. J., & Sæverot, H. (2013). Strategic education management: Outlines for a didactic planning model for exercises and training of the unexpected in high risk organizations. *Proceedings of the 22nd Society for Risk Analysis Europe (SRA E) Conference.*

Unsworth, N., Schrock, J. C., & Engle, R. W. (2004). Working memory capacity and the antisaccade task: individual differences in voluntary saccade control. *Journal of Experimental Psychology: Learning, Memory, and Cognition 30*(6), 1302–1321.

U.S. Army. (2012). *Army Doctrine Reference Publication (ADRP) 6–22 Army Leadership.* Washington, DC: Headquarters. Department of the Army.

Vātsyāyana, M. (n.d.) *Kamasutram.*

Vohs, K. D., Baumeister, R. F., Schmeichel, B. J., Twenge, J. M., Nelson, N. M., & Tice, D. M. (2008). Making choices impairs subsequent self-control: a limited-resource account of decision making, self-regulation, and active initiative. *Journal of Personality and Social Psychology, 94*(5), 883–898.

Wagner, M. T., Williams, J. M., & Long, C. J. (1990). The role of social networks in recovery from head trauma. *International Journal of Clinical Neuropsychology, 12*, 131–37.

Wallenius, C., Larsson, G., & Johansson, C. R. (2004). Military observers' reactions and performance when facing danger. *Military Psychology, 16*, 211–229.

Weiten, W. (2001). *Psychology. Themes and variations* (5th ed.). Belmont, CA: Wadsworth, Thomson Learning.

White, J. B., Langer, E. J., Yariv, L., & Welch, J. C. (2006). Frequent Social Comparisons and Destructive Emotions and Behaviors: The Dark Side of Social Comparisons. *Journal of Adult Development, 13*(1), 36-44.

Williams, A. M., & Ericsson, K. A. (2005). Perceptual-cognitive expertise in sport: Some considerations when applying the expert performance approach. *Human Movement Science, 24*(3), 283–307.

Williams, K. R. (2010). An assessment of moral and character education in initial entry training (IET). *Journal of Military Ethics, 9*(1), 41–56.

Wood, N. (1964). Xenophon's Theory of Leadership. *Classica et Mediaevalia. XXV*, 33-66.

Woodman, T., & Hardy, L. (2003). The relative impact of cognitive anxiety and self-confidence upon sport performance: a meta-analysis. *Journal of Sports Sciences, 21*, 443–457.

Yearley, L. H. (1990). *Mencius and Aquinas: Theories of virtue and conceptions of courage.* Albany: State University of New York Press.

Young, M. (2011). Patton, G. S. cited in *Follow your dreams. A book of inspirational quotes,* p. 114.

Yukl, G. (2010). *Leadership in Organizations* (7th ed.). Upper Saddle River, NJ: Prentice-Hall.

Krav Maga: How to Defend Yourself against Physical Attack

by Krav Maga founder Imi Sde-Or (Lichtenfeld) and Master Eyal Yanilov

Krav Maga, developed by Grandmaster Imi Sde-Or (1910–1998) since the 1940s, was once a method of hand-to-hand combat strictly confined to security agents and members of the Mossad and elite Israel Defense Force units. Later, it has been adapted for civilians so that everyone, of any age, gender, or physical ability, can utilize it. Based on natural reactions of the human body, the discipline is easy to learn and perform, and practical to use.

Krav Maga has rapidly gained in popularity and earned recognition by experts the world over. In the United States, South America, Europe, Australia, and the Far East, this unique method of self-defense has already been taught to and used by official law enforcement agencies, special forces and security personnel, as well as ordinary citizens.

Written by Imi Sde-Or and his most distinguished successor Eyal Yanilov as part of the Founder's Series, **Krav Maga: How to Defend Yourself against Physical Attack** is the first of two volumes presenting the techniques, key principles, strategies, and training methods of this unique and integrated system. Laid out in an accessible, step-by-step format, it covers the basics, from safety in training, warm-up, stretching, and flexibility to principles of attacks, stances, and starting positions. The authors offer solutions for every imaginable scenario: defending strikes, releases from chokes and headlocks, as well as escapes from hair, shirt, and arm grabs. Also emphasizing the psychological basis of the discipline, the book expands its usefulness with sections on mental aspects, vulnerable points, women's self-defense, and more.

Eyal Yanilov began training in Krav Maga with Grandmaster Imi Sde-Or when he was fifteen. Yanilov was the first person to begin educating Krav Maga instructors outside of Israel, and has taught special units, military and civilian students in over fifty countries.

An English-language edition has been scheduled for publication in late 2020.

Each volume contains 240 pages with over 450 b/w photos and illustrations; 16.6x23.8 cm.